ADVANCE PRAISE FOR

Critically Engaged Learning

"This book is an exciting completion of a trilogy addressing the educational needs of young people who are excluded and disengaged from school. It provides a sophisticated rebuttal to the view that marginalized youth need special programs. Instead, the book shows how critical engagement by educators, parents and young people creates educational spaces and places which all students can own and in which all thrive. Drawing on examples from a wide range of communities, the book shows not only how schools can make a difference, but how they do so—to enhance young people's learning and to build community capacity. The reader will be drawn into the communities and schools through the detailed and informative 'portraits' which illustrate the ways in which connections between young people, schools and communities are built, through familiarity with and critical engagement in local circumstances. Written with passion and with extraordinary depth of understanding, this book is a must for all educators."
Johanna Wyn, Professor in Education & Director, Australian Youth Research Centre,
The University of Melbourne

"This book is an antidote to the litany of studies marred by neoliberal beliefs and deficit thinking—a refreshing and substantive book that challenges mainstream work on engagement. Finally, a work that seriously utilizes critical democracy and the robust notions of equity and social justice to student engagement and learning that involve life to its fullest. The book's approach of creating narrative portraits is impressive."
John Portelli, Professor & Associate Chair, Co-director, Centre for Leadership & Diversity, Department of Theory and Policy Studies, OISE/University of Toronto

"In an era obsessed with school reform, it is refreshing to read a book that brings community activism and renewal to center stage."
Gary Anderson, Professor, Steinhardt School of Culture,
Education and Human Development, New York University

"An analysis of change and educational disadvantage that begins with respect for people has been long awaited. For too long education has been dominated by the emptiness of leadership and the damaging fiasco produced by neoliberal improvement and effectiveness policies. Smyth, Angus, Down and McInerney have used portraits to show how labels such as disadvantage are offensive, and how re-enchantment with learning is not only possible but vital if young people are to be made, in their words, 'powerful people'. I cannot think of another team who can pull off the interplay between scholarship and strategy in ways that demonstrate that education needs research, theory and most important of all, the energy to produce reality within the narratives of the recommended approaches for change."

Helen Gunter, Professor, School of Education, The University of Manchester

"The authors show genuine respect for youth and the multiple spheres in which their education occurs. While documenting the local, the authors take us beyond that and connect to the global. This book points us in hopeful directions that envision cultivating youthful critically engaged citizens."

Kathryn Herr, Professor, Montclair State University; Editor, Youth and Society

Critically Engaged Learning

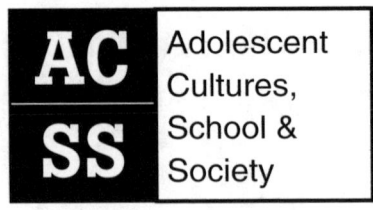

Joseph L. DeVitis & Linda Irwin-DeVitis
GENERAL EDITORS

Vol. 42

PETER LANG
New York • Washington, D.C./Baltimore • Bern
Frankfurt am Main • Berlin • Brussels • Vienna • Oxford

John Smyth, Lawrence Angus,
Barry Down, Peter McInerney

Critically Engaged Learning

Connecting to Young Lives

PETER LANG
New York • Washington, D.C./Baltimore • Bern
Frankfurt am Main • Berlin • Brussels • Vienna • Oxford

Library of Congress Cataloging-in-Publication Data

Critically engaged learning: connecting to young lives / John Smyth ... [et al.].
p. cm. — (Adolescent cultures, school, and society; v. 42)
Includes bibliographical references and index.
1. Community education—Australia. 2. Critical pedagogy—Australia.
I. Smyth, John.
LC1036.8.A8C74 370.11'5—dc22 2008017150
ISBN 978-1-4331-0156-4 (hardcover)
ISBN 978-1-4331-0155-7 (paperback)
ISSN 1091-1464

Bibliographic information published by **Die Deutsche Bibliothek**.
Die Deutsche Bibliothek lists this publication in the "Deutsche
Nationalbibliografie"; detailed bibliographic data is available
on the Internet at http://dnb.ddb.de/.

Cover design by Clear Point Designs

The paper in this book meets the guidelines for permanence and durability
of the Committee on Production Guidelines for Book Longevity
of the Council of Library Resources.

© 2008 Peter Lang Publishing, Inc., New York
29 Broadway, 18th floor, New York, NY 10006
www.peterlang.com

All rights reserved.
Reprint or reproduction, even partially, in all forms such as microfilm,
xerography, microfiche, microcard, and offset strictly prohibited.

Printed in the United States of America

Contents

Acknowledgments	**ix**
Chapter 1. Mapping the ethnographic social relations ... of community renewal and student engagement	**1**
Introduction	1
The research issues	3
What do we mean by 'critical engagement'?	5
What are the features of critical engagement?	6
Something about our orientation	8
School and community portraits	9
Wirra Wagga	9
Bountiful Bay	12
Enterprise High School	13
Marine Park High School	13
Casuarina Heights High School	14
Banksia Hill High School	15
Methodological, philosophical and research design perspectives	16
Organization of the book	20

Chapter 2. Engaging socially critical educators and community activists — 23
Introduction — 23
What does it mean to create critical spaces ...? — 27
Opening up free spaces for socially critical action — 31
Puncturing the myths: counter-narratives that go beyond pathologizing disadvantage — 34
    Story: 'We feel we can stand up and make a difference; that's what we didn't have before' — 35
    Story: 'We want a hand up not a handout' — 37
    Story: 'If you want to use it you have to fix it' — 40
    Story: 'They owned it from day one' — 42
    Story: 'It's the best thing I've done since kinder ...' — 46
Concluding comments — 51

Chapter 3. Engaging excluded communities — 53
Introduction — 53
'Dropping off the edge' — 55
Dismembering the sociological machinery of school — 58
    Story: 'If I was in a different class I would be looking to get out' — 61
    Story: 'We teach differently here' — 62
School and home as 'sites of pedagogic acquisition' — 64
Communities as resources for learning — 66
    Story: 'We gave them the option of going back to class but they decided to stay' — 69
Community-based learning — 70
    Story: 'You get what you want out of this program' — 73
The community-building school — 76
    Story: 'From little things, big things grow' — 78
Concluding comments — 79

Chapter 4. Engaging in policy and educational reform that is respectful of young lives — 81
Introduction — 81
Wirra Wagga and the neighborhood renewal ideal — 82
The limitations of community renewal — 84
The flawed logic of school effectiveness — 85
Neighborhoods and students who are 'at risk' — 89

Including community in defining the importance of education	91
Story: Community empowerment 'of the forgotten people'	93
Story: Building community by engaging with education and society	96
Story: Challenges for the Wirra Wagga Community School and educational professionals	99
Story: Curriculum and control—'teachers have to earn the respect and trust of kids'	103
Story: Imagining alternative futures and 'avoiding the shaky knees'	106
Potential reform that is respectful of young lives	109

Chapter 5. Engaging youth and popular culture — 117

Introduction	117
What's happening to young lives?	120
Connecting to students' lives and experience	124
Story: 'Starting from where kids are at'	125
Story: 'I am interested in who they are and what they do'	129
Story: 'Dumbing down the curriculum does not help kids'	130
Story: 'They were focused and proud of their achievements'	132
Story: 'Teachers had a license to experiment with pedagogy'	134
Pursuing socially critical possibilities	136
Story: 'I think it's about having a team of teachers who talk to each other'	136
Story: 'The curriculum is still subject/discipline oriented'	139
Story: 'As teachers we have to build up communication with kids and find out their interests'	141
Story: 'I feel a sense of pride in what I've accomplished at school'	144
Conclusion	146

Chapter 6. New storylines that engage young learners — 149

Introduction	149
Culture and community	153
1. Drawing on local strengths, leadership and resources	154
2. Embedding school-in-community approaches	155
Pedagogy and curriculum	156
3. Connecting to students' lives and culture	157
4. Building relationships based on trust, respect and care	158
Structure and organization	160

5. Fostering a flexible, student-focused and supportive
    school culture 160
6. Creating spaces for dialogue, reflection and innovation 161
    What next? 163
Appendix A **167**
Appendix B **169**
References **171**
Index **185**

Acknowledgments

Much of the empirical data in this book is derived from two projects funded by the Australian Research Council (ARC): an ARC Discovery Project (2006–2008), *Individual, institutional and community 'capacity building' in a cluster of disadvantaged schools and their community*, and an ARC Linkage Project (2005–2007), *School and Community Linkages for Enhanced School Retention in Regional/Rural Western Australia*. Both projects had a focus on the school- and community-related conditions that promote school retention and student engagement in disadvantaged neighborhoods.

An extensive body of research confirms the fact that students from economically disadvantaged backgrounds do not perform as well at school as their more affluent counterparts. What is less well known is what can be done to transform this situation. This research builds on previous studies, which have documented the experiences of early school leavers in Australia (Smyth, Hattam, Cannon, Edwards, Wilson & Wurst, 2000) and the educational arrangements which enhance learning for young adolescents in the middle years of schooling (Smyth & McInerney, 2007a). However, this study moves beyond the immediate school context to examine the institutional and community processes of capacity building that lead to improved learning for students. The research across the two locations was conducted by Professor John Smyth, Professor Lawrence Angus and Professor Barry Down (Chief Investigators), Dr Peter McInerney (Research Associate) and Ms Solveiga Smyth (Research Assistant).

We acknowledge the financial support of the ARC and the cooperation of the Western Australian Department of Education and Training (DET) and the Victorian Department of Education, Employment and Training (DE&T) in facilitating access to the project schools. We are especially grateful to the educational administrators, teachers, students, community activists and residents who spoke with such passion and conviction about the importance of critically engaged learning and schooling for a more just society. We express our appreciation to Chris Myers, Joe de Vitis and all the editing and production personnel at Peter Lang Publishing. Finally, we owe a special sense of gratitude to our wives and families for their ongoing support and encouragement of our work.

 ONE

Mapping the Ethnographic Social Relations . . . of Community Renewal and Student Engagement

Introduction

It seems that notions of place and space are very much on the ascendancy as resurgent theoretical categories from within which to examine social phenomena, particularly in respect of education and schooling (Gulson, 2007a; Gulson, Symes & Sumsion, 2007; Gulson & Symes, 2007). Until fairly recently, space was considered something of 'an abstract dimension or container in which human activities took place' (Tilley, 1994, p. 9). In other words, space was considered to be everywhere, and being largely 'indifferent to human affairs . . . it was largely a nothingness'. The problem with this somewhat evacuated view is that it denies 'any consideration of structures of power and domination' (Tilley, 1994, p. 9). The attractiveness of such a view is that it is no doubt less troublesome, has a degree of 'purity and simplicity', and has the potential to enable an objective plotting, mapping, measuring and locating of things according to 'the same rigorous and quantitative scale' (p. 9). An alternative but more sophisticated view, 'starts from regarding space as a medium rather than as a container for action' (p. 10)—in other words, space is socially produced, it is not innocent, but rather is invested 'with power relating to age, gender, social position and relationships with others' (p. 11). As Tilley (1994) put it:

> Spaces are intimately related to the formation of biographies and social relationships (p. 11).

What we are saying is that we don't believe there is such a thing as generalist or placeless perspectives. Attempts that purport to present themselves as if they have no perspective actually have a viewpoint—what such refusals do is obliterate (or at best diminish) the significance of local voices.

Our view is that place and space are important because of the potential they have to highlight local knowledge, celebrate local responses, and in the process, foreground the views of those to whom existential realities belong, albeit in a global context. Paul Carter (2007), an international pioneer in the field of spatial history and place making, hit the mark when he recently said that there is a continual tension being played out within places like schools and communities:

> ... where insiders are distinguished from outsiders, notably in the conflict-ridden interventions that occur whenever 'experts', 'consultants' and 'activists' improperly intrude on, and disregard, the collective domain of knowledge and experience held in trust by those who regard themselves as 'local' (Abstract).

What Carter was referring to was the notion of 'care at a distance'—a term he uses to refer to the 'conundrums collecting institutions find themselves in when pressured to repatriate culturally-sensitive materials'. This notion of 'care at a distance' is an interesting one that we might borrow and expand upon here, particularly as it might have implications for those of us who work with and are passionate about communities put at a disadvantage. As Carter (2007) says, this is a way of 'incorporat[ing] the subject position of the outsider into the place-making process' and it is a way of overtly declaring where we are coming from.

The reason notions of space and place are so relevant to our research is that what we are dealing with in this book is the concept of exclusion. Gulson, Symes & Sumsion (2007) put it in these terms: 'The language of exclusion is, by and large, spatial: who's in, who's out, at the heart, on the margins' (p. 99). In the U.S., for example, spatial notions might quite literally be extended to include the 'gated school':

> ... the one which metaphorically shields itself from populations that it regards as polluting ones, and the literal 'gates' which, with security guards and metal detectors,

shield the school from its own student population (Gulson, Symes, & Sumsion, 2007, p. 99).

We agree with Gulson, Symes & Sumsion (2007) that with few exceptions 'the ideas of space and place are more often used by social scientists as metaphors, rather than as complex theorizations of material and symbolic life' (p. 99). Gulson, Symes & Sumsion (2007) consider 'space and place as integral, yet under-examined and under-theorized, components of educational studies' (p. 100).

We are hoping to oblige in a modest way in this book by helping to turn around the importance of ideas of space and place in theorizing about the way in which educational disadvantage gets to be constructed, contested and re-constructed.

The research issues

The over-arching research issue animating us in this book and framing our efforts, is the increasing proportion of the population in Western societies that is being left behind and unceremoniously swept into the category of 'our forgotten poor' (Smith & Turley, 2007)—in the Australian case, the 9.8 percent of the population not enjoying the benefits of the alleged trickle-down effects of the good economic times, and who are living below the poverty line. They have their equivalents in other Western countries, as well.

Our more specific interests are in finding and describing the spaces and places in which community and educational effort hold out some hope of re-engaging young lives that are being so brutally and abruptly diminished by being left out. In the U.S. context, Kozol (2005) has labeled this 'the shame of the nation'.

What we are looking for in this book is what Gulson (2007b) refers to as 'temporary fixations' in educational and social policy—which is to say, a 'renovation' of educational identities (Gulson, 2005). The intent in this revitalization of 'both people and places' (Gulson, 2007b, p. 11), or as Massey (2005) invoking Amin (2002) put it, the 'temporary constellations of trajectories' requiring negotiation is:

> ...one of local accommodation, a vocabulary that addresses the rights of presence and confronts the facts of difference (Massey, 2005, p. 153).

As Massey (2005) expressed it, this is 'a politics without guarantees' in which accommodation means negotiation, and it is 'always provisional [and] may be reached or not' (p. 154).

The particular intellectual conduit by which we want to begin to confront and address the widening and proliferating exclusion of disadvantaged young people from the benefits of schooling, is via the notion of '(re)engagement'. Having said that, this is not another book about student engagement in the narrow technicist sense of reinserting alienated and disaffected young people back into the social institution of schooling—the very institution that has repelled or expelled them in the first place. To do that would be to implicitly blame these young people for their plight, and to acknowledge that the causation is young people themselves, and by implication, their families that have supposedly placed them 'at risk'. Blaming the victim misses the point about what it is that is desperately in need of repair and restoration—by that we don't simply mean individual lives, but the wider social and political forces that have contributed to placing these young people and the communities they come from at a disadvantage, and the conditions that produced their predicament in the first place.

What we want to start with are the lives, histories, experiences and aspirations of those groups in society that have been actively excluded and left behind by the experience of schooling, and allowing them to meaningfully reinsert themselves back into education on their terms.

We believe that there are two intersecting and inseparable dimensions to this: firstly, student engaged learning, and secondly, community capacity building—both of which have to be prefaced by the adjective 'critical'. That is to say, *critically engaged learning* along with *critically engaged community capacity building*. In communities blighted by exclusion, both of these have to occur in unison or in tandem—and that is a major part of what this book is about.

We want to turn now to what each of these terms means.

McMahon & Portelli (2004) identify three qualitatively different meanings of the term student engagement, or engaged learning:

i. **a conservative/traditionalist/behaviorist view**—in which the emphasis is upon 'mastery of academic work', a view of engagement that is 'goal driven', with engaged students dutifully 'attending classes', trying hard in their studies, completing their homework, and not cheating (McMahon & Portelli, 2004, p. 62). This is an essentially compliant view which according to McMahon & Portelli borders on 'indoctrination' because it adheres to an unquestioning view of what constitutes valued educational goals, and the belief that the purpose of education is to 'socialize, sort and select students' (p. 63) according to the degree to which they comply with these goals.

ii. **a liberal/progressive/student-oriented view**—the thrust here is upon an expanded and enriched view of schooling that goes beyond individual achievement to embrace connectedness to the community and the environment of the school, and along with that an expanded range of learning experiences for students. While it embraces a wider set of views about what constitutes academic work, and this view goes beyond deficit views to incorporate student voice, this perspective nevertheless still operates from within the existing order of things and does not question that order.

iii. **critical/democratic practice view**—here, engagement is located within notions of what it means to be an 'active citizen' rather than compliance as a passive 'spectator'. Engagement occurs in the daily interactions that occur between teachers, students and community members around attempts to produce democratic relationships in schools and between schools and their communities. There is a preparedness to recognize existing inequalities, to challenge authoritative discourses, to confront injustices, and to not accept the status quo.

What do we mean by 'critical engagement'?

The idea of 'critical engagement' has recently been popularized by Fear et al. (2006) working out of an agricultural extension context, and their working up of this idea derives its inspiration from Daniel Yankelovich's (1991) book *Coming to Public Judgment: Making Democracy Work in a Complex Society*. Critical engagement is code for exploring how the tectonic plates of capitalism are impacting differentially upon society and how some excluded groups might move beyond their current diminished capacity and assertively begin to push back. Part of what Yankelovich is concerned with is not only a critique of our seemingly unfettered infatuation with technical and expert values over communal values, but also a critique of how this is occurring, together with an exploration of what a democratic alternative might look like that seeks to change this situation.

As far as we can discern, there are three key aspects in the process of coming to critical engagement, namely: (1) a journey of collaborative learning; (2) a notion of the 'critical' that examines the concept of power, how things came to be the way they are, and how to improve the situation for the most excluded;

and (3) 'engagement' that asks questions about the moral imperative to engage in collegial interaction with communities in ways that emphasize visceral qualities like: self-determination; an ethic of co-ownership of processes and outcomes; open participation; distributive and decentralized leadership; and ways of working that minimize the extent of external management. Construed in this way, engagement is about the lived experiences of those pushed to the margins through no fault of their own, the conditions of their marginalization, and working to create the spaces from within which changes might occur.

What are the features of critical engagement?

There are a number of key propositions that need to be foregrounded at the outset in addressing this question:

1. In contexts of disadvantage, there is a crucial set of interconnections between students, schools and their communities.
2. We cannot examine any of the parts of disadvantage and social exclusion in isolation.
3. Deficit approaches (either explicit or implicit) have been tried in the past, and have failed dismally. That is to say, approaches that purport to identify people as categories (e.g., so-called 'at risk'), to come up with generic sets of dysfunctions, and to then 'target' these groups with programs and resources (which is not the same as saying they don't need resources).
4. Outsiders cannot possibly claim to know what the problems are in these contexts, let alone know how to frame the problem; yet they often tend to self-assuredly work as if they have the 'solutions'.
5. Outsiders need to step back from aggressive, top-down, authoritarian, and patronizing ways.
6. The centerpiece of the alternative resides in a more 'critical-democratic engagement' with the subjects.
7. The notion of 'democratic' here means more than giving people in disadvantaged situations 'a say' in their lives and destinies.
8. Being democratic and creating the circumstances of 'critical-democratic engagement' means constructing the spaces in which teachers, students, parents, community organizers, the community at large, and outsiders who work with them, can recognize how power works, for whom, how, and what a more dispersed view of power might look

like—in other words, a context that has a more critical-democratic agenda.

By focusing on the notion of engagement we are able to bring into the conversation the frequently overlooked interface between 'expert judgment and community participation' (Fear et al., 2006, p. xi) around what Yankelovich (1991) calls 'public judgment'. In other words, the delicate balance that needs to be pursued between outsiders' professional and expert judgments, and the insights, ownership and participation by communities and groups who are supposed to benefit.

What we take from all of this, is that engagement is a process by which we 'share our knowledge and learn with those who struggle for social justice ...[and] collaborate with them respectfully and responsibly for the purpose of improving life' (Fear et al., 2006, p. xiii). The sense in which engagement is 'critical' reflects the preparedness to critique ourselves as researchers (along with our insider informants), at the same time as asking probing questions about contextual histories and the wider political, global and social forces making the lives and circumstances of informants the way they are, how they got to be this way, and what works to sustain and maintain things the way they are.

The framing research agenda that infused the two studies reported upon in this book were around how to engage multiple constituencies around issues of disadvantage, social exclusion, marginalization and social justice—within an educational context. In particular:

- Engaging socially critical educators and community activists
- Engaging excluded communities
- Engaging policy respectful of young lives
- Engaging youth and popular culture

These are the four interacting central facets of this book, which focus around the question of student retention—by which we mean, the ability of schools to hold on to or retain students by virtue of energizing, enthusing and engaging them in meaningful and valued learning experiences. When schools present as unable or unwilling to embrace or understand the diversity and complexity of young lives, especially those from circumstances of socioeconomic disadvantage, then this is when students find school to be inhospitable places, and they disconnect from school. Our argument is that while there are clearly pedagogical, relational, curriculum and educational policy issues that have to be addressed, there are also significant areas requiring attention around

8 ❖ Critically Engaged Learning

the wider aspects of the community in which the schools are located.

Something about our orientation

Before we come to the substance of the book, or even the context in which we undertook our research, it is important that we say something about one of the defining hallmarks of the approach we have used. Throughout the book we have drawn upon, extended, and gained a good deal of sustenance from Lawrence-Lightfoot's (1983; 2000; 2005) and Lawrence-Lightfoot & Davis' (1997) notion of 'portraiture' as a form of textual representation as well as a 'method of documentation, analysis, and narrative development' (Lawrence-Lightfoot, 2005, p. 3). This is a strategy we have used extensively in our earlier work (see: Smyth et al., 2000; Smyth & Hattam, et al., 2004; Smyth & McInerney, 2007a), and it may be helpful to give the reader a sense of the 'lie of the land' in respect of portraiture, to invoke Carter's (1996) spatial and topographical metaphor.

Sarah Lawrence-Lightfoot (1983) first used the approach of portraiture in the early 1980s in her study of six U.S. high schools in trying to capture what it was about the 'institutional character and culture . . . and the mix of ingredients that made good schools' (Lawrence-Lightfoot, 2005, p. 5). She admits to searching for a form of inquiry that would enable her to capture both the complexity as well as the aesthetic nature of human experience. What she wanted, she said, was:

> . . . to create a narrative that bridged the realms of science and art, merging the systematic and careful description of good ethnography with the evocative resonance of fine literature (p. 6).

What she came up with was an approach that owed much to a long lineage and a 'rich history of dialogue and collaboration between novelists and philosophers, artists and scholars' (p. 6), but above all, it was an approach that reflected:

> . . . [a] cross between art and science [with] a blend of aesthetic sensibilities and empirical rigor, [along with] its humanistic and literary metaphors (p. 6).

As we might expect, cutting new ground like this was not without its critics and detractors. While portraiture was 'welcomed, and resisted, embraced and criticized by the scholarly community' (p. 7), what was most significant for Lawrence-Lightfoot (2005) were 'the fault lines of opportunity and risk' (p. 7). While questions of authenticity and legitimacy, and the 'power of paradox' were never far away, it was the self-scrutiny and self-analysis that came with the kind of boundary crossing involved in portraiture, that gave this approach its real potency:

> The process of creating narrative portraits requires a difficult (sometimes paradoxical) vigilance to empirical description *and* aesthetic expression and a careful scrutiny and modulation of voice ... [T]here is never a single story [and] ... what gets left out is often as important as what gets included ... (p. 10).

What we like about Lightfoot's approach is not only its healthy skepticism, but its refreshing honesty and commitment to transparency in an era of rampant paranoia, concealment, obfuscation and outright dishonesty, with demands for research to be 'scientific' and 'evidence-based'. In the context of fakery and lack of authenticity, courageous approaches like that of portraiture, hold out true hope for what Featherstone (1989) labeled 'a people's scholarship' in which 'scientific facts gathered in the field give voice to a people's experience' (p. 376).

School and community portraits

Our research into the issues of school retention and student engagement was carried out in two somewhat disparate Australian sites: an elementary and a middle school in the small suburb of Wirra Wagga and a cluster of senior high schools in the much larger Bountiful Bay Education District. The project schools were all government (public) schools operating under administrative and curriculum guidelines laid down by state and commonwealth governments. What follows is a snapshot of the schools and their communities.

Wirra Wagga

It's a hot summer day as we make our way through the working-class suburb of Wirra Wagga for an orientation meeting with a community renewal team. Like much of southern Australia, the region is in the grip of a severe drought and water restrictions mean that many gardens and public reserves are parched and drab. But there are signs of vitality in this neighborhood. A brightly colored mural adorns a bus shelter. Many homes have been given a fresh coat of paint. Fences have been restored. Young children have a new playground and the older children have a BMX [bicycle motorcross] track. In the midst of a somewhat dilapidated shopping center a local woman runs a computer club for young people. We hear about a men's shed and a community house. Something exciting is happening here and we are keen to find out how it all connects to education.

Since 2001 Wirra Wagga has been a priority site for a state government-funded neighborhood renewal project that aims to strengthen social institutions and improve the well-being and economic opportunities for residents. An investment in this community is long overdue. Developed as a public housing estate following the postwar migration boom of the 1950s, Wirra Wagga is a community of some 2,500 people on the outskirts of a regional Australian city. In many respects, the population is remarkably homogeneous. There are very few Indigenous Australians in the community and only a handful of Asian migrants. The vast majority of residents have an Anglo-Celtic ancestry and many are third generation settlers who feel a strong attachment to the community.
In addition to cultural influences, a strong sense of neighborhood identity has been forged by a shared experience of poverty and social exclusion. Bounded by an industrial zone on the north, Wirra Wagga has a history of protracted disadvantage, with high levels of unemployment and welfare dependency. Only 7% of public housing tenants cite 'a wage' as the primary source of income (Neighborhood Renewal Evaluation Framework 2002–2003). Like 'excluded communities' everywhere, the people who call Wirra Wagga 'home' have to contend with negative and disparaging portrayals of their lifestyles and identities from outsiders.

It is certainly true that Wirra Wagga has its fair share of social problems. Along with other 'rust belt' neighborhoods it has born the brunt of globalization and neoliberal policies that have ripped the economic heart out of low socioeconomic communities. But as we were to discover during our many visits, demonizing discourses about dysfunctional families, criminal behavior and educational aspirations are largely sustained by myths, ignorance and prejudices. Our initial meeting with the renewal team heralded the beginning of a counter-narrative to a prevailing deficit discourse. 'People [in Wirra Wagga] don't like to be called disadvantaged . . . they don't want hand-outs', explained a resident networker. What began to unfold during our conversations was a largely untold story of a resilient and caring community with a strong sense of identity and pride. In the words of a recently arrived resident, 'newcomers are accepted for who they are rather than judging them by their past and appearance'. We heard about a reservoir of (largely untapped) community assets, of an ethos of volunteering and the enormous potential of local leadership to enhance social networks and build community capacity. We also heard from local residents about a change in attitude on the part of government officials. In the past there was a tendency to tell people what they needed instead of listening to them. A capacity to listen and respond to local people marked a new approach on the part of government officials to neighborhood renewal. In cooperation with government agencies, residents prepared an action plan to guide development in the areas of housing, community well-being, learning, employment and education, community safety, and community works and environment. Community renewal has proceeded through an extensive network of committees, neighborhood meetings and community projects that have harnessed the talent and skills of residents, developed a capacity for local leadership and increased the level of neighborhood participation in decision making.

So what has all this got to do with education? We quickly found out that education was right at the heart of community renewal. Long-term sustainability was seen to be highly dependent on the community improving educational facilities and opportunities for children as well as adults. Although parents can enroll their children in schools outside of Wirra Wagga, the community is principally served by three elementary schools with a total of 850 students, two of which we studied—Hillview Elementary and Rose Park Elementary—and a high school, Provincetown High, which was also part of our study, with some 600 students from years 7–10. Given the social and economic profile of the community, it is hardly surprising that the neighborhood schools are categorized as 'disadvantaged,' with the vast majority of students receiving some form of government assistance. The complexity of schooling is compounded by a significant proportion of enrolled students with disabilities and diagnosed learning difficulties. Few children have experience of pre-schooling and attrition rates are well above the state average, with a high proportion of students failing to complete formal schooling requirements. Many parents are concerned that their children are unable to handle transition points in their schooling either into elementary school or from elementary school to high school, and there has been a call for a radical review of current arrangements in an effort to reconnect young people to schooling.

The challenge is a quite daunting. A major step has been taken with the demolition of a run-down elementary school and the construction of a community school incorporating kindergarten to year 8 learning communities, adult education facilities, a gymnasium, library and shared community facilities, and a more integrated approach to the delivery of health and community services. With support and cooperation from the Wirra Wagga Community House, government departments and local businesses, the high school has developed a community-based program aimed at re-connecting early school leavers to education.

Community engagement lies at the heart of school reform in Wirra Wagga. A manifestation of this can be seen in the growing realization that teachers need to draw on community knowledge. In a very real sense, community renewal and school reform are seen to go hand-in-hand. How achievable are these goals? To what extent can community renewal be sustained without major structural adjustments to the economy and an ongoing investment from governments? We will revisit these issues further into the account when we look more closely at the concept of capacity building and student engagement, but we want to conclude with some optimistic reflections from a resident who was initially skeptical about the benefits of the project. 'In a few years Wirra Wagga will be a great place to live. It will be a community that believes in itself, an inclusive community that everybody will want to live in'.

Bountiful Bay

Some 3000 miles distant from Wirra Wagga, educators and residents in the Bountiful Bay Education District are also struggling with issues of school retention and student engagement. At first glance this might seem somewhat surprising. Bountiful Bay is a resource-rich region with a strong economic base and a unique maritime heritage. Tourism, agriculture, fishing, mining, petrochemical production, steel fabrication and a host of manufacturing and service industries all contribute to the development of a prosperous and expanding urban region. As we drove along the foreshore of one of the prominent coastal towns it was apparent from the proliferation of high-rise apartments that the wealth generated by the state's mineral boom had penetrated the region. However, pockets of affluence on the seafront mask the extent of poverty in the hinterland. These beautiful coastal locales may be playgrounds for holiday makers and week-end trippers but they are also home for working class families who have largely missed out on the 'new money'. Compared with state averages, Bountiful Bay townships have low levels of weekly earnings, low levels of adult workforce participation, low levels of parental education, reduced levels of life expectancy, a greater percentage of single-parent families, high levels of welfare dependency and a youth unemployment rate of 12%.

These statistics point to a considerable degree of educational disadvantage in the four senior high schools serving the Bountiful Bay district. What follows is a brief portrait of each school detailing some of the educational concerns confronting the community and the organizational and curriculum responses.

Enterprise High School

With student enrolments exceeding 1000, Enterprise High School is the largest high school in the Bountiful Bay Education District. Aboriginal students account for 3% of the school population and the vast majority of children come from English-speaking backgrounds. The school serves a resource-rich region but pockets of poverty and welfare dependency prevail. Some 40% of students receive government assistance to offset the cost of educational materials. Although the school offers a comprehensive education, much of the curriculum focus is on work-related studies and enterprise education. Only one in five senior school students undertake courses leading to university entrance. 'Private schools cream off the smart students', explained a teacher. The issues confronting the school are complex and demanding. We were told that students have limited cultural experiences and many parents tend to devalue education partly as a result of their own negative experiences of schooling. In an effort to improve student engagement, buildings have been refurbished to accommodate middle school practices and a daily timetable of five 65-minute lessons creates opportunities for extended learning activities, subject integration and pastoral care in years 8–10. The school attempts to broaden students' horizons through an extensive range of cultural exchange programs, outdoor education activities and co-curricula options. Specialized sporting and artistic programs have been established to attract and retain students with particular gifts and talents and a special senior school course has been developed for students considered at risk of failing in the mainstream. School retention rates have improved but tensions remain, not the least being the tendency to stream and sort students into academic or vocational courses in the middle years thereby restricting future pathways.

Marine Park High School

The beautiful coastline of Bountiful Bay is a wonderful educational resource for the 900 students attending Marine Park High School. Indeed a good deal of the school's reputation has been built around its coastal studies program and links to maritime industries. A popular tourist destination, Marine Park has the external appearance of an affluent seaside resort but the city has an unemployment rate of 12% (twice the state average) and high levels of youth unemployment. The school is organized around three sub-schools, each with a particular curriculum focus, namely (a) Coastal Studies (b) Science and Technology (c) Arts and Humanities. An Educational Support Center caters for students with disabilities and 20 Aboriginal students who are supported by an Aboriginal Liaison Officer. In common with Enterprise High, teachers have to deal with negative perceptions of the school and community by the mainstream media and outsiders. Attracting and holding academically able students amidst the drift to private schools is particularly challenging. 'We have to sell our sub-school structure and special programs' explained the principal. Maritime Park High has programs to engage Indigenous students and well-coordinated vocational education program incorporating structured workplace learning and Technical and Further Education (TAFE) options. One of the features of the school was a willingness on the part of teachers and counselors to negotiate courses with students—to make the course fit the student. As we shall show in Chapter 3, community-based studies play a crucial role in promoting student engagement and school retention.

Casuarina Heights High School

Natural bushland cushions Casuarina Heights High from a rapidly growing industrial zone near Bountiful Bay. Built as a Junior High School in the 1950s, the school is undergoing a major redevelopment with the construction of a middle school campus, senior school campus and TAFE facilities which will cater for 1200 students. The school provides a comprehensive education in years 8–12 for 700 students most of whom come from low socioeconomic backgrounds. Aboriginal students constitute 13% of the school enrolments and students with diagnosed physical and cognitive disabilities make up a further 5%. The school runs a breakfast program and a peer support and work-related training courses for Indigenous students. Many of the educational concerns discussed in earlier portraits surfaced again in Casuarina Heights. We were told that 'kids don't see that they have a future', 'there's a stigma attached to living in the area', 'many kids have low self-esteem and a poor work ethic', 'parents see the school as a VET [Vocational Education and Training] school—not for the academically inclined'. According to a school leader the challenge for staff is to develop the 3 Rs—rigor, relevance and relationships. The school has managed to improve options for senior students through on-line (Internet) learning and networks with other schools and TAFE institutes. Students are involved in enterprise activities including a cafe and plant nursery, and there has been a move towards more integrated curriculum in years 8 and 9, where teachers work in teams to develop programs that are more attuned to the needs of individual students.

Banksia Hill High School

With a current population of 800 students, Banksia Hill is one of oldest and the most culturally diverse schools in the Bountiful Bay Education District. Indigenous students make up 12% of enrolments, and some 52 ethnic groups are represented in the school, including recently arrived Asian immigrants. The school has a low socioeconomic index and runs an after-hour homework center and a breakfast program. Although retention rates are improving, Banksia Hill is experiencing declining enrolments and is under pressure to attract students from across the region. Maintaining viable programs and a range of subjects for academically oriented students in the senior years is especially challenging. Recent changes have led to a move away from faculty-based school organization to sub-schools and cross-curriculum teaching teams. There is a much greater emphasis on pastoral care and a more integrated approach to teaching and learning in the middle years. In common with the other high school in the region, Banksia Hill attaches a lot of importance to vocational education and work placement programs. Student engagement is further enhanced by an expansive extra-curricula program incorporating cultural, artistic, sporting, recreational and social activities. 'Kids are encouraged to *go* for things', a school leader remarked.

It is apparent from the portraits that all four schools placed a good deal of emphasis on developing a stronger sense of community through the formation of sub-schools or middle schools. Sometimes these took on a special curriculum focus, such as vocational education, maritime studies, the arts, science and technology, and sporting programs. Schools invested resources in student counseling and welfare services. We saw evidence of productive school/community partnerships. Curriculum leadership roles were increasingly oriented to curriculum and pedagogy rather than administration. We heard a good deal about individual learning plans and tailoring instruction to meet the needs and aspirations of students. We met teachers who were 'hanging in' with difficult students, developing trustful relationships and a sense of belongingness. Many were drawing on popular culture and community-based studies to enliven learning for their students. Others engaged students in entrepreneurial activities linking classroom learning to student lives. A growing spirit of cooperation between the four schools meant that students across the district had access to a pool of resources and personnel to support school and career options. But as we shall relate further into the study, a good deal of angst and tension accompanied these school reforms, not the least being the difficulties of navigating a pathway between system-driven accountability requirements and educators' knowledge of what really works for students in schools.

Methodological, philosophical and research design perspectives

Before we say something about the more specific content and organization of the book, it is appropriate that we say a little about the set of preferences that are animating our research in this book. In particular, we need to say something about our methodological approach of 'creating data' or what we term bringing it into existence—which is quite contrary to the conventional view of 'collecting data', as are our views about how to make sense of such data.

Returning to our opening comments about the resurgence of the importance of space and place in contemporary forms of social exclusion, we find Sibley's (1995) category of 'geographies of exclusion' to be most helpful. According to Sibley:

> Because power is expressed in the monopolization of space and the relegation of weaker groups in society to less desirable environments, any text on the social geography of advanced capitalism should be concerned with the question of exclusion (p. ix).

Sibley's over-arching argument is that examining the way 'exclusionary practices' operate is 'important because they are less noticed and so the ways in which control is exercised in society are concealed' (p. ix). The reason notions of socio-spatial exclusion become so important is that moving beyond opaque explanations of how such exclusion works 'require[s] an account of barriers, prohibitions and constraints on activities from the point of view of the excluded' (Sibley, 1995, p. x).

Our positioning in this book, and we readily admit to having a position, is unashamedly within the 'critical' tradition—which is to say, that we believe in the importance of research as a way of challenging the existing social order, questioning dominant practices and discourses, and interrupting the asymmetry of the way things are and the trajectory by which they came to be that way. We also believe quite passionately that, however modestly, a new and more just social order is possible. Alvesson & Deetz (2000) put this idea succinctly when they said:

> Critical research generally aims to disrupt ongoing social reality for the sake of providing impulses to the liberation from or resistance to what dominates and leads to constraints in human decision making (p. 1).

This is not to suggest that we believe in adopting a negative, fault-finding or carping view simply in order to be difficult or to be troublesome. To a degree, we endorse the view that all research ought to be 'critical' in the everyday sense of demanding the existence of reason. But we believe that research ought to go a lot further than this in contributing to the construction of a fairer, more equitable and just world. We agree with Alvesson and Deetz (2000) that the former refers more to 'criticism', while the latter is more about 'critique'.

To stick with Alvesson and Deetz (2000) for a moment longer, we also concur with them that it is not possible 'to tak[e] the native's point of view seriously without [also] questioning the wider context of it or the processes forming it' (p. 1). In this we also part company with some well-known critical theorists who roundly eschew the idea of getting their digits dirty by puddling around in the real world and who are 'known for their lack of interest in conducting empirical work' (p. 2). We strongly believe that in the pursuit of research it is only possible to makes sense of the world through 'careful empirical work' (p. 2), and that theories of critique only have robustness when they are informed by rigorous and careful analyses of the everyday lives and practices of people. Critical social science, which is the larger set of ideas that go beyond criticism and fault finding, has a number of quite explicit platforms, or as Brookfield (1987) put it, four major components:

1. identifying and challenging assumptions behind ordinary ways of perceiving, conceiving, and acting;
2. recognizing the influence of history, culture, and social positioning on beliefs and actions;
3. imaging and exploring extraordinary alternatives, ones that may disrupt routines and established orders;
4. being appropriately skeptical about any knowledge or solution that

claims to be the only truth or alternative. (summarized in Alvesson & Deetz, 2000, p. 8).

The study reported upon in this book is in the style of a 'multi-locale *critical* ethnography' (Marcus, 1998) in the sense that we were trying to immerse ourselves in two quite disparate research sites, while trying to transcend the limitations of 'place-focused, single site ethnography [which] provides very partial views of social processes with which it might be concerned' (p. 49). Our style, in the vein of Marcus' (1998) multi-sited ethnographies, is very much of a 'pastiche' (p. 49) kind that is looking for 'complex connections' (p. 53).

According to Marcus (1998), multi-sited ethnography of the kind we were attempting, promises a 'sense of wholism' (p. 5), or at least a study that aspires to 'imaging the whole', in ways that might not otherwise be possible. What also occurs is the creation of a kind of 'research imaginary' (p. 6) that provides something of a license to experiment or engage in 'circumstantial activism' (p. 6), rather then be constrained by a somewhat rigid research methodology. The kind of 'estrangement (or defamiliarization)' (p. 14) necessary for this to occur, can only come about by working across boundaries. Furthermore, as Marcus (1998) argues, because multi-sited ethnographies focus attention 'on mapping ... [the] complex spaces into which fieldwork literally moves' (p. 19), there is less of a danger of 'overtheorization' as the voices of informants are 'allowed to 'breathe' ... before theory kicks in' (p. 18).

From this vantage point we posed a number of investigatory probes that helped frame our thinking and inquiry as we sought to understand how the most educationally disadvantaged, marginalized and excluded groups of young people might be recuperated in ways that enabled them to improve their life chances through the benefits of education. We framed these probes at the level of some 'how to' or 'how come' questions of the following kind:

- how do disadvantaged schools and their communities 'read' the issue of disadvantage and its impact on their educational outcomes and futures?
- how do disadvantaged schools and their communities situate, understand and confront the wider 'causes' of educational under achievement?
- how do disadvantaged 'insiders' develop alternatives to the 'official' deficit views of educational disadvantage?
- how can educational debate be refocused away from so-called 'students at risk' towards more optimistic scenarios of how to enhance learning

within which local voices can be heard and have significant ownership in shaping young educational destinies. What we present here are some counter-narratives that puncture the long-perpetrated myth of a pathological view of disadvantage. Quite to the contrary, what we find emerging are community strengths and assets built around an optimistic set of views, not withstanding some setbacks, that belie the stigmatized, one-dimensional and stereotypical views often portrayed about disadvantage that make it difficult for such people to maintain a collective sense of courage, pride, and hope.

2. *Engaging excluded communities around knowledge* (Chapter 3): in this chapter we explore how at the level of a group of schools in the community of Bountiful Bay, what occurs within and through the community has a profound effect on the way young people perceive themselves and value their community. From a situation in which disadvantaged communities often tend to 'stand off' or distance themselves from (or be actively 'distanced by') schools for understandable reasons, this chapter explores when schools regard communities as having strengths which can be used to (re)engage young people in learning. Both the school and the home are presented as 'sites of pedagogic acquisition', in which the problem of educational wastage of working-class potential is confronted head-on by acknowledging the 'funds of knowledge' (Moll, et al., 1992) possessed by these communities. We explore how this is worked through in Bountiful Bay schools through a place-based pedagogy that draws the community into the school.

3. *Engaging in policy and educational reform that is respectful of young lives* (Chapter 4): this chapter pauses to reflect on some of the major concepts drawn upon in the book so far, and in doing so it deconstructs and analyzes the meanings behind some of the taken-for-granted and apparently benign terms like 'community', 'social inclusion' and 'educational reform'. It steps behind some of the unexamined shibboleths like 'neighborhood renewal' and explains why we need to exercise a modicum of caution. Likewise, it exposes the flawed logic behind the current dominant ideology of 'school effectiveness' and argues that it is only when we create dialogic space that marginalized and excluded communities can challenge and expose the faulty deficit logics within which they have become encased. Through the voices and stories of the informants in Wirra Wagga, this chapter displays something of the layered complexities across school and community boundaries that

need to be traversed if real and meaningful change is to occur. To put it in a single word, this chapter is about 'respect' in all of its multi-faceted aspects.

4. *Engaging youth and popular culture* (Chapter 5): there can be no more tangible testimony as to whether a school is truly connected to its students from backgrounds of disadvantage than whether it is prepared to let go and genuinely embrace the lives and aspirations of its students, and put these at the center of what the school does. This is not a matter of embroidery! This chapter illustrates how the Bountiful Bay schools were prepared to take this courageous step, because the alternative is schools that have metal detectors, and security guards, and that go into lock-down mode. As this chapter shows, this is not only an issue of trust, but it is also a profound act of courage in a climate that believes that all manner of deviance in schools can be settled by means of managerialism and accountability, preferably within a context in which the market is allowed to have the final say. There can be absolutely no doubt that for schools like those in communities like Wirra Wagga and Bountiful Bay, and their equivalents in other countries, that there is a need to start in a very different place—one that builds relationships and pursues educational rigor from within rather than against young lives. For young people who find schools toxic or antagonistic, there can be no other way—it is either that or join the exodus!

In the final chapter, Chapter 6, we draw the ideas presented in the book to a close, and join in a resounding round of applause for the schools and the communities in our research that were prepared to step outside the square and to imagine, paraphrasing Counts (1932), how they might 'dare [to] . . . build a new social order'.

 TWO

Engaging Socially Critical Educators and Community Activists

Introduction

Many millions of words and pages of text have passed through publishing houses and over journal editors' desks over the past couple of decades supporting the need for socially critical educators as well as community-minded advocates able to do great feats in disadvantaged and urban schools. It is almost as if, to use the words of Peck and Tickell (1994) we have been in search of some 'new institutional fix', yet educational practice would suggest that we seem to be getting further rather than closer to this most elusive of ideals.

The purpose of this chapter is threefold: (1) to explore through a *community voice* perspective what is meant by the idea of democratic community engagement; (2) to explore the nature of the relationship between community renewal and school reform *for* disadvantaged young people; and (3) to explain how notions of community renewal and educational organizing for school reform (Fruchter, 2007, p. 136) are crucial to advancing *critically engaged learning that connects to young lives*. In pursuing these three inter-related purposes we want to try and advance what we believe to be the role of critically minded educators and community organizers in trying to produce the conditions for breaking the debilitating cycle of educational disadvantage and social exclusion.

With this in mind we want to argue in this chapter that part of the problem with the elusive but fruitless search for the next institutional fix is not only its misleading simplicity, but also the compelling absence of a theoretical, sociological or philosophical category capable of carrying or propelling such a significant agenda. To invoke Brown (1990), maybe what we need is some 'genre-stretching' (pp. 57–58)—by which he means, ways of departing from accepted rules, ways of thinking, paradigms, and forms of representation so as to construct new and exciting meanings, relationships and language with which to know and represent reality. Brown (1990) refers to 'genre thickening' as the opposite, in which accepted ways of thinking and acting atrophy because they are based on 'tightly coded descriptions, and semiotic denseness' (p. 57). According to Brown (1990), 'Genre stretching or mixing fosters scientific or artistic revolutions, the shaping of new paradigms, the creation through articulation of a reality in formation' (p. 58).

In pursuing what might be involved in engaging educators along with community members in socially critical action in disadvantaged schools and communities, we want to start this genre-stretching by borrowing from and building upon the notion of 'free spaces'—a term first popularized by Evans and Boyte (1986), and that has since been used by sociologists—but not with much traction it would seem—'to provide [the] institutional anchor for the cultural challenge that explodes structural arrangements' (Polletta, 1999, p. 1).

According to Polletta (1999), free spaces, as the term has come to be used, refers to:

> ...small-scale settings within a community or movement that are removed from the direct control of dominant groups, are voluntarily participated in, and generate the cultural challenge that precedes or accompanies political mobilization (p. 1).

The essence of what is meant by the concept of free space, was put by Evans and Boyte (1986) in terms of public places in the community:

> ...in which people are able to learn a new self-respect, a deeper and more assertive group identity, public skills, and values of cooperation and civic virtue. Put simply, free spaces are settings between private lives and large scale institutions where ordinary citizens can act with dignity, independence and vision (p. 17).

We are concerned here with what Polletta (1999) argues are not the counter-hegemonic ideas that come from 'free-floating oppositional consciousness',

but rather ideas and ideals that are rooted in 'long-standing community institutions' (p. 1). In other words, the theoretical appeal of a term like *free space* lies in the fact that 'not only does it discredit a view of the powerless as deludedly acquiescent to their domination' (p. 1), but on the contrary, it posits that they are capable of creating and pursuing through rich interactive networks, alternative visions of the future. Put most directly:

> ... the free space concept shows that the oppressed are not without the resources to combat their oppressions ... [and that they] are able to penetrate the prevailing common sense that keep most people passive in the face of injustice ... (p. 3).

Free spaces have the potential to:

> ... insulate the challenging group from the rationalizing ideologies normally disseminated by society's dominant group (Hirsh cited in Polletta, 1999, p. 3).

It hardly comes as a new revelation that metaphors powerfully shape how we think and act, and at the moment there is considerable attention being paid in the social sciences to the notion that 'space matters' (Massey, 1984, p. 14) in enabling or constraining social action and change. Indeed, in understanding urban poverty, Gotham (2003) argues that we need to move beyond the benign view of 'space-as-container ontology' (p. 723), to a much more politicized view of space being an active player in shaping meaning, action and behavior. The reasons this is necessary Gotham (2003) argues, is that 'socio-spatial relations and conflicts can illuminate our understanding of change' (p. 723). To put this another way, 'spatial boundaries, identities and meanings are negotiated, defined and produced through social interactions, social conflict and struggles between different groups' (p. 723).

The potency of the 'spatial turn', as Soja (2000) described it, lies in its 'in-between[ness]' or the capacity it provides for those of us in education, to work 'in the space in-between' (p. 171), or 'to work with the tension, the relationship in-between' (Vadeboncoeur, Hirst & Kostogriz, 2006, pp. 171–172).

The merits of the kind of theoretical turn being canvassed here, for researching and advancing knowledge around the little understood boundary between *community renewal* and *school reform or reinvention*, lie in:

- recognizing that dynamic, fluid and turbulent relationships require moving beyond static or fluid approaches;
- acknowledging that multiple identities are continually in the process of being deformed, re-formed and re-normed;

- grasping potentially more inclusive and empowering ways of re-imagining a set of relationships that have historically been characterized by hierarchy, domination, subservience, denigration and dependence;
- shifting from centralized ways of thinking, to 'regions, districts, communities, schools and classrooms' (Kostogriz, 2006, p. 179) so that these become the new 'nodal points' of knowledge production; and
- focusing on 'boundaries as sites of learning' in ways that present forms of critical and collaborative analysis that go beyond patterns of 'domination' and 'resistance' (Kostogriz, 2006, p. 188).

To put the argument contained in these points most directly. Rather than running after yet another elusive 'new institutional fix', as Peck and Tickell (1994) so aptly put it, what we need instead is to confront and change situations of entrenched social and educational disadvantage, through better ways of thinking and acting across boundaries. In reviewing Anyon's (2005) seminal work *Radical Possibilities*, Shirley (2007) argued that contesting inequalities in urban and disadvantaged schools present us with 'a major political problem' (p. 503), the nature of which is the schism or disconnect between school reformers and social and community activists. As Anyon (2005a) put it:

> School reformers and community organizers, in fact, rarely talk to each other; they typically operate in different social circles. Most school reform groups are from university, funding, or government arenas, and community organizers are usually from neighborhood or political activist spheres. There is little communication or co-operation (pp. 185–186).

The result, according to Anyon (2005a) is that:

> ...most urban school reforms are not successful in part because the community is not behind them, and often actively mistrusts them (p. 186).

It is clear, therefore, that we need to be talking and acting much more in terms of what Mediratta and Fruchter (2001; 2002) and others (Shirley, 1997; 2002; Fruchter, 2007) refer to as 'education organizing'—which is another way of saying, a fusing of 'community organizing with educational change' (Shirley, 2007, p. 503), or an approach in which 'street-level problems' rather than being parked at the school gate are actually regarded as 'classroom problems', and vice versa.

To summarize the direction of the argument we are developing in this chapter: In the first instance, we want to render problematic the notion of 'community renewal' and the unproblematic use of the 'metaphor of 'community' to imagine the social relations of mutuality and reciprocity' (Kostogriz and Peeler, 2007, p. 110). We want to do this within a context of the lived experiences of a group of 'disadvantaged' schools, their teachers, students, parents and community members.

Secondly, we want to develop a reading of these matters from the vantage point of the lived experiences of these participants, of how they experienced the politics of exclusion and marginalization, as well how they understood an attempt at inclusion through a process of school and community renewal.

Some early questions that suggest themselves for interrogation are:

- how have participants come to understand the label of 'disadvantage'?
- how do they present themselves in ways other than as victims?
- how have they created spaces for themselves as active agents?
- how have they been able to work in the tensions between relationships?
- how have they been able to collaborate with agencies in creating spaces for community activism? and
- what part do teachers and community activists play as socially critical educators?

What does it mean to create critical spaces for socially critical educators and community activists?

In the context of how a process of school and community renewal can act as a focal turning point in a community that has experienced inter-generation disadvantage, we want to argue that creating socially critical spaces involves a number of distinct orientations and dispositions that include:

- being prepared to endure discomfort by 'speaking the unpleasant' (Chavez & O'Donnell, 1998)
- admitting our own implicatedness in social injustice
- having the conviction and the courage to ask how inequality and disadvantage are perpetrated and maintained
- placing the interests of the most excluded and marginalized individuals at the center

- asking questions about who benefits and who loses from particular arrangements
- preparedness to interrupt comfortable and habitual ways of doing things and to be regarded by others as out of sync or out of fashion
- finding ways in which outside agencies, teachers, students and community activists can sustain conversations about these matters in a context of solidarity
- continually asking the question: how can a community and its young people be given social power? i.e. how to make them powerful people
- continually promoting the view of the school and its community as a 'capababilities-oriented' institution?
- working in ways that equip such communities to not only survive but to work against the grain
- above all, having a wider vision about what is important.

As we will try to demonstrate shortly through the voiced accounts of community and school participants, these are ideological positions that need to be understood and continually foregrounded in the way things happen.

To return for a moment to our opening argument about the need to find critical spaces within which to work in contexts of disadvantage, we believe that what is centrally involved here is a process of locating the contradictions within educational policy, and then finding viable ways of inhabiting and capitalizing on them.

An example of what we have in mind that illustrates the space that can emerge within educational policy contradictions is captured by Troman, Jeffrey and Raggl (2007) in their UK research into the ways in which cultures of performativity, on the one hand, shape the work of elementary teachers. By performativity they mean policies that bear down upon and that require teachers to 'perform' in terms of enhancing international economic competitiveness—through complying with target setting, inspection, national testing, league tables, performance management, merit pay, etc. On the other hand, this policy trajectory is seemingly undermined by what Troman et al. (2007) note in the UK is an emerging countervailing policy tendency framed in terms of a discourse of creativity. This latter tendency is being fed by a realization in the wider 'knowledge industries' that 'the creativity of the worker is the new resource of labour power to be tapped for increased performance and prosperity in the twenty-first century' (p. 556). In short, promoting creative learning, they argue, revolves around key notions of 'relevance, control, ownership and innovation' (p. 556).

At one level the message for teachers in all of this could not be clearer; namely, making teaching and learning relevant means 'devising activities in which learners take control and ownership and facilitating learners' innovative opportunities' (p. 556). However, at a practical level the message is by no means unequivocal—it is not a case of teachers being given the licence to stop responding to the unremitting emphasis on performativity and standards and being urged to start embracing creativity. It is rather a case of continuing to embrace the former while also embracing the latter, and 'woe betide anyone who doesn't' (Webb & Vulliamy, 2006, p. 5).

Bringing about substantial and sustained change necessary with the most educationally marginalized and excluded students requires a much more sophisticated and nuanced approach than that embodied in the performativity agenda. It inheres much more in the issues identified by Troman and Woods (2001), around:

- student ownership of learning
- students seeing the relevance of what they learn
- an acknowledgment that disadvantaged students learn in varied and multiple ways, and teaching needs to be innovative
- the needs of these students have to be addressed through multi-agency approaches.

Against this policy background, it is demonstrably the case that students from contexts that put them at an educational disadvantage require highly creative educational responses rather than a one-size-fits-all approach. Teachers need a teaching context other than one of 'unremitting performative pressures', one that is characterized much in terms of working with 'local communities by building social capital' (Troman et al., 2007, p. 552). Creative educational responses in contexts of disadvantage are required because:

- students often present with multiple and complex forms of disadvantage—health, poverty, housing, transience, etc
- their home backgrounds are often grossly at variance with the middle-class ethos and message systems of schools
- parental backgrounds (and often expectations of schools), have been formed by incomplete experiences of schooling, along with less than satisfying or rewarding experiences
- there are often issues of student care and safety that have to be accorded precedence and high priority

- the overall demeanor and disposition of the middle-class notion of schooling does not always connect with notions of disadvantage in a consistently positive way.

The Joseph Rowntree Foundation's (2007) wide-ranging analysis of children's experiences of poverty and educational disadvantage makes the point that:

> A key message of the evidence summarized here is that equality of educational opportunity cannot rely solely on better delivery of the school curriculum for disadvantaged groups, but must address multiple aspects of disadvantaged children's lives (p. 3).

Comer's (1996) notion that it requires the rallying of a whole village to raise a child, is in the metaphorical quarter and nicely sums up what we are talking about when considering the issues of educating students in contexts of disadvantage. It does require a critical level of engagement across a broad spectrum with a number of distinct commitments that include:

- a preparedness to understand students' lives and to place this knowledge at the center of pedagogical efforts
- a willingness to work with students as well as the communities they come from
- a respect for background and differences, no matter how complex
- regarding students as having assets and strengths different from middle-class students, rather than considering what they present to school with as 'deficits'
- building curriculum and learning around the experiences of students in the communities they come from; in other words, regarding the community as a potentially 'rich resource'
- working to create and recreate a positive community and affirming student identity
- actively listening to hopes and aspirations in order to jointly construct viable educational visions and pathways for students' futures
- incorporating student voice and ownership of learning into educational approaches.

The consistent message from the UK research is that children from less advantaged backgrounds feel 'less in control in school, because they [are] under pressure to perform required tasks in which they lack confidence'. These children see schools as places that are 'controlling and coercive' and that do not 'give them the space to build co-operative relationships with teachers and other adults' (Joseph Rowntree Foundation, 2007, p. 7).

These are all matters that pertain in a central way to confronting and tackling issues of protracted educational disadvantage in Australia, as well. In reinforcing a point that is central to this chapter, the Joseph Rowntree Foundation (2007) synthesis of research found that the most compelling imperative in re-engaging young people in learning and keeping them so, was:

> ... to build close relationships, not just with young people but with the families, addressing the family circumstances as well as the child's learning needs, and making education a shared enterprise between family, educator and child (p. 8).

The starting point as Anyon (2005a) cogently put it, is one around enabling young people and community members to understand that poverty and disadvantage 'arises from systemic rather than personal failings' (p. 189), and that re-constituting community identity begins with a process of documenting, 'mapping' and analyzing the community's inventory of 'gifts, skills and capacities' (Kretzmann and McKnight, 1993, p. 5). These become the basis for a community to re-invigorate its view of itself, and they also become educative candidates or an 'opportunity structure' (Anyon, 2005a, p. 191) around which students can begin to explore the resourceful nature of their community.

Opening up free spaces for socially critical action

If there is a single idea that encapsulates what was occurring in the disadvantaged community of Wirra Wagga around school and community renewal, then it can best be expressed in terms of de-institutionalizing relationships. By this we mean decoupling, unshackling, deconstructing and above all challenging the debilitating 'deficit' ways of thinking (Valencia, 1997) about disadvantage, and replacing them with a process of imagining alternatives that are located in the experiences of the people in these communities themselves, including young people. This means addressing pervasive mythologies and unsettling dominant positions, and pursuing Evans and Boyte's (1992) question:

> What are the structures of support, the resources, and the experiences that generate the capacity and the inspiration to challenge 'the way things are' and imagine a different world ? (p. 2).

Above all such approaches involve rejecting and exposing the manifest limitations of the flawed 'culture of poverty' theory (Lewis, 1961) which continues to be sustained through the work of contemporary American educational entrepreneur, Ruby Payne (1998; 2002) and Payne, DeVol and Smith (2006).

Critiquing Lewis' work and the way it has been appropriated by policy makers because of its apparent simplicity, Foley (1997) points to its major flaw as lying in its view that:

> ... people living in poverty tend to create a unique, self-sustaining life-style or way of life marked by a host of negative values, norms and social practices. The culture of poverty that is allegedly passed on to successive generations consisted of 70 traits which can be compressed into four clusters: 1) basic attitudes, values and the character and structure of poor people; 2) the nature of the poor's family system; 3) the nature of the slum community; and 4) the poor's social and civic relationship with the larger society (p. 115).

This is not the place in which to do a full-blown critique of Lewis and by association Payne (see for example, the following who have done that: Gorski, 2005; 2006; Bohn, 2006; Bomer, Dworin, May & Semingson, 2008; Osei-Kofi, 2005; Ng & Rury, 2006). Suffice to say that what is most problematic about this 'cultural traits' view of poverty is that it:

> ... evokes a powerful negative image of poor people as a lazy, fatalistic, hedonistic, violent distrustful people living in common law unions, as well as dysfunctional, female-centered authoritarian families who are chronically unemployed and rarely participate in local civic activity, vote or trust the police and political leaders (Foley, 1997, p. 115).

Its ultimate limitation lies in the 'powerful metaphor [it] spawns [of] a sweeping, holistic image' and the accompanying danger, in that it 'provides public policy makers and the general public with a relatively nontechnical, yet 'scientific' way to categorize and characterize all poor people' (p. 115).

When we refuse to accept such simplistic, demeaning, patronizing, individualist, victim-blaming and dependent mentalities, then we open up a very different space within which agencies can work with communities of disadvantage. The defining hallmarks are ones that acknowledge dignity, respect, complexity, diversity and the assets, strengths and agency that actually resides in these communities. Foley (1997) argues that when studies of disadvantaged communities are informed by a cultural anthropology perspective that is not embedded in a view of hapless and hopeless communities, then the 'solutions' are much less driven from outside, and are characterized much more by unacknowledged internal strengths. He says: 'Far from being passive and fatalistic . . . [they] are active in civic and school affairs and draw upon a rich fund of community knowledge' (p. 124).

The kind of cultural production perspective that researchers like Zou and Trueba (2001) and Levinson, Foley and Holland (1996) and others adopt, is one in which 'subordinate groups are actively constructing positive individual and cultural identities' that emphasize 'cultural pride and community practices which empower individuals and groups' (Foley, 1997, p. 124). What more hopeful and optimistic approaches like this do, is to effectively deposit 'the culture of poverty concept of culture and deficit view of thinking in the dustbin of history' (p. 124)—notwithstanding its self-serving resurrection by opportunists like Payne.

To draw this discussion to some closure; when we refer to de-institutionalizing relationships what we mean is a process of actively stepping outside of the language and deficit practices that subordinate and devalue communities of disadvantage, and present them as having to be more tightly controlled and in a sense re-made by those who supposedly know better.

The broader context within which the term 'institutionalization' sits is the international development literature, and in particular, those aspects that derive from notions of 'colonial rule' and the 'implantation of metropolitan education institutions in the colonized world' (Samoff, 2003, p. 53). These were models that drew heavily upon 'borrowing and imposition' and invoked 'authoritative leadership' and 'tacit acquiescence' (p. 61) as the way of 'solving' problems through the resuscitation of so-called 'modernization'. The tactics involved explanations of problems as residing in the 'characteristics and (in)abilities of the poor' (p. 58). In other words, 'solutions' were seen as being akin to the 'medical metaphor' of teams of 'visiting clinicians [who] diagnose then prescribe . . . [and] the patient (i.e., the country) must be encouraged, perhaps even pressured, to swallow the bitter medicine' (p. 51). The consequence, according to Samoff (2003) is that 'learning disappears from view, buried by the focus on finance' (p. 51).

In our work relating to education, we put it like this:

> . . . when schools are assailed with policies, regulations and requirements that demand increasingly institutionalisation of relationships, then some degree of relational corrosion with students is inevitable. In other words, when there is increasing formalization of relationships between students, teachers, the administration of the school and system policy-makers, there is a depersonalization as each layer is pushed to communicate with other layers through officially sanctioned discourses. Policies, practices and strategies are not of teachers' own making, and over which they have only limited

discretionary control (Smyth & McInerney, 2007a, pp. 156–157).

Against this discursive backdrop, we want to turn now to what sense the members of the Wirra Wagga community made of the opportunity to become involved in a process of school and community renewal and the portents this holds for the wider project of educational engagement of disadvantaged young people. While the over-arching theme is one of de-institutionalizing relationships, the sub-themes embedded within it were ones around:

- Community ownership
- Taking responsibility
- Direction, hope, possibility and purpose.

Rather than trying to artificially extricate these themes, we will leave them in the embedded narratives of the school and community members in Wirra Wagga.

Figure 2.1: Themes in critical community and school engagement

Puncturing the myths: counter-narratives that go beyond pathologizing disadvantage

The stories we want to present next, are in stark contrast to the stereotypical stick figure portrayals and pathological views of disadvantage and poverty offered by people like Ruby Payne. What they reveal is something about what happens within a context of externally fostered community and school renewal, when there is a commitment to respect and dignity. It shows people who are certainly struggling as a result of circumstances they have been dealt, but these stories also reveal a strong sense of history and pride in their community, and aspirations and hopes for the future for themselves and their children. There is a sense that the community renewal process was opportune in Wirra Wagga in that it provided a timely focus with which to open up spaces for dialogue and action, and in some instances, legitimation and affirmation for community and self-identity, something that was not well understood outside the community.

Story: 'We feel we can stand up and make a difference; that's what we didn't have before'

We need to be careful not to over-romanticize the effect of community renewal or to buy too far into the 'romance of civil society' (Shirley, 2007, p. 503), and in the process to inadvertently disempower the community by suggesting that nothing of value existed before, because that would be far from the truth. There have certainly been advances as a result of the community renewal process in Wirra Wagga, but to suggest that it was all hopeless beforehand, would be to play to ill-informed perceptions. A fourth generation community resident, Sally Lomax, who works in the community project as a communications officer, argued that the project has provided the vehicle for focusing and legitimating community pride:

> I'm very passionate about renewal but things have happened because the foundation was already there; neighborhood renewal has been the vehicle for change.
>
> There are a lot of unfounded perceptions about Wirra Wagga—about the lack of pride in the community, high crime rates and safety concerns. For me there has not been a great change since the community renewal program began because our family has always been involved in the neighborhood and we've known about the strengths of the community. When people say that there are people that don't come out of their houses and that there is a transient population that's not accurate at all. There have been changes that drive it but this has gone through periods before. People take more pride in their properties and they have fences now that's changed, but the heart and the soul is the same. It's always been there . . .

Sally is also quick to point to the way the media has in the past delighted in conveying and reinforcing simplified and stigmatized stereotypes, to the detriment of more positive images:

> Unfortunately the whole community gets labelled because of the bad effects of one or two families. The media thrive on this. If someone finds a dead dog in a dumpster the media really beats it up, even though anyone could have put it there. They should be giving some coverage to all the positive effects of the renewal program but it just won't happen here. There has certainly been a perception that this is not a safe community and that we have police here all the time, but it's an insult to the community. The crime rate is not high and we don't have safety fences around our school. . . . We hear all the talk about 'those low lives' and 'they can't do this and they can't do that'. Our children do get bullied and those sorts of things do happen. But this generation of children will tell anyone who will listen that they are from Wirra Wagga and maybe that's what this renewal project has done. It's given them pride.

Residents in communities like Wirra Wagga can spot fake ownership, having experienced past government efforts that had left them excluded or let down. On this occasion, they made it clear they would not accept token participation. They left no doubt as to the conditions on which community renewal was to proceed. Speaking about their suspicion of 'government speak' that did not translate into action, Sally put it like this:

> I think without the visual things it's harder because the government comes to us and says that this is what we are going to do for you but you never see where the money has gone. In the community they said that 'yes this is another government project and nothing will happen and we won't have a say'.
> The government came back with a large action plan and we just put it in the bin. The one you have [pointing to a document] is the second one which the residents put together. We said that we would put it together. We wrote our vision and interviewed the residents and we decided on the format, not a great big boring document—when it went back to government they didn't want our logo on it but we had this big fight and got our logo on it. That action plan was very important to us and everything that happens has to come from the residents and if we don't like it it's just not going to happen.

Contrary to the view that people in disadvantaged communities are all fractured and fragmented and without any sense of civic pride or desire for participation, Sally raised the specter of the real risk of volunteer 'burnout' and the frustration that comes with democratization, as the tension around extended talk results in delays in seeing tangible results.

> Over about 18 months we had a lot of meetings and we were all burned out. There was a lot of talking and not much happening. The people needed to see

things happening in their community. Some of the things that have made a difference are the park, the shops and the fences which have given privacy—you don't have the next-door neighbor driving across your lawn.

What is above all most significant about this story is the sense of pride in community expressed by Sally that is quite at odds with the stigmatized and denigrated perceptions held by outsiders. Rather, there is a sense of undeserved 'put downs' that fail to recognize or acknowledge community strengths that might be different from those of the dominant surrounding middle-class community. A history of a lack of respect towards communities like Wirra Wagga does not augur well for the self-confidence necessary to foster educational aspirations in the young in communities like Wirra Wagga.

Spatial aspects are not irrelevant here either. With a long-standing well-defined geographic boundary distinguishing it from more affluent nearby suburbs, Wirra Wagga has always been susceptible to the kind of 'othering' discourse Lister (2004) refers to as a way of demarcating and distinguishing 'them from us'. This is the means, she says, by which 'the more powerful 'non-poor' construct the 'poor' as Other' and 'Othering may be most marked where inequality is the sharpest' (p. 102). Reflecting the sentiments of Sally's comments, Lister (2004) says:

> It is a dualistic process of differentiation and demarcation, by which the line is drawn between 'us' and 'them'—between the more and less powerful—and through which social distance is established and maintained (p. 101).

Lister (2004) argues that this is not a 'neutral line, for it is imbued with negative value judgments that construct 'the poor' variously as a source of moral contamination, a threat, an 'undeserving' economic burden and an object of pity or even as an exotic species' (p. 101). The discursive shift 'from othering to respect' (Lister, 2004) and the accompanying construction of a more appropriate policy agenda 'to address children's and family poverty and exclusion, is not well developed' (Cass, 2007, p. 4) in countries like Australia. The reality is that low-income families are not by and large being given a voice in articulating their aspirations, the multiple obstacles they confront, or what might need to be organized differently for them.

Story: 'We want a hand up not a handout'

Fundamentally re-working institutionalized relationships that had traditionally characterized communications between people in this community and outside agencies and wider perceptions of the community, in ways that debunked unhelpful stereotypical images, was regarded as being crucial to the community identity formation process that was underway here.

Despite being warned by his case worker against moving to this community, Warren Kane moved to Wirra Wagga in 2001 with a life history of substance abuse, drug dealing, crime and imprisonment that had left him with little sense of agency and an angry attitude towards society. The turn around for him was the opportunity to become involved in the committees created by the community renewal program. Not only did Warren become an enthusiastic supporter for the program, but he also became the principal spokesperson for the community at local, regional and state forums.

He offers a counter-narrative about the joys of living in a community where people really care for each other and accept newcomers for who they are rather than judging them according to their past or their appearance. Warren is quite emphatic about the capacity of people to rejuvenate their community with the support of external agencies and the importance of rejecting the welfare mentality.

> I found that the people here accepted me for what I was, not what I looked like and all the drugs I did in the past.
>
> Today it's 4 years 10 months and 4 days since I have taken drugs. I haven't had a drink for 28 years when my younger son was born. Alcohol made me very angry. I went to Pentridge prison [high security prison] and joined AA [Alcoholics Anonymous] and instead of using that as a crutch I went on downers and that. Yes, for the first time in 36 years, I thought, I could do this without medical help. When we had the first committee meeting and I was sitting opposite two policemen and a person from the department of justice and they were videoing this, I knew that they would go and find out who Warren was. But I could see that this program was going to work because these people just accepted me. I thought they might think 'what is this going to be like with a junkie on the committee'. I thought 'Well I could piss in a bottle for you'.

Warren speaks eloquently about the confusion he encountered when he first experienced de-institutionalized relationships in the community renewal project. After of lifetime of loss of power and agency he was understandably confounded when he was not only treated respectfully but his opinions were sought and valued.

> At the beginning I used to get angry with the women at Community House [local center for community education programs and neighborhood activities].

> Whenever I asked a question they never answered it; instead they sent me away with more questions for myself. They never told me to do anything. I was used to being told to do everything, even go to the toilet when I was in jail.

Warren summarized how community ownership was inscribed in the renewal process right from the start through the remarkable vision of a local state politician who had a worldview beyond a 'them versus us' mentality. What had to change were people and attitudes, even though improving housing and the environmental surrounds might have been a convenient vehicle.

> [They] spent two years setting this up to make sure that residents were involved. They wanted the residents to have the input and make the decision. They put a face to the department of housing that made this possible. When there was razor wire around the office of housing it was a case of us and them. Then it just all seemed to come together. Originally a lot of the job programs aimed to beautify and improve the environment, but its not just bricks and mortar, it's about people. It was about building us, not just our houses. In the long run, it enabled us to call our houses our homes. They found that we were not just idiots. 'Consult us don't insult us' we said.

Warren's story gives us something of a unique window into the relationships rebuilding process that is so crucial to the renovation of communities like Wirra Wagga and indirectly, the educational engagement of its young people. When all of the hype and rhetoric surrounding the notion of 'capacity building' is stripped away, what we are left with are stories like those of Warren. What his experience demonstrates is the capacity of people in poverty to reinvent themselves when they are provided with the space in which to move out of the straight-jacket of institutionalized constraints and relationships that have been held in place through stigmatizing and stereotyping.

Warren's story is illustrative of what was being attempted in the UK 'voices for change process' that occurred through the Commission on Poverty, Participation and Power (2000) *Listen Hear: the Right to be Heard* report. The focus in that instance, as in the one Warren found himself in, was not exclusively on issues of poverty per se, but rather on 'issues surrounding the participation of people experiencing poverty in the decisions and policies affecting their lives' (del Tufo & Gaster, 2002, p. 88). All of this is by way of making the significant point that it is crucial to focus on issues of participation and power as they are connected to poverty. Warren's experience is a reflection of what can happen when there is a genuine commitment to achieve change based upon 'involving people with a direct experience of poverty' (del Tufo & Gaster, 2002, p. 2).

Story: 'If you want to use it you have to fix it'

There are often stereotypical portrayals of people in disadvantaged communities as being firebrands, as being conflictual, and as having a predisposition towards dealing with matters in direct and head-on ways. Critiquing the values and beliefs behind Ruby Payne's 'culture of poverty' and the view she has of a subculture perpetuated from one generation to the next, Osei-Kofi (2005) exposes the uni-dimensional problematic behind Payne's views as residing in:

> ...a way of life characterized by an inability to delay gratification; a belief in fatalism; a present orientation and an inability to plan for the future; a lack of emotional stamina; a high tolerance and acceptance of physical violence, crime, mental illness, and sexual promiscuity; a preoccupation with entertainment and humour; and a lack of value placed on education (p. 369).

What black and white representations like this obscure, of course, is the nuanced way in which people like Brigid Lavinsky, in the next story, often play out quite complex contradictory scenarios in serendipitous ways. We see here how events can quite unexpectedly unfold in ways that shape identity and character. The story is a nice one because of the way it shows what happens when institutional relationships are put aside and people deal with one another at a humanized person-to-person level.

Brigid is a local public housing resident who became involved in the community renewal project almost by accident through an altercation she was having with the Department of Housing. During a visit to her house by the local community renewal project manager, Brigid's self-taught skills in computers became the point around which to defuse the tension over her housing issue. It led on to an incredible partnership in which Brigid shifted from being a feisty critic to a powerful ally, as she launched a computer club in the community which engages young people who have dropped out of schools (from ages 8–20) in rebuilding and repairing computers.

> I got involved in the renewal program through a dispute with the department of housing. I'm in public housing and proud of it. I had a window you could stick fists through and when I couldn't get any action from the department I took it all the way to the premier. I took on the government on the radio and it closed three times from all the calls. I then met Carol from the Community Renewal Center and in our discussion about the problem she said she had 60 computers that she didn't know what to do with. She knew I had some computing skills and when she came to check the house she asked if I could share my knowledge with the community. So that's how we met. We make a good team.

> Everyone thinks everything is roses, but it only gets changed because it isn't roses. I'm now running computing classes in the shopping center. Information technology scares people—so we call it a computer club.

In the way she works with young people, Brigid is also adamant in that she is not going to get caught up in the power games traditionally played between teachers and students and the power she has is of being a long-term resident and knowing the community and being respected by it. But she also sees herself as being something of an advocate.

> It's the kids' choices that they are here with me. I don't have to put up with their crap. I'm not their teacher. I've lived here since I was one year old so I know the community. I've got respect . . . I know what it's like to have $2 in your pocket. What I'm doing is helping these kids—to stand up for them . . . A lot of kids just need confidence . . . No one is the boss [here]. The social aspect of the club is huge. Kids develop confidence and pretty soon they are holding their heads up. People feel comfortable coming here.

Understanding poverty from having experienced it first hand is important to Brigid's way of presenting herself, as well as her stoic working-class way of writing off her own adversity.

> I've got two young kids no other family and I've had some spells in the hospital. I'm ok as long as I can walk—if you are not on your hands and knees dragging yourself across the floor it's a bloody good day. So far as my computing goes, I'm mostly self taught although I learnt a little from my uncle. I can't have three computers in my house and have the money to fix them . . . When people come in and say they need a computer the first thing I ask them is what you need it for . . . Too many people get ripped off by service providers. There's just not the money in this community so people have to learn to build their own computers.

If we step back a little and transcend the particularities of Brigid's case, her story provides some broader insights at several levels that hold important implications about the connections between students, schools, learning, and community. The connections are certainly not direct ones, and in many respects their very indirectness may be their major virtue.

It is clear that Brigid's case is an exemplar of what Kretzmann and McKnight (1993) refer to in the title of their book as *Building Communities from the Inside Out*. What Brigid is doing, metaphorically speaking, is 'working the ruins' of 'stuck places', to invoke the language of feminist ethnographer Patti Lather (1998, p. 488), through seizing the opportunity to reconstruct the damaged lives of young people who have been exiled from school (or exiled themselves), by having them reconstruct computers. In a very real way, Brigid is powerfully re-engaging these young people with learning but in ways that are considerably outside of the institutionalized relationships that contributed to damaging them in the first place. In the process, Brigid is also reconstituting a working-class identity in the eyes of the young people of Wirra Wagga, largely through the respect she has earned because of her knowledge and firsthand experience of having 'lived' poverty.

The message to early school leavers here is that learning can be a hands-on, grassroots, practical and fun activity that connects to the practicalities of real life, like computers. This is a powerful message to be learned by these young people. The fact that one of the enduring characteristics of protracted poverty is low levels of access to the Internet and diminished possession of personal computers, adds further poignancy to Brigid's case. Using the internal resources of the community, its young people, to turn around two protracted problems provides a further important message about the possibilities of making a productive local civic contribution. Above all, Brigid's case is one that underscores Kretzmann and McKnight's (1993) point that how people are positioned in communities like Wirra Wagga, whether at the margins as 'clients [who] have deficiencies and needs', or at the center as 'citizens [who] have capacities and gifts' (p. 13), matters profoundly.

Story: 'They owned it from day one'

The other crucial story to be told here is from the vantage point of what Lipsky (1980) calls the 'street-level bureaucrats'—the personnel from government agencies, in this case, whose job it was to find the spaces within which community ownership could be fashioned. They had to enact a crucial balancing role moving adeptly between dilemmas, contradictions and paradoxes, while exercising the right amount of leadership, orchestrating outcomes, and facilitating genuine community ownership. Street-level bureaucrats, as distinct from managers, are involved in work with high levels of uncertainty and unpredictability, enacted in contexts of inadequate resources, where deliverables are notoriously difficult to measure. As a consequence, street-level bureaucrats have 'high degrees of discretion and relative autonomy' (p. 13). What they are trying to achieve is too complex to be amenable to programmatic formulae, and the nature of the work requires high levels of human interaction in ways that make these people 'de facto policy makers' (p. 24) in the way they have to creatively resist organizational pressures while making it up for their clients as they go.

On the question of ownership, the community renewal co-ordinator, Carol Georgiadis, said there was clarity on this right from the start, although that was not the same as knowing exactly how it might operate:

> It's all very well to have visions but it was up to the residents to have the light go on. We could tell them the repercussions, but the rest came from them. They had to reach the decision themselves.

Helping a community that has historically been 'down on its luck' or that has been 'put down' often mercilessly by outsiders for generations, is a formidable and multi-layered task. Challenging stigma and stereotyping has to occur around a community moving beyond its own self-sustaining diminished expectations of itself, by actively affirming 'who we are', and in the process developing confidence in where they are going. Part of this involves outside agencies who work with the community, developing a 'listening' rather than an 'expert' or 'telling' stance. On this occasion it happened over a period of around two years in successive rounds of community meetings and committee talk-fests.

Equally important in community identity-building is the way the community presents itself to the outside world. In this community, outsiders working with the community don't speak *for* the community, as Carol put it:

> We have a very clear understanding with this community that we won't stand up and represent them. One of the first things that happened was all the 11 secretaries of all the [government] departments came here as part of a whole-government approach to community renewal. The residents presented them with all the things they wanted and outlined the things that were wrong. They owned it from day one and they would never let us talk on their behalf. It's a normal community. No one could stand up in [my community] and speak for me.
>
> Community renewal is from the bottom up and from the top down and we are the bit in the middle. We pick out people that we think can do it and they do a few things and before you know it, that person becomes a bit of a voice for the community. One of our biggest challenges was getting other residents to take part in things.

This serves the purpose of both demonstrating skills they did not acknowledge themselves as having and advancing leadership skills in the community, while at the same time debunking or puncturing simplistic outside-held stereotypes. In Carol's words:

> The more people we take outside and people don't see that they have two

heads and horns . . . and getting people to come inside here to Wirra Wagga . . . Some people embrace the term Wirra Wagga-ite and the sense of a little bit of defiance that goes with it. Some people just consider themselves to be ordinary, and there are others who have taken on the victim role. That's the hardest thing we have had to do is to take them out of the victim thing.

Just because 98% of the people in a community are cardholders [subsidized lunch program] and 46% of the houses are government owned and there are practically no people who earn income from wages, is not to say that this is not a robust and proud community with an identity of itself. According to Carol, the government lost out when it tried to do cosmetic surgery on the community by attempting to change its name:

> The community is clearly defined. If you live here you can't escape it. They tried to rename it before the renewal program was set up, but the people wouldn't have it. I think it's to do with the social fabric that has built up over the years.

That is not to say that everyone agreed with what was being attempted through the renewal process or that there were not understandable suspicions of a takeover, given the previous history of outside agencies in this community. From Carol:

> This renewal program has polarized the community. Some people thought that the Community House was being taken over and people were feeling threatened, but it was really about understanding the importance of shared facilities.

In contrast to past ineffectual efforts to either do things *to* or *for* disadvantaged people, the way Carol envisaged her job was as acting as a kind of bureaucratic insurgent—using power and knowledge of how the system operates, to work for the local community. As she put it:

> One of the best skills I bring to this community is that I was a corporate human services manager. I know what I can get away with and what I can't and I know about the paper work.

Part of the process for people like Carol is to recast the role of the outsider in authentic ways, and trust has to be earned, as the following incident indicates:

> You have to be really honest with people in this community. They have big bull

Engaging Socially Critical Educators and Community Activists ❖ 45

> shit detectors. When we first started our community discussions we tried to make people feel at home and we provided plates of sandwiches and drinks. To begin with it seemed a brilliant idea because it brought in the people. We were honest with them and we told them we would feed them, but then we started hearing things like 'How much of our 3 million dollars [the community renewal grant] is left?' So we pulled back on the food, and then we changed the meeting times.

This involves demonstrating in very tangible terms that the basis of the relationships is not a master-client one, but a true partnership:

> It's an important process to sit down with these people. Sit down and eat an apple with them, and they get confused, especially if they think that you are up here [pointing upwards]. We said we were going to call ourselves bureaucrats, but we're going to turn it into a nice word.

A major aspect of working in this way is knowing when your job is done, and the tricky business of making a dignified and honorable exit in which power is truly handed over:

> I think I still have something to give to the community and I have to be big enough to step aside when I think I have reached my use-by date.

What we see being enacted in Carols's story of a self-confessed reconstructed bureaucrat, is what might be termed a thickening of the concept of engagement around what Portelli and McMahon (2004) appropriately label a 'critical-democratic conception of engagement' (p. 40). By this they mean moving beyond a thin view of engagement that collapses down to a 'set of techniques, strategies or behaviours that are meant to be universally replicable regardless of context' and that result in what Martin (1992) describes as 'spectator citizenry' (Portelli & McMahon, 2004, p. 40). Martin (1992) argues instead for 'critical spectators' (p. 171) who are not detached and captivated in seeing and living the world though the eyes and thoughts of others, but rather active critical citizens who have learnt 'to know when to question something, and what sorts of questions to ask' (McPeck, 1981, p. 7).

The kind of critically educative process Carol is implicitly involved in with the residents of Wirra Wagga is a transformative and democratic one based on relationships that question purpose and intent and that ask 'engagement for what?' and 'in whose interest?' (Portelli & McMahon, 2004, p. 43). While Carol's interests are primarily in working with residents, her agenda is one that clearly has 'permeable boundaries between schools and communities' (p. 44) based on the recognition that there are multiple communities and that leadership in contexts of critical democratic engagement is always 'emancipatory and inclusive'. If we backward map for a moment, it is not hard to see how what Carol is doing in her critical democratic work with residents is closely connected to the need to ground the learning experiences of children in communities like Wirra Wagga in what Portelli and Vibert (2001) call a 'curriculum of life'—that is to say, that is located in students' 'immediate daily worlds as well as in the larger social and political contexts of their lives . . . [an approach that] breaks down the walls between the school and the world' (p. 63).

We will see how this works out in more detail in the next story.

Story: 'It's the best thing I've done since kinder'. 'It's about engagement at the point of need'

One of the strong markers of educational difference between young people from middle-class backgrounds in contrast to those from contexts like Wirra Wagga, is the extent to which they feel autonomous and in control of their lives, versus the extent to which they feel like they are 'people to whom things happen' (Solomon & Rogers, 2001, p. 341). Paradoxically, this is occurring in a wider context in which young people express confidence in making active choices about their lives and futures. In other words, they don't see themselves as mere cyphers being moved along by somebody else's agenda. Ball, Maguire and Macrae (2000) explain this apparent tension in terms of the 'greater diversity of . . . life experience and prolonged and extended opportunities to participate in education and training, [but of this] tend[ing] to obscure the structural and material continuities which patterned their 'choices'' (p. 4). In other words, while many young people don't think in terms of structural conditions shaping their lives, 'at least some of them perceive that they have very little autonomy and control over events or, to some extent, their own actions' (Attwood, Croll & Hamilton, 2003, p. 80).

One of the key ways this is played out in disadvantaged contexts is in terms of young people exercising choice to prematurely exit school even against their own long-term economic interests and in ways that produce social exclusion. A key instigating factor in this early exit from school is around poor relationships—with peers in terms of harassment and bullying, with teachers around perceived irrelevance of curriculum, and more broadly the inability to connect to the institution of schooling. Issues of relationships, respect, trust and care are the flashpoints that feature most prominently in the complex array of explanations around why disadvantaged young people leave school early (see: Smyth, et al., 2000; Smyth & Hattam, et al., 2004). They are also the points at which turn-arounds are most likely if these young people are to be re-engaged in learning (Smyth & McInerney, 2007b; Smyth & Fasoli, 2007).

One of the successes in Wirra Wagga has been the turn-around achieved amongst a group of young people from within the wider context of Provincetown for whom schooling has been an alienating and damaging experience. Labelled Connexions because of its obvious reference to linking up with young people who have fallen between the cracks, it provides a pathway back into learning outside of the formal institutional structures of schooling even though they receive accreditation through a high school.

From an initial start-up group of 20 students 4 years ago, the group has expanded to nearly 160. Young people are not required to formally attend a school, but rather enter into learning contracts with adult tutors who help them map out a program and monitor achievements. The program focuses on three aspects: (i) experiential learning—designed to improve confidence and self-esteem; (ii) a literacy and numeracy component; and (iii) project work around negotiated learning.

A central defining aspect of Connexions is the way in which it de-institutionalizes relationships between young people and the contexts in which they learn. This is considered crucial because it is the major reason in most cases that they have given up on formal schooling. It can be argued that Connexions de-institionalizes relationships in several ways:

- it does not require formal attendance, although there is a close monitoring of learning progress through case management
- there is no rigid timetable of the kind that occurs within the structured setting of a high school
- progress is assessed through learning portfolios and through personalized learning contracts rather than through testing regimes
- there is an acknowldgement that there can be many obstacles and interferences to learning in young people's lives, and that these need to be seriously taken into account if learning is to occur. In the words of one of the most passionate advocates and a teacher in the program, 'It's about engagement at the point of need', in the words of one of its most passionate advocates.
- there are no requirements to comply with other institutional norms that can be a major source of aggravation and distraction for many young people around school uniforms, discipline policies, substance

use, punctuality, and the like. The emphasis is upon mutual respect rather than blind adherence to rules and regulations.
- there is a belief that for these young people the restoration of confidence and self-esteem has to take precedence over formal academic achievements, at least in the first instance
- there is a genuine commitment to negotiating learning with young people around a valued learning pathway they see themselves heading along
- the most prominent defining hallmark of the approach is 'taking you as you are', in the words of one young informant, rather than to exclude, stigmatize, disparage or punish on the basis of past reputation or history.

Here are some comments from Paul Kilborn the regional school improvement officer responsible for the program, but his starting points are particularly revealing:

> Some kids it seems are hard wired for failure because of the things that happen at home. A lot of our Connexions students come from low socioeconomic backgrounds but the ones for us that are particularly difficult are from dysfunctional families. . . . school it is toxic for a lot of students.
>
> The model of instruction we have in schools—especially high schools—is an industrial model that works around a timetable set for the convenience of everyone except the people it was designed for. Schools are like prisons in some respects with long corridors, rooms on both side, and the ghettos are the lockers where things get stolen. The timetable has little to do with student outcomes—it's more about keeping things tidy. You'll find that most staff will teach towards the kids who will pay attention—that might be 15 in a class of 30. The furniture is arranged to discourage some students in that class from making contact with the teacher.
>
> Teachers in most schools tend to focus their energies on compliant/attentive kids rather than the disengaged. There is a need to develop more respectful structures and settings, especially for those kids who simply don't fit the system.

Paul's last point about more respectful structures and settings for young people who don't fit is a key launching point for Connexions. His starting position is learning 'within a setting that's more respectful of everyone', but it is important to be clear about what Connexions is not. As he put it:

> Connexions is not a dumping ground for those who can't succeed in the main-

stream. It's an extension program and these kids will go on to university or business or wherever.

The question of relevance loomed large for these young people and was cental to their re-engagement in learning, but as Paul was quick to point out, this had to be done outside of institutionalized arrangements that looked like schools:

> Pathway planning [career and future education options] became an issue for us because it had to be of benefit to them further down the track. We couldn't get them all in the same place at the same time because this was like creating a school which we wanted to avoid, so we organized different times for different students—personalized timetables—and a very basic e learning web site.

In Paul's mind there is a distinct philosophical orientation here:

> The key to our work is cooperation, perseverance, and persistence. We develop students on a continuum of need and start from where they are.
>   Each student has an individual education plan of where they are at, what were the issues at school and where they want to be. This is supported by a daily, weekly, or monthly worksheet of what they are achieving. We also have a running tally sheet of what they have done every day.

He saw the underlying commitment and aspiration as being to:

> . . . value add to their lives now, and give them the opportunity to make decisions from a position of strength . . . they can then value add back into society. It's a small price to pay.

He summed up the effect of the Connexions program by invoking the words of one young person, with an added question, when he said:

> 'it's the best thing I've done since kinder'. You have to wonder what the rest of his life has been like.

A self-confessed radical ex-teacher who was denied the opportunity of getting his ideas up in the 1980s, Ian Partridge saw himself as getting something of a 'second chance' through his involvement as a tutor in Connexions, while giving these young people some opportunities denied them during their upbringing for various reasons:

> I was attracted to Connexions because it was trying to do something for those

whose self-esteem was at rock bottom . . . kids who had the crap belted out of them . . . who were bullied in school . . . who were excluded . . . disconnected kids who carried an enormous amount of baggage.

As a local government councillor, Ian prides himself in being able to cut through the bureaucratic redtape and at the same time harness the resources of the business community to help these young people get restarted in their learning:

> I used my contacts at UFS (a pharmacy business) and told them that this was good for their company. They gave us their head beautician for a morning for 6 weeks. The girls go through makeup and hair care and they get to take home hair care products. A girl was crying at the hairdresser saying this was her first haircut ever. She was 14 year of age. Next week we are starting deportment classes at minimal cost. Students will have a portfolio at the end of the 10 weeks and they will graduate.
>
> To see some of the results we have had in the last six to seven months has been staggering.
>
> Six weeks ago these girls would have been punching the crap out of each other. Now they were sitting together having pancakes and laughing with each other. I had a strong belief in the 80s that this is the way things should have been happening but they wouldn't let me do it, so this is my second chance.

There was a high level of consistency too in the stories young people told of their reasons for not completing schooling, and the subsequent benefits they had derived from and experienced in Connexions.

While these young people's comments are only fleeting glimpses, they tell us much about the flashpoints that cause them so much angst, as well as the more affirming relationships that enabled them to re-engage with learning:

> From Melany:
>
> They take you as you are at Connexions.
> School wasn't a happy time for me. I went to 6 different elementary schools. Mum has schizophrenia and when my brother and sister moved out I had to look after her and two Pit bull terriers—they're gentle dogs if you train them.
> At school you get a bit lost in a big class and I was too easily distracted by my friends. My teachers were always telling me I was dumb except my maths teacher who used to get me on the highest level in maths. She treated me like an adult instead of a kid that didn't know anything. Most teachers didn't pay attention to us, but it's a lot different here.
> Connexions has been great for me. Before this I couldn't even look people

in the eye, but it's really easy now. I'm a lot more organized and confident.

If I had a magic wand I would get rid of schools and send everyone to Connexions. Schools put you down about everything but they take you as you are at Connexions. At school everyone is dumb but here everyone wants to learn.

Body image is a crucial element in the identity formation of young women. Jacinta was low on self-esteem when she left school but she made friends and learnt to get along with people when she joined the Connexions program. As she became more confident and self-assured she began to see the relevance of subjects like maths in her new courses of study. The turn-around in her emotional state seems to have had a positive impact on her aspirations and attitude towards education and work.

I was having trouble at school. I was in year 9 but I wasn't going to school. Connexions is easier and it's funnier than school and it's not as crowded. I don't do well around crowds. I couldn't do any of the work.

I used to be really quiet and I didn't talk, but they listen here.

The first thing I did was the beauty course and I got a certificate; I've never had a certificate before. I felt better much better about myself. We learned about makeup and cleansers and keeping your face clean. It was good and they gave you heaps of freebies. Ian (a Connexions tutor) got me into two hairdressing courses. I finished one and I am doing another one across the road with Jessica. We learnt how to wash our hair and all about hair styles. I'd like to do hairdressing and Jessica said she would give me an apprenticeship if I proved myself to her—like turning up on time and doing things without being asked.

Me and my friend talked about going back to high school next year. She tried it but she only lasted about three weeks and now she is back here. It's that school. I just didn't like it. The problem is there's a lot of bullying. . I was shy but never really picked on.

I was never good at maths at school but I can see that you need maths in hairdressing. What am I good at? I listen really good and hairdressers need to be good listeners.

Concluding comments

The need for multi-faceted approaches to analyzing entrenched disadvantage were illustrated in this chapter in what was occurring in the community of Wirra Wagga. We saw how this was being attempted on two inter-related fronts: one, in the form of an alternative kind of school reform, the Connexions initiative, and the other, in terms of community renewal in which residents were being given spaces in which to exercise responsibility and take up opportunities. The centerpiece of both community renewal and Connexions was the attempt to rework, reinvent, recast and de-institutionalize relationships in ways that gave residents and young people greater agency. On the one hand, it was to develop new map and shape the direction of their community, and on the other, to re-engage in meaningful forms of learning.

The endeavor in both cases was to regard *income poverty*, which intergenerationally can only be turned around in the long-term through raising the levels of educational participation, and *social inclusion*, which is about opening up and expanding vistas of opportunity—as really intersecting aspects of the same problem, namely a pronounced inability to participate fully and meaningfully in society, and as Hirsch (2006) argues, both have to be tackled together.

In the next chapter we agree with Warren's (2005) assessment that communities of disadvantage constitute more than 'bundles of pathologies' (Warren, Thompson & Saegert, 2001 cited in Warren, 2005, p. 134) to be 'fixed'. Rather, communities like Wirra Wagga and Bountiful Bay have assets and resources that provide an important basis upon which to create partnerships between schools and families that can be mutually beneficial. They can enhance the identity a community holds of itself and that it can present to the wider world, as well as providing young people with a more informed view of how they fit within their community. What gets mobilized here are crucial forms of what Warren (2005) refers to as 'relational power' (p. 136), in the form of trust and co-operation between people.

 THREE

Engaging Excluded Communities

Introduction

In chapter two we gained a glimpse into school and community renewal through the lives and experiences of people in the suburb of Wirra Wagga. Giving center space to resident's stories of hope, pride, struggle and courage, we presented a counter narrative to the pathologizing and dispiriting discourses of disadvantage that abound in much of the community development literature. In posing the question, 'What does it mean to create spaces for socially critical educators and community activists?' we began to open up the discussion about the ways in which schools can work with (rather than against) local communities to develop trusting relationships and build curriculum around the lives and experiences of students.

In this chapter we turn our attention more directly to the curriculum and pedagogical features of school–community engagement. Specifically we ask:

- How might schools utilize and value community assets to develop engaging and relevant curriculum for students?

- How, in turn, might community-based learning enhance social capital, promote civic engagement and strengthen the social and cultural fabric of local communities?

We begin with the observation that schools are social organizations embedded in 'communities of difference' (Tierney, 1993). They are not hermetically sealed from society, nor are they immune from the cultural, economic and political forces that intrude on our daily lives. As most teachers can testify, inequalities, injustices and oppressive behaviors penetrate classrooms on a regular basis. Young people's identities, values and attitudes are shaped by family background, social class, ethnicity, peer groups, religion, and a multitude of social and cultural influences that lie outside the classroom. Despite the crucial importance of these factors, schools have shown a tendency to work in isolation from the communities that they serve and often fail to involve parents and local residents in decision-making processes. (Mills & Gale, 2004) or to incorporate their concerns and interests into classroom learning.

What we are arguing for in this chapter is a community-engaged approach to schooling which:

- challenges the adequacy of the prevailing school effectiveness discourse on education reform
- attempts to break down the institutional barriers to learning for students from disadvantaged backgrounds
- regards the community as a potentially rich source of knowledge and ideas for curriculum development
- views schools as resources for the larger community and sites for assisting students to gain an understanding of what it means to exercise rights and responsibilities as critically engaged citizens.

Empirical data informing this chapter is largely derived from a study of school retention and student engagement in a cluster of senior high schools in the Bountiful Bay Education District. As outlined in the school and community portrait in Chapter 1, many students in these neighborhoods experience a high degree of educational disadvantage and social exclusion as a consequence of poverty, Aboriginality, ill health, disability, minimal parental education levels, a high degree of transience and family trauma. Although the district was not engaged in the kind of government-sponsored renewal program that we witnessed in Wirra Wagga, there were signs of active community engagement in all four schools, most notably through school-industry partnerships, place-based learning, co-curricula programs and community-oriented studies.

The chapter begins with a brief analysis of the dominant policy response to issues of social exclusion and educational disadvantage and proceeds to a critique of traditional schooling arrangements for young people. We then discuss the theoretical and practical dimensions of community-engaged schooling with reference to civic education, local literacies, environmental studies, service learning and other forms of community-based learning in Bountiful Bay. Finally, we look at the ways in which schools can function as sites for community capacity building.

'Dropping off the edge'

We use the term 'excluded communities' to refer to those communities that have been marginalized from the mainstream of social, economic and political life. A report mapping the distribution of disadvantage in Australia found that, despite the nation's strong economic growth over the past decade, hundreds of rural and urban communities are 'dropping off the edge' in terms of school attainment, employment, health and social cohesion (Vinson, 2007). Conducted by Jesuit Social Services, the study noted that in the state of Victoria almost one-third of communities suffer from entrenched social disadvantage. The degree of social exclusion in these communities is compounded by the prevalence of poverty, welfare dependency, intergenerational unemployment, low levels of home ownership, greatly reduced access to communication technologies, poor health standards, a high incidence of children with multiple and severe disabilities, restricted public transport and community services, and low levels of education.

Typically, residents are subjected to negative labeling, stereotyping and stigmatization on the basis of social class, family and cultural background. As described in the previous chapter, prevailing myths about criminal activity, unsafe neighborhoods, fractured families, drug abuse, lack of community pride and poor work ethic reinforce community prejudices and create a sense of 'otherness' when it comes to social relations. Often excluded from community decision making, they are, in many respects, communities that are 'done to' as recipients of 'governments know best' policies. More than any other groups, they have borne the brunt of shifts in global capitalism and neoliberal policies which have led to a decline in manufacturing industries, underemployment and casualization of the workforce, the undermining of industrial awards and more stringent requirements of welfare-to-work policies.

Patterns of exclusion bear down on schools. Teachers in Bountiful Bay schools spoke of the impact of poverty, unemployment and welfare dependency on the lives of children and their families. They talked of the pressures to perform in a highly competitive environment in which public schools were often struggling to retain their share of academically able students. We heard about the difficulties of raising community expectations of education, contesting deficit views of working-class students, motivating and engaging significant numbers of seemingly apathetic young people (especially in the middle years of schooling) and dealing with the fractured lives of students and intrusions of violence and antisocial behavior into their classrooms. We were told that maintaining student interest and engagement in the senior years of schooling was becoming quite problematic following the state government's decision to raise the school leaving age to 16 years of age—a decision which appears to have been taken with little teacher consultation. A teacher in one of the low socioeconomic communities explained the concerns as follows:

> We have a major problem with retention with year 10, which has dropped from 90 per cent to about 80 per cent attendance over the past few years. We are concerned about the effects of the raising of the school leaving age. A lot of kids are at school because they have to be, not because they want to be. This causes teacher stress and lots of behaviour management problems. (Teacher)

There was a strong view that such coercive measures were unlikely to succeed without a major investment in resources to support curriculum development, school organization and teachers' learning. In the absence of viable pathways and engaging courses, students commonly withdrew their labor from the learning process. Although they were often unsure how to tackle the seemingly entrenched problems of school retention and student engagement, many teachers recognized a need for much stronger school–community links. A teacher commented:

> Our school could make better use of community resources, and a lot more networking needs to be done. The local council should have an education liaison officer who lives in the community and who has a good knowledge of schools. (Teacher)

The extent and persistence of educational disadvantage suggests that current approaches to schooling are not working for a significant proportion of young people. However, rather than addressing exclusionary structures and practices, there is a tendency to 'demonize, stigmatize and pathologize young people whose identity is not consistent with the middle-class institution of schooling' (Smyth, 2006, p. 33). In other words, it's the students and not the school or education system that must change. Regrettably, much of the thrust of educational reform in Australia and elsewhere is on policies aimed at making schools more accountable through prescribed curriculum, testing regimes, national benchmarks and performativity measures. To a large extent, teachers and local communities have been excluded from a policy discourse which extols the merits of parental choice but laminates over social class and the deeply entrenched inequalities in society.

The lack of a critical sociological reading of what is happening in schools and society is deeply disturbing. Australia is becoming an increasingly polarized nation, with low-income households, single parents and the unemployed bearing a 'disproportionate burden of the costs of globalization with few if any resultant benefits' (Di Bartolo, 2005, p. 65). We are now witnessing a distinct spatial sorting of city dwellers into areas of relative advantage and disadvantage that is reflected in a growing educational divide and entrenched patterns of social exclusion. However, mandated solutions to issues of student engagement, participation and school retention often take little heed of the appalling conditions under which many children live out their lives.

Writing about the limits of school reform in the United States, Berliner (2006) claims that the most powerful policy for improving student achievement is likely to stem from measures which involve a reduction in family and youth poverty. Because schools and families are generally situated in neighborhoods that are highly segregated by social class and racial background, efforts which focus solely on teacher quality, curriculum change and school organization are unlikely to make substantial difference to the alleviation of educational inequalities. The bigger challenge envisioned by Berliner (2006, p. 988) is to set about 'building a more economically equitable society'. In a similar vein, Warren (2005) poses two provocative questions:

> What sense does it make to try to reform urban schools while the communities around them stagnate or collapse? Conversely, can community-building efforts and development efforts succeed in revitalizing inner-city neighborhoods if the public schools within them fail their students? (p. 133)

Although Warren is writing specifically about the failure of educational reforms in the United States, his arguments are also applicable to an Australian context marked by growing disparities in income distribution, economic opportunities and social capital (Greig, Lewins & White, 2003). Warren reminds us that the fate of individual schools and their communities are inextricably linked and that any attempts to improve education for young people must engage simultaneously with the cultural, organizational and pedagogical features of schools as well as the structural inequalities that pervade communities so graphically illustrated in the writings of Anyon (2005b) and Kozol (1992; 2005).

Clearly there are some limits to what educators can achieve in ameliorating educational inequalities, but as a starting point we need to acknowledge that schools cannot teach children well if teachers do not understand the culture and lives of their students and their communities, or worse still, if they see them in a deficit light (Warren, 2005). The situation also demands a closer scrutiny of the institutional policies and practices of schools that reinforce educational inequalities.

Dismembering the sociological machinery of school

A key theme emerging from our research has been the importance attached to education in transforming young lives and supporting adults to become more literate, socially engaged and community-minded. Notwithstanding their own unhappy experience of school, low-income parents generally spoke optimistically about the possibilities of schooling making a real difference for their children. However, there was a broad agreement that existing arrangements were not working for a significant proportion of students. Parents and teachers expressed concerns about high drop-out rates from the primary to secondary years of schooling, students' lack of connectedness to school (especially in the middle years), poor attendance and participation figures, safety and well-being issues and, low levels of achievement in literacy and numeracy.

We believe there is an urgent need to critically examine the role of current schooling arrangements in perpetuating educational disadvantage. The hierarchical structure of high schools, the ordering of knowledge in subject disciplines and an absence of student voice, can be especially disempowering for students in low socioeconomic communities. Young people in our field studies often complained about being treated like children and having few opportunities to negotiate important aspects of their learning. Technologies of exclusion operating through sorting and streaming practices and inflexible student behavior management policies tended to reinforce the practices of exclusion that are writ large in the lives of many students. (Smyth and McInerney, 2007a).

There is a disposition on the part of middle-class educators to harbor low expectations of working-class students, to consign them to non-academic courses, or worse still to offer a 'pedagogy of poverty' (Haberman, 1991), in the form of compensatory education programs. Deprived of their agency and subject status it is not surprising that these students are inclined to engage in oppositional behaviors that ultimately exacerbate their degree of educational disadvantage. Appropriating Foucault's notions of power and resistance, Field and Olafson (1998) claim that teachers and students alike are caught in a sociological machine that strangles pedagogical relationships and inhibits meaningful learning. This is particularly so in the middle years of schooling where institutional resistance is generally framed in terms of individual students, 'leaving little room for examining the social conditions that contribute to becoming resistant' (p. 51).

All too often it seems that young people experience schooling as something which is 'done to them' rather than an opportunity to become more independent and engaged learners. Meier (2002) makes the point that learning is often so disconnected from young people's lives that it ceases to have great relevance and meaning. She argues forcefully:

> [w]e've invented schools that present at best a caricature of what the kids need in order to grow up to be effective citizens, skilful team members, tenacious and ingenious thinkers, or truth seekers. They sit, largely passively, through one after another different subject matter in no special order of relevance, directed by people they can't imagine becoming, much less would like to become. The older they get, the less like 'real life' their schooling experience is—and the more disconnected and fractionated (Meier, 2002, p. 12).

Perhaps Meier's criticism is rather sweeping and a little too harsh on the many committed and community-minded educators who strive to make a difference for students. However, it appears that an 'institutional boundary between family and school' (Nixon, Allan, & Mannion, 2001) is inclined to foster a 'them' and 'us' mentality, especially when the school is seen to be working against, rather than with, local residents.

We agree with Fielding (2006) that we need to move from a bureaucratic to a person-centered approach to schooling that combines an ethic of care with an integrated and student-led approach to learning. 'Respect' was one of the words that kept recurring in conversations with parents, teachers and administrators. Respect encompassed a number of realms, ranging from the personal and pedagogical to the institutional and cultural. In the words of one of our informants the very structure of the high school made for disrespectful relationships.

> There is a need to develop more respectful structures and settings, especially for those kids who simply don't fit the system. The model of instruction we have in schools—especially high schools—is an industrial model that works around a timetable set for the convenience of everyone except the people it was designed for. (Education administrator)

The importance of 'relational trust' (Bryk & Schneider (2002) and 'dialogic decision making' (Shor, 1993) can't be underestimated in creating schools that students want to be part of. In their study, Field and Olafson (1998) concluded that a good deal of oppositional behavior on the part of students occurred around tasks and activities imposed by teachers. Not surprisingly, they discovered that most successful learning took place when:

- both students and teachers spent time talking about the ways they learned best, the tasks and activities they found difficult or unappealing, and the conditions under which they could produce quality work
- the curriculum was expanded beyond simple learning from the textbook, and tasks were structured that required them to think, make and do
- [students] were given the opportunity to generate their own ways of representing their learning (p. 54)

These observations illustrate the importance of what Goodman and Kuzmic (1997) call a 'connectionist pedagogy'—one which links classroom learning to the diverse lives, backgrounds and aspirations of their students. Ayers (2004) claims that knowing students as learners is an important starting point in teaching and suggests that educators should approach their pedagogical journey by asking such questions as:

> What experiences, knowledges, and skills do children bring with them to school? What kinds of thought and intelligence are there to challenge and nurture? (p. 21)

What Ayers is alluding to here is the notion of a critical engagement that foregrounds the lives of young people, their communities and their cultures as the basis for curriculum. However, creating the conditions for critical engagement requires a willingness on the part of teachers to back away from authoritarian and patronizing approaches that have generally failed the most marginalized students. In essence, it means breaking down the rigid institutional barriers between students and schools and offering young people a sense of purpose, hope and direction in their education—elements that are revealed in the following stories from Bountiful Bay senior high schools. In the first instance we hear from potential early school leavers, Mick and Johnny, who are involved in a courtyard project under the direction of Rob White, a teacher with a special interest in horticulture and science.

Story: 'If I was in different classes I would be looking to get out'

'Tell us what you've been doing this year and what's been good about it'. Johnny gets in first, 'We've been getting out of class and building walls and things; we are starting a TAFE (Technical and Further Education) course and we know that we are not doing it for no reason' ' Yeah we've been having a fun stuff', chips in Mick. 'What have you learnt this year?' 'I've learnt most about maths, says Johnny 'it has really helped' and he adds, 'Mr White has taught us all that. If the teacher doesn't know and a student does then everyone helps each other'. 'Did you do any writing?' I ask. Mick replies, 'Yes three times a week we had to write in our journals—it helps us reflect over what we have been doing'. 'How does this type of learning compare with sitting in a classroom with a teacher sitting out the front?' 'We don't like it', says Mick forcefully. 'If you ask anyone in our class we learn better with hands on'.

'How did you go about constructing that courtyard?' Mick responds, 'we we got split up in groups and we had to write up a report for the principal—a proposal. She was going to choose one or two but she let us do the whole lot. We had to cost out all that we were going to do and she asked a lot of questions. Mr White told us what we had to do to present it to her'. 'Once you got the money what did you do?' 'We got the quad ready and that involved a lot of cleaning' explained Johnny, 'we ordered all the trees and we had to measure everything—it took forever'. 'Do you think this is going to be useful in the future?' 'Oh yes', exclaims Mick, 'it is going to be very useful'.

'What's good about the way Mr White works with you?' Johnny replies, 'he doesn't tell us, he ask us to do things; he treats us like adults'. How does that differ from other schools?' 'They get on your case', continues Johnny, 'they treat us like kids. Sometimes when you ask other teachers they just ignore you. Most of the time you would just rather get it wrong than have to ask over and over again. How can you do something that you haven't got an explanation of how to do it'. 'Where would you be if you didn't have this program?' 'We would be here', says Mick, 'but we wouldn't be liking it at all'. 'If I was in different classes I would be looking to get out', adds Johnny, 'other classes are hell. The difference in other classes is that you get heaps and heaps of assignments, but we get to do big projects. Maybe the teacher gets something out of me doing an assignment, but I don't get anything out of it. When you have finished a project you are proud of it'.

'What was it like when you started the courtyard project?' Mick replies, 'we thought it was slave labor at first—getting us to fix up the school for nothing'. It's like I'm at school and you want me to shovel all the stuff—ok right. But we learnt a lot. We did the long jump pit and learnt about measuring and angles and I've used that again. We had to order the sand' 'Did you have to do any writing?' 'We had to do the scale diagram ', says Johnny, but we didn't have to do a proposal for this because they came to us and asked us to do it'.

What would you tell me if I wanted to go to this school? 'I would tell you to do this class because in the other courses it's pen to paper all the time', remarks Mick. 'All the smartest kids they had a maths problem and they took two weeks to do it but we just took two days. The stuff here is hands-on but small bits of pen to paper'. 'You can see the purpose and the end objective', I suggest. 'Yeah' they nod in agreement. (Mick and Johnny, July 27, 2005)

Whether young people choose to continue with their schooling is highly dependent on the relational aspects of schooling. Mick and Johnny had effectively given up on schooling in year 9, and the school had given up on them, until Rob White came on the scene. The transformation in attitude on the part of the boys came about largely through their relationship to the teacher who engaged them in a community-based project that encouraged them to develop a sense of ownership, agency, purpose and fulfillment. Not only did they appreciate the hands-on approach to learning but they discovered that the contextualized nature of their study gave them a deeper understanding of mathematical concepts than their peers in the so-called 'smarter' classes. The kind of learning promoted by Rob White gave them a reason for staying on at school and brightened their aspirations for the future.

A crucial element in this account is the way in which the teacher was able to de-institutionalize pedagogical relationships for a group of disadvantaged boys. The theme is picked up again in the second story, which offers insights into critically engaged learning from the perspectives of teachers and girls involved in a community studies course in a senior high school.

Story: 'We teach differently here'

Helen and Elizabeth, work as a team with a group of year 11 students enrolled in a community services program. Helen says that the girls have made a choice to do the course and they want to come to classes. 'We make things relevant and develop skills that people can use in their lives. The work is hands-on and varied. Within negotiated limits, kids can work at their own pace. We teach differently in here', she exclaims. 'We try to create a homely atmosphere', adds Elizabeth. 'Kids can make themselves a cup of coffee at any time. Because it's a small class we get to know each other very well. We build up high levels of trust. The girls can talk about most things.' 'Sometimes we hear things that we'd rather not know about', Elizabeth says. Most students will complete a TAFE accredited Certificate 3 course (taught by the school) by the end of year 12. Helen and Elizabeth explain the extensive nature of community links in this course. Students have an ongoing association with a nearby special school where students work with severely disabled children, and a local aged care home where they were involved in garden make-over. They have also spent time getting to understand the nature of the work in a day care center and a youth refuge which some girls have actually used themselves. Some girls work in a local elementary school supporting kid's literacy and getting to know more about teaching methods, curriculum and reporting. Helen explained how the class had visited a funeral parlor and spoke to the director about funeral rites, grief counselling and the issues involved in organizing a funeral. This was especially relevant for some of the students because they had lost family members and friends through car accidents and suicide. Unravelling some of the myths about a taboo subject was seen as especially valuable by the teachers.

'We provide a lot of emotional support for these girls', says Helen. Students have their own space in the class—a place they can call home—and time for socializing with teachers and their peers. It's an advantage having two teachers working with the girls because the load can get very heavy'. Helen and Elizabeth have had two pregnant girls enrolled in the course and estimate that some 20 young mothers and pregnant girls would join the group with more support. They have put in a submission for a crèche for schools and tertiary institutions in the area.

Students talked openly about positive aspects of the community studies course and their relationships with their teachers. A girl stated 'I like this course because you get a certificate out of it—for jobs this is important. The teachers keep you motivated and they push you along. I've worked in respite care and a hospital for disabled children. I feel a sense of pride in what I've accomplished at school. My mother is very proud of me. My parents have high expectations. They were a bit shocked about me working with disabled kids but I've learned a lot about autism, Down syndrome and other disabilities from the year 4 kids at the special school.' Another student commented, 'I'm enjoying this course a lot. I've had work experience in a hospital and a nursing home. I think I'd like to be a nurse. You can do that through TAFE or university. My friends out of school keep me motivated with my studies. They tell me to stay on at school and complete my courses . . . not to leave early like some of them did.' (Elizabeth and Helen, August 3, 2005)

Two salient features of critically engaged learning emerge from this vignette. Firstly, although there is a strong vocational orientation to the community studies program, it does extend beyond the acquisition of employment skills to incorporate a good deal of service learning that is recognized and valued by the school. Moreover, students develop a great deal of knowledge and empathetic understandings about social structures, programs and primary care organizations such as schools, day care centers and hospitals. Most importantly, they feel they are making a worthwhile contribution to the social and economic well-being of their communities through voluntary work. Secondly, not only do these teachers feel a moral obligation to hang in with students in disadvantaged circumstances, but they have developed pedagogically engaging strategies that motivate and encourage them to persist with their studies. It was most apparent from our conversations with the girls that Helen and Elizabeth had gone some way to dismembering the sociological machinery of schooling by creating spaces for young people to talk about their concerns and aspirations, and by fostering a sense of community in the classroom. 'Teaching differently' in this instance also involved a reorientation to curriculum which positioned homes and communities as sites of pedagogic acquisition (Bernstein, 2004).

School and home as 'sites of pedagogic acquisition'

More than four decades ago British sociologist, Basil Bernstein (1961), began his research into educational disadvantage with a desire to find ways to prevent what he called 'the wastage of working class educational potential' (p. 308). Initially, he developed a theory of social and educational codes and their effect on social reproduction but later focused on the discourse and pedagogic practices in schools, in order to create a more systematic outline of the 'what' and the 'how' of education (McFadden & Munns, 2000). Through an analysis of the macro and micro setting of classrooms, Bernstein demonstrated how pedagogy and curriculum are integral to processes of devaluing and excluding people in disadvantaged social positions and how student identity is constructed both in response to education and because of it (Bernstein, 1996).

Bernstein claimed that what teachers teach, how they teach it, and the way that student learning is evaluated conveys powerful messages to students about what society and schools consider to be important and valid knowledge. A 'hidden curriculum' is played out through the language code that children use. One code (elaborated) is the norm for middle-class adults and their children whilst another (restricted) is the prevailing norm for working-class adults and their children. Because middle-class children are more likely to have been socialized in a home environment that creates an elaborated language code, they and their teachers tend to speak the same language in school. If the school insulates itself from the family, working-class children are likely to be doubly disadvantaged, firstly because the orientation to elaborate meanings required by the school may not be encouraged by the family, and, secondly because the contexts, contents and rhythms of the school are out of kilter with the family's pedagogic practice.

Bernstein's theorizing adds weight to the view that schools are generally oriented toward middle-class values, interests and aspirations and are often dismissive of the funds of knowledge in low socioeconomic communities. Not only is curriculum disconnected from the lives of working-class students but, there is a tendency on the part of some educators to view these students, their families and their communities through a deficit prism, as indicated in the following teacher comments from our research sites: 'we don't have a lot of academic kids in our school'; 'many of our parents don't value education'; 'staff often tell me that our kids are not motivated'. When a history of failure characterizes students' schooling it is not surprising that many come to the realization that they do not fit the system or that school is not for them (McFadden & Munns, 2000). Competitive, grade-oriented methods of assessment and didactic teaching approaches are implicated in this process of disengagement. Equally, 'pedagogical methods that leave no space for students to insert their culture, experience or language ... can amount to an educational lock out (McFadden & Munns, 2000, p. 6).

An alternative approach is to view schools, families and communities as 'sites of pedagogic acquisition' (Bernstein, 2004). Researching effective pedagogies in a low socioeconomic and culturally diverse urban area, Singh (2007) claims that significant progress occurs when teachers connect school knowledge to the learner's background and lifeworld. Beginning with something familiar, these teachers broaden students' horizons and move to more powerful representations of knowledge. Singh concluded:

> teachers who make explicit the routines of learning, that is both the regulative and instructional discourses of learning, are more likely to achieve student engagement and improved learning outcomes (Singh, 2007, p. 19)

For teachers, the challenge is to bring students' lives, backgrounds and cultures into purposeful engagement with the officially sanctioned curriculum.

Such an imperative demands that teachers get to know the physical, cultural and economic features of the local area but more importantly that they develop an understanding of the significant issues for the community. It was apparent in the Bountiful Bay schools that a core of teachers had enormous pride in, and respect for, their communities and were strong advocates for their schools and for public education in general. These teachers were prepared to contest the deficit views of young people and their families that were sometimes expressed by outsiders and even their own colleagues. In many instances, teachers had chosen to live in the neighborhood and were active contributors to civic life and community organizations. According to a teacher, this had tangible benefits for the school and community:

> When you live in the community you get to know the kids and their parents outside of school. They see you doing the things you are passionate about. I've made lots of contacts with industry and commerce. I love where I live. . . . Most of my links with the community have come through personal friendship. I'm planning to talk to council about a marina proposal and Technical and Further Education (TAFE) / School programs. I have become more politically motivated in trying to push a school agenda. (Teacher)

Teachers, like Helen and Elizabeth, were aware that some of their students had additional demands on their time because of family care responsibilities and part-time employment. Without reducing the academic demands on students they showed considerable flexibility in the scheduling of learning activities and assessment tasks. Important as these sensitivities were, what stood out in the Bountiful Bay schools was the amount of learning that took place beyond the walls of the classroom. For many students the community was not only a place to learn but a resource for learning.

Communities as resources for learning

> From the standpoint of the child, the great waste in the school comes from his [sic] inability to utilize the experience he gets outside the school in any complete and free way within the school itself; whilst on the other hand he is unable to apply in daily life what he is learning at school. (Dewey, 1959, p. 76)

More that a century ago John Dewey wrote about the disaffection of students with learning that was disconnected from their lives and communities. The great waste referred to in the quote above is very much in evidence today as schools grapple with questions of curriculum relevance and engaging pedagogies amidst a push for standards-based curricula, national testing regimes and a greater emphasis on vocational education. Yet the evidence to support Dewey's contention is compelling. The Queensland School Longitudinal Study (Hayes, Lingard and Mills, 2000) identified four dimensions of productive pedagogies that can make a difference for student learning: intellectual quality; supportive classroom environments; engagement with difference; and connectedness to the world beyond the classroom. The last of these pedagogies highlights the crucial link between student learning and community engagement.

Although the notion of communities as resources for learning is broadly accepted in schools serving middle-class neighborhoods, there is a tendency to dismiss or downplay the assets that reside in low socioeconomic communities. Historically, policy makers, including school reformers, have adopted a needs-oriented approach to school–community renewal in which poor urban communities are conceived as problems to be solved by outside experts. McKnight and Kretzmann (1996) sum up the prevailing attitudes and policy responses as follows:

> [M]ost Americans think about lower income urban neighborhoods as problems. They are noted for their deficiencies and needs. This view is accepted by elected officials who codify and program this perspective through deficiency-oriented policies and programs.... As a result, many low-income urban neighborhoods are now environments of service where behaviours are affected because residents come to believe that their well-being depends upon being a client. They see themselves as people with special needs to be met by outsiders. (p. 1)

One of the effects of this deficiency-oriented social service model is that local people 'are often subjected to systematic and repeated inventories of their deficiencies with a device called a 'needs survey' (p. 4) which often ends up as a map of the community's social problems—criminal activity, drug abuse, teenage pregnancy—that simply reinforces this deficit view. This kind of thinking also permeates schools through the categorization of particular groups of young people as being 'at-risk' of not completing formal schooling requirements. However, as we have documented through the stories of Wirra Wagga residents in Chapter Two, 'excluded' communities possess 'funds of knowledge' (Moll et al., 1992) in the largely untapped, skills and wisdom of community organizations such as churches, sporting bodies, women's groups, businesses and the collective creativity and talent of residents (Chaskin, 2001; Kretzmann & McKnight, 1993). In their study of household and classroom practices within working-class communities in Tucson, Arizona, Moll et al. (1992) describe the broad range of underutilized cultural and cognitive resources and the importance of developing relationships between schools and families through household visits. Commenting on lessons learnt from the next phase of their studies, the Puente project, Gonzalez and Moll (2002, p. 623) state that 'instruction must be linked to students' lives and that details of effective pedagogy should be linked to local histories and community contexts'. They go on to argue that 'building on what students bring to school and on their strengths' is an especially effective teaching strategy (p. 627), especially when students are engaged as active researchers (ethnographers) within their own communities. Pursuing the notions of local ownership and community engagement, Ayers (2004) notes:

> We must remake schools by drawing on strengths and capacities in communities, rather than focusing obsessively on deficiencies and difficulties. We must name our problems as shared and social and our solutions as collective and manageable. We must note that the people with the problems are also the people essential to creating the solutions, and we must act accordingly. (p. 21)

Discussing school reform in the United States, Wood (1992) claims that schools often underutilize community resources, partly because teachers are so encumbered by bureaucratization and standardization of the curriculum that text book learning is an easy way out. Yet, a few feet from classrooms 'is a treasure trove of resources both physical and human' (Wood, 1992, p. 207) that can enrich students' educational experiences. The value of local funds of knowledge was not lost on the Bountiful Bay high schools. A principal commented:

> We have 52 regular partners that work with our school. They add value to our school in terms of sponsorship, resources, personnel, work sites for kids. Our partners actively support some 18 scholarships in year 11 and 12 that encourage our year 10s to stay on at school. These are financially rewarding for students but also link to curriculum focus areas, for example, science for women and opportunities for students in local industries and local government. (Principal)

Beyond the school-business partnerships, which were perceived in some quarters to have limited curriculum impact, innovative teachers utilized the knowledge and skills of Aboriginal elders, school chaplains, community arts personnel, local historians, service groups, sports coaches, environmental activists and those involved in the maritime leisure activities, to develop educational programs. Developing close links with Indigenous communities was a priority for schools with a significant proportion of Aboriginal students. A teacher described how student engagement and school retention was improved with the support of local elders, Aboriginal liaison officers and cultural awareness programs.

> The local Aboriginal community is fairly strong and we get a lot of support. We feel lucky because a couple of the elders have had kids that have passed through the programs and they speak highly about the school in the community. They are proud of their kids' achievements in regional and state sporting competitions. The Aboriginal liaison officer (0.8) plays a prominent role in promoting dialogue with Aboriginal parents. Her two children have passed through the basketball program and she talks up the benefits. We have a cultural awareness program. They have a Wadjala (white fellow) day where the Aboriginal kids all play sports but they're allowed to bring along a white fellow. (Teacher)

Schools in Bountiful Bay had also established partnerships with parents, elementary schools, inter-agency support teams and community organizations, such as the Smith Family and Department of Community Development (DCD). What this involved in practice was a more holistic, community-based approach to supporting children and families with social and economic problems.

> Smith Family is a program of support for families initiated through DCD. Members of DCD, juvenile justice, police, etc. come together to try to resolve issues. When we have major issues with families the whole group get together to work out what we can do to support kids and families. (Teacher)

The Bountiful Bay district had extensive funds of community knowledge. In the following snapshot, Jennifer, a teacher in charge of English describes the reactions of a group of students who participated in a social history project which involved students in researching the history of the school, the town, local Aboriginal people and oral histories. In the process, students used a range of primary and secondary sources of data collection as well as interviews, journal writing, and video recordings.

Story: 'We gave them the option of going back to class but they decided to stay'.

> The students are fascinated by some of the research they are doing. They really love Chris, a community helper, who is very much a part of the project. Last week she took the oral history kids—she knows what she is doing with them. They have that contact with her which wouldn't have happened

elsewhere. We plan on interviewing people who are ex-students and want to develop a Power-Point presentation and attach it to the school web site. We also want to create some panels and a time capsule. We opened one a few years ago and then set the next one into the ground and we want a written one. The regional library is really keen to get hold of what we produce. I'm an English teacher but I'm a National Trust person. The students know that their teachers are excited about this. They became really excited when they found some maps. We gave them the option of going back to class but they decided to stay. You know you are doing something if you engage with the kids apart from the things you just have to do. (Jennifer, August 2, 2005).

Critically engaged learning in this project involved students in a study of locally produced texts and artifacts but more importantly it created an opportunity for them to become authors in their own right. Research of this kind encourages students to view their local community as a source of knowledge and ideas and to see themselves as makers and interpreters of history rather than passive objects of text book versions of the past. Emerging from the social history project is the pedagogical value of community-based learning, a theme we now explore in some detail.

Community-based learning

Why not discuss with students the concrete realities of their lives . . . establish an intimate connection between knowledge considered crucial for the curriculum and knowledge that is the fruits of the lived experiences of students as individuals? (Freire, 2001 p. 36)

In spite of Freire's exhortation, many young people experience schooling as an alienating and irrelevant phenomenon that is often disconnected from their lives and communities. Writing about the United States, Goodman and Kuzmic (1997) claim that highly individualized forms of instruction and subject specialization act as barriers to the development of a more connectionist pedagogy 'that places one's connection to the lives of all human beings and other living things on this planet at the center of the educational process' (p. 80). Perhaps we could draw the same conclusion about the lack of respect for students' knowledge in many Australian high schools, but it was most apparent from our research at Bountiful Bay that many teachers were making considerable efforts to engage with the lifeworlds of students and assist them to explore their own personal interests and those of their neighborhoods.

> In my senior English class we are doing community investigations. We've looked at the school as a community, the suburb as a community, the city as a community . . . the state . . . the nation etc. The students tend to choose something quite local, such as bullying, the skate park, foreshore development, water restrictions, road rage, and redevelopment of the local shopping center and so on. We are involving the kids a lot more in the community and their place in the community. There is real animation in kids' discussion now when they report on what they have found out from their investigations. Students get to see some of the complexities of the political issues involved in development issues. (Teacher)

Bringing students' lives into the curriculum in this way is a major challenge in a policy context which seems intent on reducing teachers' work to technical and prescriptive forms of instruction. Nonetheless, it was apparent that a number of teachers were striving to break entrenched barriers to learning through participatory and cooperative forms of instruction which give students greater power and control over their learning through the notion of negotiated curriculum (Boomer, 1982). How teachers incorporated generative themes arising from youth identity and popular culture into the curriculum is discussed in some detail in Chapter Five, but suffice to say that some teachers were encouraging students to think more critically about the media and consumer society.

Community-based learning encompasses civic education, service learning, work-based studies, heritage and cultural studies, environmental education and other programs and strategies that assist students to build a strong sense of connection to their communities. However, beyond community connectedness this form of learning carries with it a number of pedagogical principles and practices that challenge conventional classroom teaching and contribute to more critically engaged learning. Melaville, Berg and Blank (2006) summarize these as follows:

- students' communities are the source and focus for learning across the curriculum
- young people are valued as active agents of their own learning and given a voice in determining what and how they learn
- learning goals connect personal achievement to public purpose as students are involved in learning activities that promote community development, civic responsibility and a commitment to the welfare of the planet
- students receive ongoing assessment and constructive feedback that supports them to evaluate their own progress and the impact of their

learning
- community partnerships and social networks increase the resources and relationships available for student learning and action. (pp. 2–20)

Understanding how young people read the world is a crucial aspect of student engagement. Freire (1994, p. 107) makes the claim that 'unless educators expose themselves to popular culture across the board, their discourse will hardly be heard by anyone but themselves'. However, Freire also stresses the importance of engaging students in curriculum which 'challenges them to build a critical understanding of their presence in the world' (Freire, 2004, p. 74). Beane (1990) argues for a curriculum based on the integration of the personal concerns of adolescents and larger issues facing our world. Drawing on Freire's critical pedagogy, Shor (1992) proposes an approach to curriculum making in which teachers, in dialogue with students, develop curriculum around 'generative themes' from everyday life, 'topical themes' that have local, national and global significance, and 'academic themes' that lie in the traditional disciplines and curriculum areas.

In recent years many of these forms of community-based learning have become subsumed under the title of place-based learning because they attach a strong emphasis to the notion of place as a key construct of teaching and learning. Working on the premise that students make sense of their world through the places in which they live, place-based learning uses the local community as a primary context for learning. Although this may seem a perfectly obvious strategy, Gruenewald (2003, p. 620) claims that contemporary school reform with it's emphasis on state-mandated standards for teachers and students takes little notice of the concept of place. Instead there is a tendency to work towards uniform learning outcomes that can be measured by standardized testing processes with little regard to local contexts. School curricula often endorse the acquisition of knowledge, skills and understandings deemed relevant to the economy and business interests rather than the local community.

Teachers involved in a place-based approach to learning design curriculum that allows 'students to connect what they are learning to their own lives, communities, and regions' (Smith, 2002, p. 587). This is not to be interpreted as sanctioning parochialism; rather, the intent is 'to use local knowledges to examine more distant and abstract knowledge from other places'. In other words, the local becomes a point of entry into the regional and global community. Ideally, learning experiences contribute to community development and are often supported by partnerships with community groups and organizations. Learning is generally interdisciplinary in nature and tailored to local contexts and audiences. By 'authorizing locally produced knowledge' (Mills & Gale, 2001, p. 10), teachers enable students to see that their everyday lives and experiences are relevant to learning and success at school. Furthermore, students are involved in 'real-world problem solving activities' (Smith, 2002, p. 589) and frequently utilize 'funds of knowledge' within communities (Moll et al., 1992) as illustrated below:

> Students participated in rap dancing and graffiti art organized by the local city council Youth Arts Officer. Council gives schools a community artist to assist with banner competition. Students learn a lot from these people; they see art as a profession. (Teacher)

To highlight the potential of community-based learning to improve student engagement and school retention we have chosen a case study of a horticultural program run by an enterprising and socially engaged teacher, Bill Green.

Story: 'You get what you want out of this program'

I'm a qualified environmental scientist. I've worked on mine sites and I've done pastoral assessments. That was my passion, but due to family reasons I didn't want to travel away any more. My wife has been a teacher for 12 years and she suggested that I do my one-year training on top of my science degree and go into teaching. When I'd finished I got a phone call from a school asking me if I was interested in running a horticulture course for students at risk. The principal at the time said 'This is your baby; you've got a free rein to develop a course'. We need to keep these kids at school so do what you want with them. I met the kids and shook their hands and they just looked at me. I asked them what they wanted to do in horticulture. 'Grow marijuana', said one boy. I told them that I would support them in whatever they want to do within reason. My message from the start was 'You get what you want to out of this program'.

The horticulture program has been running for five years now and the numbers have grown so much that last year we set up an application system to get into the course. So it's gone from the students as risks to the higher achievers. I find there are some kids who struggle in the classroom but when you take them outside their attitude changes and they treat their peers better. I would say that 80% of the student excel when working with their hands. They get a bit of self-belief and then they start producing a little bit of work. Kids often tell me 'I'm too dumb,' but out there in the workplace their egos get a boost. A lot of them enjoy the atmosphere so much that by middle of year 11 they are far more comfortable with the classroom learning. The written and theory work makes more sense and they turn the corner.

We run a number of enterprises. We take orders from industry and grow the plants and every year we supply these industries with plants. We have done plant displays, supplied the plants and put on the displays. We ran a 'rent a plant' project for classes in the school. Kids get rewards in form of vouchers, T-shirts etc. but no payment. We have done a rehabilitation study and decided what plants can be planted. We have jobs in the horticulture section at school, and students have to apply for positions like horticulture manager and ground manager. Students run the whole place and I just watch what they do. They come self-motivated and they take responsibility for it all. Students know that to get funds for equipment that they have to produce plants to an industry standard. They have a purpose to what they do over there and get some realism into their learning. We also operate a café twice a week in conjunction with the hospitality program. We grow our own produce and take the orders for the cafe.

A lot of these kids come from working-class homes. Most of them don't even get fed or showered—they are basically poor. I've been doing one early morning start for my guys now. They moan and groan but we put on breakfast. The best building block with the kids is honesty. I paid for the breakfasts the whole first term and the kids know they have to sell plants or whatever to get money to pay for bus trips etc. I don't think civic responsibility is something that is learned by these kids. We have to teach life-skills. (Bill Green, August 1, 2005)

Bill is convinced that all students can be successful learners with the right kind of encouragement and opportunities for personal development. Critically engaged learning in this instance combines connectionist pedagogy with a large measure of student ownership of learning and an entrepreneurial approach that allows students to envision an optimistic future in the workplace and community. Bill displays empathy for his students but does not allow this to degenerate into paternalism or teacher dependency. Although students are encouraged to take responsibility for their own actions, he is under no illusion that civic responsibility is something that students have to learn through their studies.

The view of 'curriculum in the community' outlined in this chapter has been described by Orner (1996) as 'situated pedagogy' because it attaches primary importance to the pedagogical implications of local contexts, histories, languages and cultures. However, as Orner explains, learning is not merely about maintaining the status quo, rather students should be encouraged to:

think about their own local contexts—work, home and friends—and to think about how they might intervene in one or more of these contexts in order to interrupt business as usual and generate alternative understandings and engagement with issues and events. (Orner, 1996, pp. 72–73)

Interrupting student's insular and prejudicial views of other people and cultures was seen as an especially challenging task for teachers in Bountiful Bay schools, as indicated in the following remark:

> A teacher who is doing a unit on Asia has run into the attitude that we get all the time 'We hate Asians'. Kids say 'they're all 'povo' [poor] or 'SALVO' [Salvation Army welfare recipient]. 'Why do they have rice every meal' they ask. It's not the kids' fault that they're like that. You have to challenge understandings and stereotypes. (Teacher)

In this instance, the teacher had attempted to broaden her students' experiences through exchange programs, excursions and cultural activities, although she acknowledged the difficulties of tackling entrenched racism. Although community-based learning has the potential to improve student engagement the challenge for educators is to move beyond mere endorsement of the local to foster a commitment to the values of critical citizenship, democracy and social justice. How schools approach workplace studies is a case in point. All too often it appears that vocational education courses fail to engage students in a critical examination of the role of trade unions, practices, workers' rights and responsibilities, the changing nature of work, structural unemployment, power relations, health and safety, child labor, industrial legislation, and wages and conditions (Simon, Dippo & Schenke, 1991). From our observations these and other political issues are largely silent in the school curriculum. We highlight these concerns because we believe that any attempts to improve education for young people must necessarily engage with poverty and the structural inequalities that pervade society. In this context, critically engaged educators can make a worthwhile contribution to the social, economic and cultural development of communities and towards the growth of a more socially just society. (McInerney, 2004)

What are the pedagogical implications for this approach to teachers' work? Discussing the moral purposes of education, Goodman (1992, pp. 27–29) claims that school reformers need to emphasize educating children in a way which will develop their capacities for altruism, cooperation, civic responsibility and commitment to working for the welfare of our planet not just their own individual gain. This requires the cultivation of a connectionist prospective that places ones connection to the lives of all human beings at the center of educational practices. Goodman argues that teachers can create islands of democracy in their own classrooms and, through the judicious choice of curriculum content and learning experiences, can promote democratic sensibilities in young people. Above all, it demands a critical pedagogy that engages students in a critical reading of the world (Freire, 2004) coupled with the possibility of social action to improve their world (Shor, 1992). A socially critical approach to community-based studies not only gives students firsthand experience of local life but more importantly involves them in 'the political process of understanding and shaping what happens there' (Gruenewald, 2003, p. 620). Using a critical lens, teachers and students might pose the following questions about their local communities and living spaces:

- Whose heritage is valued in this community? What cultural groups are underrepresented or rendered invisible in the community heritage?
- What might be done to ensure a more balanced and inclusive approach to public heritage?
- What is the quality of our environment? (water, air, soil, native fauna and flora)
- What might we do to conserve our environment and to work for a more sustainable future?
- To what extent does our school model good environmental practice? What might we do to improve the situation?
- What are the social, economic and cultural assets of the community? How fairly are they distributed within the community?

This transformative view of education shifts the scope of teaching and learning beyond the perimeters of the school. It opens up the possibilities of forming alliances with organizations working for social justice, ecological sustainability, cross-cultural understandings, reconciliation with Indigenous Australians and community welfare. It also positions the school as a potential resource for community capacity building.

The community-building school

Warren (2005) argues that if urban school reform in the United States is to be successful, it must be linked to the revitalization of the communities around schools. In other words, school reform and community renewal must go hand-in-hand. What is being proposed in this chapter is the idea of the school as a resource for community building. Schools have a potential to enhance social capital—'the processes between people which establish networks, norms and social trust and facilitate co-ordination and co-operation for mutual benefit'

(Cox, 1995, p. 150). Part of this social capital derives from the fact that government schools are involved in creating a set of public goods that extend beyond imparting knowledge for the benefit of individuals. Because schools help to foster belongingness, educative relationships and a sense of community, they clearly have a capacity to develop educational, social and cultural networks that extend into, and strengthen, local communities. Capacity building can be further enhanced through a curriculum which provides a model of ecological sustainability and socially just practices for the community.

The notion of the community-building school carries with it the need for teachers and schools to develop educational experiences that are sensitive to context at the local, national and global level. Making the community curricula creates opportunities for students to utilize community funds of knowledge, study community texts, access vernacular theories of knowledge and gain recognition for community service and out-of-school learning. Schools of this kind attempt to break down the institutionalized distance between school and community—a distance that operates through entrenched structures and bureaucratic and professional language. As Bastian et al. (1985) explain, this is especially important in excluded communities where

> [s]chool isolation works to deny students a link between what they learn in the classroom and the environment they function in outside of the school. The lack of relevance and integration is particularly acute for minority and disadvantaged students whose social and cultural background is not reflected, or negatively reflected, in standard curriculum based on a white, middle-class mainstream. (Bastian et al., 1985, p. 47)

Community-building schools are able to draw on the intellectual, cultural, economic and social resources of government and nongovernment agencies and community organizations in addressing such issues as poverty, racism, homelessness, health initiatives, human rights and the environment. But most significantly, they are committed to working with local residents for the betterment of the community. We have described some of the ways in which this occurred in the Bountiful Bay high schools through service learning, community arts programs, local history projects and environmental studies. This idea of civic engagement is well captured in the following account of a cross-curricula project which involved a group of disengaged students in a tree planting project of particular significance to Australia's wartime heritage. Organized by Jason McIntyre, a teacher with a passion for horticulture and an interest in Australia's military history, the venture brought students into educative dialogues with a war veterans association, conservation groups and plant nursery employers.

Story: 'From little things, big things grow'

> Last year we started a Lone Pine Tree project with the year 9 students—predominantly boys. The original scope of the project was to put up a shade house and to grow Lone Pine trees from seed supplied by Yarralumla Nursery in Canberra. The seeds, which come from the War Memorial Gardens in Canberra, were originally brought back from Gallipoli by returning World War One soldiers. [So called because of the solitary tree standing amidst the carnage of battle, Lone Pine is the site of the official Australian war memorial at Gallipoli and is of special significance because of the high casualty rates suffered by the Australian Imperial Forces. Until recently, quarantine restrictions had stopped seeds from being imported into the state but this has changed. Our aim was to grow and distribute the trees throughout the state. Students will be assigned to Returned Services League groups that want one of the trees propagated from the seeds. Students will look after the plants and hand over trees on Anzac Day [A public holiday originally set aside to commemorate those who gave their lives in the Great War 1914–1919.] This will become a major science project, but kids will also learn about history so it's a good opportunity for cross-curricula study.
>
> From little things, big things grow. The project has expanded well beyond our original plan and has brought many benefits to the school and community. We now have an accredited nursery in our school and students have opportunities to develop skills which may lead to employment in the field. Students have gained community recognition for their work in assisting the Department of Conservation and Land Management and other organizations in the raising of endangered flora for reintroduction into the wild. (Jason, August 3, 2005)

The Lone Tree project illustrates the ways in which schools can function as vital institutions for community and democracy—a long-held vision of philosopher John Dewey (Warren, 2005). Jason's students were involved in doing worthwhile and valued work for the community whilst developing knowledge and awareness of the environment, their heritage and the workplace. Critically engaged learning in this instance involved a degree of enterprise education but it was also coupled with service learning and community involvement. Making a strong case for the notion of the community-serving school Wood (1992) states:

> If the mission of public education is to make democracy possible, then a spirit of pubic service, of commitment to the community, must be part of the school's mission. (p. 216)

Wood goes on to show what this commitment looks like in Central Park East High School, New York, where students spend up to three hours per week in a community service program built around work placement and experience in elementary schools, nursing homes, a museum and a newspaper business. Although the school aims to develop students' workplace skills, the main purpose is to provide opportunities for students to contribute to the community now, not at some time in the distant future. In the process, they learn to interact with adults and begin to appreciate the wealth of the cultural, civic, social and educational resources in the community. Most importantly, they learn more about themselves and their capacity to contribute to the betterment of society. In an era when public schools are under relentless pressure to narrow the curriculum and to teach to the test, it is encouraging to see that there are schools that have not given up on ideals of democracy, civic engagement and community building.

Concluding comments

Much of our discussion in this chapter has centered on the curriculum and pedagogical aspects of school–community relations. Whilst recognizing the crucial importance of building parent partnerships, improving participatory decision making and developing local leadership, we have endeavored to show how schools and teachers can promote critical engagement through the avenues of local funds of knowledge and community-based learning. In rethinking the question of school reform and educational disadvantage, we have argued that we need to move away from a school effectiveness paradigm to a community engagement approach that recognizes the interconnectedness of schooling and community. But beyond mere engagement, the bigger challenge is to reposition the school as a vehicle for community capacity building. In seeking to improve the education for young people we need to be guided by local sensitivities as to what is needed, rather than by a needs-oriented approach which says 'we know what's best for kids in poor communities'. What this amounts to is a capacity on the part of teachers to listen to what parents, students and community members have to say, a willingness to construct curriculum around the knowledge and lives of young people, and professional judgment about what is needed to expand students' horizons. Above all, it requires public policy that is respectful of young lives, an issue we take up in the next chapter.

FOUR

Engaging in Policy and Educational Reform That Is Respectful of Young Lives

Introduction

The previous chapter has illustrated, through a range of 'counter-perspectives', that concepts like community and disadvantage are problematic, particularly because they tend to be incorporated into a policy discourse that is characterized by deficit assumptions. We want to emphasize that we are not merely making a pedantic point about language use here. Our point is a political one; namely, that the meanings attributed to concepts like 'community', 'social inclusion', 'educational reform', and 'students at risk' have powerful effects. The disrespectful deficit logic that we have noted in relation to issues of inequality is insidious because deficit assumptions are implicated in such seemingly neutral discourses and generally are not challenged except through the kinds of counter-perspectives we want to present here.

It is precisely because these concepts are so insidious in policy language, and because they convey seemingly 'common sense' and benign intentions, that they are so powerful. Power works in such low-key and largely unnoticed ways through representations in seemingly 'common sense' language without anyone necessarily intending to wield power (Foucault, 1980). Hence, while we want to unpack and analyze, or deconstruct, such language and concepts, we also want to be careful not to simplistically or uncritically attribute blame for educational inequality to particular individuals for what we see as policy failures in education. Instead, we want in this chapter to build counter-perspectives that can challenge current orthodoxy and advance the broader interests of communities. Such interests, we argue, are not likely to be realized within current policy orthodoxy for a number of reasons, but particularly because of policy assumptions about neo-liberalism, the efficacy of accountability regimes, and a general 'enchantment' with management and leadership. We attempt to present such a challenge in this chapter through a close analysis of the policy language and assumptions associated with both 'neighborhood renewal' and 'school effectiveness' in Australia.

Wirra Wagga and the neighborhood renewal ideal

The policy concept of 'neighborhood renewal' is presented by governments as something much more positive for, and inclusive of, disadvantaged communities than the 'community development' models of the twentieth century that are now often accused of having resulted in welfare dependence. Neighborhoods undergoing 'renewal' are neighborhoods in which the policy expectation is that there will be normative change in the prevailing values of the community members. Programs of Neighborhood Renewal are typically applied in areas in which there are pubic housing estates, and which are characterized by high rates of poverty and unemployment and low rates of school success. These are communities that typically also suffer from poor health, particularly mental health, and anti-social activities such as crime, vandalism and graffiti. They are places like Wirra Wagga.

Various State governments in Australia place a great deal of emphasis on the necessity of 'social capital' in bringing about neighborhood renewal. Social capital is a concept that is central to the work of Robert Putnam (2000) and which refers to the normative ideal that social cohesion is best developed through building community trust and social ties. Putnam (2000) maintains that, in disadvantaged neighborhoods, 'social networks are not nearly as dense or effective' (p. 317) as they were in the 1960s; they 'have less social capital nowadays than they once did' (p. 317). This is because:

> [People] who grow up in socially isolated rural and inner-city areas are held back, not merely because they tend to be financially and educationally deprived, but also because they are relatively poor in social ties that can provide a 'hand up'. (Putnam, 2000, p. 319)

The optimistic expectation of neighborhood renewal policies, therefore, is that through the development of social capital the self-confidence and self-esteem of local residents will be enhanced, as will their community-building capacity, social entrepreneurship and local leadership. In the 'renewed' community, shared bonds of trust will contribute to a social vision and improved individual and community livelihoods (McClenaghan, 2000). Through 'joined-up government' and a 'whole of community' approach, and by developing partnerships between the community, government departments, and the private and voluntary sectors, the process of 'renewal' will motivate and 'empower' the citizens of the community and result in improved social and economic outcomes (Millar & Kilpatrick, 2005; Quinn 2005). Such a process is arguably consistent with prevalent neo-liberal aspirations, which pervade state and commonwealth governments in Australia, in that the approach is intended to move disadvantaged communities from a welfarist dependence on government and, instead, galvanize residents to lead their own renewal with the enabling support of the government and welfare agencies (Lilley, 2005).

In other words, the policy intention is that the residents of neighborhoods like Wirra Wagga and their local service agencies will join together in partnership with government and be supported in becoming self-sufficient, at which time they will be empowered to act collectively to improve their own lives and well-being as well as the social and economic viability of their neighborhood as a whole. There is an emphasis in such programs on identifying the range of skills that exists within the community and deploying these skills (and the people who possess them) to generate employment and training opportunities in the area. The overall aim is to empower residents through such processes so that they become actively involved in decision-making forums within the neighborhood and develop sufficient collective social capital to enable them to sustain ongoing community building and to promote social entrepreneurialism. Such coming together of the community, it is anticipated, will promote positive attitudinal change of its members, a spirit of cooperative and mutual support, trust and reciprocity, and will generally enhance the community's levels of well-being and confidence in the future, and, ultimately, the individual livelihoods of community members.

The limitations of community renewal

The perceived local benefits and expectations of neighborhood renewal programs are clearly extremely high and possibly overly optimistic for the people of Wirra Wagga. Their neighborhood has been stigmatized and demonized since it was established as a housing estate for recently arrived migrants from the United Kingdom in the mid-1950s. Any notion that the neighborhood can be dramatically turned around through a process of 'community renewal' would seem unlikely. Unsurprisingly, there is a great deal of skepticism among critical scholars about the likelihood of successful 'neighborhood renewal', 'community building' and 'social capital' bringing about substantial social and economic change for the downtrodden of society. Part of the point of this chapter is to test whether the optimism about community renewal of the advocates of social capital, or the skepticism of the critics, is warranted.

The notion of 'community renewal' can certainly be criticized for its lack of clarity (Lilley, 2005). Indeed, Smith (1996) associates the discourse of 'community' with the dreamy, romantic language of 'Wonderland', in that 'it can mean just what you want' (p. 250). More importantly, it is not clear exactly how the community renewal approach can even address, much less resolve, causes of inequality and social, economic and educational disadvantage that are rooted in entrenched structural features of the society and economy. The language of 'community' and 'community renewal' is therefore problematic because it does not confront systematic inequalities that, although embedded and manifest in particular spatial contexts, are not simply the result of internal community dysfunctions. It is hard to see how a 'community renewal' approach, for example, can respond to the multidimensional nature of disadvantage and all the macro-factors such as power and the economy that shape processes of advantaging and disadvantaging.

The voluntarist discourse of 'renewal' implies that local people, despite their circumstances, have the solution to their marginalization and deprivation in their own hands. They just have to accept norms of community-awareness, trust and reciprocity, and be willing to take individual and community responsibility for fixing their dysfunctions and becoming more like the middle-class mainstream. The deficit logic of this position presumes that, although the identities and lives of community members are defective, they can be fixed if the community gets behind the new direction. This has the effect, as Osei-Kofi (2005) puts it, of 'pathologizing the poor' (p. 267) and reinforcing the popular middle-class belief that 'the perpetuation of poverty [results] from particular values and beliefs held by those in poverty, thus ultimately making the poor responsible for their own condition' (p. 269). Therefore, when it comes to the relationship between neighborhood and schooling, according to Cummins (2002):

> The groups that experience the most disproportionate school failure ... have been on the receiving end of a pattern of devaluation of identity for generations, in both schools and society. Consequently, any attempt to reverse underachievement must challenge both the devaluation of identity that these students have historically experienced and the societal power structure that perpetuates this pattern. (p. 651)

As we argued in the previous chapter, paternalist assumptions about the capacities of people in poverty to lift themselves out of their dire circumstances have largely become normalized in the supposedly neutral, apolitical discourse of community renewal, which has the effect that entrenched structures of privilege, power and class (which we would argue are the fundamental causes of inequality and social disadvantage) need not be considered. The inevitable conclusion to such logic is that all that is required of people in situations of disadvantage is that, in essence, they industriously attempt to become more middle class. A similarly flawed logic infects prevailing notions of 'school effectiveness' which seem to dominate education policy in Australia.

The flawed logic of school effectiveness

A particular notion of 'school effectiveness' is currently rampant in many counties, particularly in much of the English-speaking world (Angus, 1993; Thrupp, 1999; 2001; Hursh, 2005). Any attempt at school reform in Wirra Wagga must therefore be conducted under the shadow of the dominant school effectiveness discourse and its problematic notions of standards, accountability, evidence-base, knowledge-base, high-quality instruction, performance data, national benchmark data, performance targets, effective schools correlates, effective practice, effectiveness attributes, effective leader characteristics, performance and development culture, compliance and audit issues, and the like, which are all characteristic of the school effectiveness discourse. The underlying core of school effectiveness approaches is an accountability regime in which the 'performance' of a school system is presumed to be measurable against a particular kind of 'student achievement' that is based on common, large-scale test results.

During 2007, the State Education Department published an important policy document titled *School Improvement: A Theory of Action* (Fraser and Petch, 2007), which includes heavy usage of all the terminology just mentioned. This document has been distributed to all principals of government schools in the State 'with the express purpose of describing . . . the work that has been undertaken as part of the school reform agenda since . . . 2003'. The document and the educational approach it describes are based largely on 'The Effective Schools Model' (p. 11), the template for which is adapted from an English summary by Sammons, Hillman and Mortimore (1995) of school effectiveness research. The model lists eight of the vague, predictable 'effectiveness factors' (such as professional leadership, accountability, high expectations) which are said to 'have an evidence-based correlation with improved student outcomes' (p. 11). While there is reference in the document to 'children from disadvantaged backgrounds' (p. 15) and brief mention of 'equity funding . . . that is deployed to benefit those students who are most at risk' (p. 15), the only specific reference to 'inclusive education' is in relation to a 'Program for Students with Disabilities' (pp. 15–16).

In other words, the *theory of action* presented in this official document is derived from the particularly thin theoretical base of the school effectiveness literature (see Angus 1993 and Thrupp 1999 for theoretical critiques) which, in a somewhat pseudo-scientific manner, concludes that particular recipes or prescriptions for teaching amount to 'best practice' that should become standard practice. These prescriptions are then presented to teachers and principals, in the name of 'quality', as 'authoritative directives to be followed, not ideas to be examined' (Hinchey, 2004, p. 6).

Yet these concepts and prescriptions clearly deserve to be examined critically when, as researchers such as Teese and Polesel (2003) show, the least 'effective' schools in Victoria (i.e., those with the highest rates of failure and early school leaving) are generally those that have the highest proportions of students in the lowest socioeconomic group. These authors explain that significant 'performance gaps' between relatively rich and poor schools apply even when students at a 'poor' school perform better than would be predicted for young people of their low economic status:

> When a poor school is assessed as effective relative to the standard predicted by its intake characteristics—that is, at least as good as could be expected—this leaves open the question of why it is not better than a rich school. Failure to raise this second question is dangerous. It risks lowering expectations to a norm that is merely the relative position of the groups served by the school in the social universe of the school system. (Teese & Polesel, 2003, p. 199)

Such is the logic of school effectiveness that differential achievement relative to social class is endorsed and accepted as simply part of a natural order. As Teese (2004) points out:

> By focusing on the things that make an impact in socially comparable settings, [school effectiveness research] overlooks the gaps between socially *different* settings. This is a failing of grave consequence. For it blinds us to the depths of inequality which exist at all levels in our school system and it pushes us towards policies which promise only relative relief. (emphasis added) (p. 14)

The differences in achievement among social-economic status (SES) groups are stark. Teese (2004) demonstrates that, in Victoria, more than three times as many young people from low SES background as high SES background fail to complete high school. And of the students who actually *do* complete, 37% of those from the lowest SES band receive grades in the lowest quintile compared with only 6% of students in the highest SES band. Moreover, only 9% of the lowest SES students who complete high school receive grades in the highest quintile compared with 44% of the highest SES students. The inevitable conclusion to be drawn from such evidence is that schools low on the hierarchy, which are therefore characterized by a high concentration of socially disadvantaged students relative to other schools, have particular difficulties in improving academic results (Teese & Polesel, 2003, p. 197). As Teese (2004) states: 'This is not the death of class: it is the death of opportunity due to class'. (p. 19)

Such conclusions indicate that educational reforms that are intended to make schools more democratic, engaging and equitable places will not be assisted much by school effectiveness research because such research 'does not take account of the complexity of the personal, social and cultural world in which teachers and learners move, or of the thinking processes, both conscious and subconscious, that inform their pedagogy' (Atkinson, 2000, p. 323). Atkinson's (2000) research leads to the conclusion that there are more important influences on the thinking of practicing teachers than the rather instrumental 'theory of action' (Fraser & Petch, 2007) afforded by the school effectiveness literature. It would seem that progressive teachers approve of 'reflection and the development of personal theories' (Atkinson, 2000, p. 324) that are typically influenced, not by instrumental models like school effectiveness, but by exposure to the 'big thinkers' in education such as Dewey, Piaget, Rousseau, Vygotsky, Chomsky, Bernstein, Bourdieu, Willis, Connell, Gardner, and the list could go on.

To demonstrate the day-to-day relevance of such thinkers and theorists to teachers in their everyday practice, Atkinson (2000, p. 325) points out that 'it would be hard to find a teacher who did not believe in the value of concrete experience, the power of language, the importance of adult interaction and support, or the recognition of developmental stages in children's learning'. Even though such concepts might have become embedded in teachers' 'tacit rather than explicit knowledge', Atkinson (2000) shows that they continually influence the thinking, shared ideas and debates, reflection and experience of practicing teachers. But while the repertoire of teachers' thinking therefore seems to be much more expansive, more complex and much deeper than the narrow, utilitarian concern with 'what works' that is characteristic of school effectiveness mentalities, Atkinson's fear is that the privileging in education policy and accountability requirements of 'school effectiveness' concepts, particularly the obsession with so-called evidence-based best practice, may result in a narrowing of the thinking and experimentation of teacher-inquirers. Atkinson (2000) is therefore rightly concerned that

> . . . a narrow focus on 'what works' will close the door that leads to new possibilities, new strategies, new ways of re-framing and reconceiving the educational enterprise. 'What works' looks back, in reality, to what has worked for some people in the past. (p. 328)

Of course, the people for whom 'what works' has worked best are, not surprisingly, those whose social and economic advantages are most likely to be consolidated by, and least likely to be disrupted by, the *status quo* position of school effectiveness thinking. This conclusion is certainly consistent with the emphasis in many education jurisdictions on the role of teachers as merely deliverers of 'high-quality instruction' (Fraser & Petch, 2007). Yet, clearly, such an approach has little regard for education as 'an ethical activity directed towards morally defensible or socially transformative ends' (Carr, 2003, p. 15) such as greater equity, justice and democracy in education. Instead, school effectiveness thinking 'reinforces contemporary views of pedagogy as knowledge dissemination and consumption, and takes attention away from notions of pedagogy as relational practices of cultural exchange and exercises of power' (Edwards, 2006, p. 125).

In other words, the school effectiveness mentality militates against the kind of efforts that we argued in the previous chapter are necessary to make schooling more relevant and appealing for the young people of disadvantaged neighborhoods like Wirra Wagga.

Neighborhoods and students who are 'at risk'

Neighborhoods that are considered to be in need of 'renewal' invariably contain substantial numbers of young people who are deemed to be 'at risk'— particularly of early school leaving and unemployment. That is certainly the case in Wirra Wagga. Neighborhood renewal meets school reform in the task of managing 'youth at risk', a term that Kelly (1999, p. 204) describes as 'a continuation of the historical process of constructing certain populations of young people in terms of deviancy, delinquency and deficit'. As we have already argued in this chapter, and to some extent in the previous one, deficit thinking is quite explicit in 'neighborhood renewal' policy and is also explicit in 'youth at risk' discourse. In both cases there is an implicit assumption that disadvantaged or marginalized individuals and communities lack the knowledge, skills, aspiration and motivation to take advantage of opportunities for social and economic advancement to which they should be continually, and naturally, striving (Bessant, 2002; Kelly, 2007; te Riele, 2006). That is why they have to be helped to 'renew' themselves. But such a benevolent and patronizing intention betrays the uncomfortable tension in 'youth at risk' and 'neighborhood renewal' policies between their 'social justice' and 'social control' mentalities. Wishart and her colleagues reflect on this tension and its logical conclusion:

> [T]he concern that policy interventions related to YAR [i.e., youth at risk] will emphasize individual pathology over the role of institutional practices in producing risk is real. In particular, 'risk factorology' discourse works to objectify a group of youth, which is then subjectified through practices and techniques that link experts in local sites to the calculations of those in the center. Within education, YAR discourse may be more about minimizing the risk posed by disadvantaged students to the mainstream than about addressing the risks faced by disadvantaged students. (Wishart et al. 2006, p. 294)

Bessant (2002, p. 46) argues that 'we need to ask whether we are addressing [through such policies] the actual causes of problems such as unemployment' that communities and youth 'at risk' have to deal with, for, as te Riele (2006) explains:

> The way in which policy has constructed some individuals and groups as being 'at risk' of not completing high education has led to an overly narrow focus on technical intervention strategies perceived to fix students' personal problems. Thus, the dominant conceptualization of 'youth at risk' draws attention to what is wrong with youth, rather than what might be wrong with schooling. (p. 141)

This conclusion brings us back to one of the starting points of this chapter; namely, that there are deep structural, economic and cultural causes of social and educational disadvantage. And school reformers in Wirra Wagga and elsewhere need to consider whether current forms of schooling might be in part responsible for youth and communities being at risk in the first place. We saw in the previous chapter that the architects of the Connexions program, Paul Kilborn and Ian Partridge, have concluded that schools are 'toxic' places for many young people and that any attempt to engage marginalized youth in serious educational experiences will require changing the broadly accepted 'education system'. They are trying to offer a more empowering alternative that commences by treating young people with respect regardless of their experiences and situations. In these respects they are in agreement with te Riele (2006) who argues that:

> To serve marginalized youth, policy needs to change its focus from 'fixing students' to providing high quality education. To ignore the role played by schools and society in marginalizing students may be a reflection of the self-interest of governments, since it absolves them of taking a more complex level of responsibility and the consequent need to take more wide-ranging action. (p. 141)

Despite the obvious force of this argument, in the broader political and education sense such reform issues are clearly not on the educational and community policy agenda. The current policy thinking in terms of community renewal and school effectiveness, in particular, can give advocates of social justice and equity in schools and society no optimism that government-led efforts to renew and empower communities like Wirra Wagga will result in much, if any, positive change. The current approach to managing youth at risk would seem equally unlikely to result in positive change for marginalized young people. Yet, as we have already demonstrated to some extent in the previous chapter, and shall further illustrate through the remainder of this chapter, there is a strong sense in Wirra Wagga, particularly among both residents and service professionals, and to a lesser extent among educators, that positive things are happening that are good for the neighborhood and for young people. The fact that so many local participants agree that 'good things' are happening in Wirra Wagga would seem to suggest that the optimistic advocates of social capital and feel-good Neighborhood Renewal proponents are right and that critical, theoretical skeptics with their materialist concern about embedded structural inequality are wrong. We suspect that the truth of the matter is somewhere in between.

In the remaining pages of this chapter, we attempt to interrogate the data provided by participants in the Wirra Wagga reforms in order to identify just what it is about the interpersonal and institutional dynamics of the community renewal process that has led to apparently positive changes in the neighborhood and an increasing sense of confidence for the future. We also try to explain why it is that such relative optimism is being asserted by local residents without there being evidence of any significant structural change. We conclude the chapter with an analysis of the potential of these perceived 'positive changes' to contribute to genuine democratic reform that may result in improved livelihoods for the people of Wirra Wagga.

Including community in defining the importance of education

As we made clear in the previous chapter, Wirra Wagga is not a prestigious address. The houses are recognizable as typical 'Housing Commission' [public housing] dwellings of the 1950s and 1960s; although in the north-western section of the area the houses are of brick rather than the more common timber construction elsewhere on the estate. This distinction sets up something of a social divide even within the community. In recent years about half of the housing stock on the estate has been sold by the state government and now the 'best' streets are said to be those in which a substantial number of houses are occupied by their private owners. The 'worst' streets are said to be those in which a substantial number of houses are owned by absentee landlords. Many of the renters of these houses are referred to as 'ferals'—transients with problems whose reported violent and illegal behavior is said to give the whole of Wirra Wagga a bad name. Certainly, throughout the city of Provincetown, there are plenty of stories that put the people of Wirra Wagga (the 'Wirras') in a bad light. There are tales of children riding their bikes right around the borders of Wirra Wagga rather than daring to pass through. One resident jokes that, 'Some friends are still too scared to drive through Wirra Wagga in case they get carjacked'. Most locals resent the negative labeling.

The centerpiece of the Neighborhood Renewal Program has been a long time on the drawing board. At the time of writing this chapter, in early 2008, construction is well underway of the planned community precinct that will become the 'Community Hub'. This is taking shape as an extensive network of buildings, including a futuristic elementary and junior high school, constructed on the site of what was previously one of the community's two elementary schools. The two schools, Hillview Elementary and Rose Park Elementary, have now amalgamated to form the Wirra Wagga Community School during the building of the new school within the Community Hub at the old Hillview site, staff and students of both schools have been concentrated in Rose Park Elementary School. Once the new school, to be called Wirra Wagga Community School, is completed, the other school will be demolished and the grounds will become public space. The different possibilities for the use of this space are quite exciting.

Importantly, as part of the community partnership approach, the new school is intended to cater for a range of community education purposes. There will also be a kindergarten, community education center and a new community house. The various agencies will also be located in the Community Hub, which will host a range of community activities. In many ways, the Hub is expected to become the focus of the community. Already, it is being regarded as an object of community pride and, seemingly, will symbolize the worth of the 'renewed' community and its achievements.

'Neighborhood Renewal' in Wirra Wagga is strongly associated with government intervention. The idea is that a range of government agencies will deliver services in the neighborhood as an example of 'joined-up' government. The most visible elements of the program so far are the Renewal Office and a number of new front fences and carports. A number of residents have been able to get temporary work in the construction of these and other minor renovations of estate houses, such as kitchen improvements and the installation of security lighting and better footpaths. Surveys have been conducted to generate data for a 'skills audit' of the local area and to identify residents' needs and attitudes. Again, residents have been employed to distribute and collect surveys and to conduct interviews. There has also been a range of educational and recreational programs offered through the Community House, some of which have been funded by the private sector.

As we emphasized in the previous chapter, initial government speculation about 'neighborhood renewal' in Wirra Wagga as early as 2001 was, not surprisingly, met with a great deal of initial suspicion from locals. A resident puts concisely the general lesson learnt from previous experiences with government: 'Anything we have had from the government or the council we have had to fight for'. Small wonder, then, that we heard many comments from residents who were initially highly suspicious of anything to do with government, bureaucracy or 'officials'. An important mediator between the residents and various officials during this time has been the district's popular member of State

Parliament, Olive Kennedy. One of the resident leaders in the Wirra Wagga community, Warren Kane (referred to in previous chapters), has been quick to recognize the importance of the groundwork done by Olive and other senior bureaucrats who were willing to listen to the community this time:

> Olive Kennedy and Molly Ward, who was head woman of one of the agencies, they spent two years in setting this up to make sure that residents were involved. They wanted the residents to have input and make the decisions. They put a face to the department of housing that made this possible. . . . But it's not just about bricks and mortar, it's about people—they found that we were not just idiots. . . . When people started to see [things] happening then they started coming on board, and now we are very well supplied with people being part of it—volunteers.

Notwithstanding reservations we might hold about the history of policy attempts of this kind in the past, at the level of the experiences of the community there was hope that, with a commitment to some democratic principles and a real modicum of ownership by residents, things might be different.

Story: Community empowerment 'of the 'forgotten people'

Olive Kennedy is the local Member of Parliament in the state government and a staunch advocate for the Wirra Wagga renewal program. Before entering parliament in 1992, she was a welfare worker with a local agency, a role that brought her into close contact with what she calls 'the forgotten people', those who struggle with poverty and the consequences of reduced services, privatization and individualistic policies of neo-liberalism. Olive is a grassroots politician with a strong sense of connection to her local community. As the original chair of the Wirra Wagga renewal committee, she played a vital role in shaping the direction and goals of the program. For Olive, neighborhood renewal is all about community empowerment. She has been involved in the general development of Neighborhood Renewal policy in government, and compares the Wirra Wagga experience with other attempts at Neighborhood Renewal:

> Neighborhood renewal is Labor party policy but at the beginning no one knew what shape it would take. In some places the bureaucrats went in and decided what they thought the community needed with little or no consultation. When consultation did happen there was often no money left.

Olive was determined that such would not be the case in Wirra Wagga:

> Things were different in Wirra Wagga. I was keen on renewal, given the history of disadvantage and stigma of the area. People talk about the 'Wirras' and their moccasins. When [funding for the Renewal project] was announced, the bureaucrats came to see me with a blueprint—a committee of 30 with me as chair and not one resident. I said, 'No way! There has to be community consultation'. I knew some people in Wirra Wagga and we ran a series of public meetings where we talked about the idea of renewal. They were very suspicious and not at all trustful. 'We've heard all this before', they said. These discussions took about six to eight months.

Olive then held a series of public meetings in Wirra Wagga at which, she says, the community members were very suspicious but, particularly as a few influential residents got involved, started to get interested. As one resident puts it, 'The renewal got a few residents on side and those residents spread good gossip and they got others on side'. Olive Kennedy targeted some individuals in the community and generally kept pressing residents to participate. She promised that 'the only thing they couldn't change was having me as chair'. This approach contrasts directly with the community's experience of officialdom in the past when, as one resident puts it, 'there was too much *telling* what we need, instead of *listening* to what we need'. Olive continues the story of winning over the community:

> We discussed the idea of subcommittees and a residents' group and what they would like to see in these groups. Safety was a big issue. The conveners of the subcommittees and the residents group all sat on the committee. We had a flow chart, and so there was consultation at all times although it was not easy sometimes. The community meetings were well attended . . . during the consultation we found that practical things like fences and security lighting were their main priorities. There has been a good interaction between the housing owners and the non-housing owners. We have taken a whole of community approach to restoration. If we go in there with a service it is offered to everyone, whether they are public, private or renting.

It was not all plain sailing, however. For example, as progress was being made and Department officials put together a Renewal Plan after consultation with the various resident committees and subcommittees that were being established, the residents found they needed to become more assertive. Members of the Renewal Team seem to have responded by redoubling their efforts to promote a facilitative and supportive front to the residents. They accept the view that their role is to facilitate community development in which the local people take the lead. One Renewal Team member asserts that the 'big difference' between the current community reforms and previous attempts at change is the level of trust that has been developed in the community this time:

> The government has been doing things to people here forever. They could never engage with them. So much is about trust. It's a real privilege to work here, it's that level of trust . . . this is different and a lot of people don't get it. It's about putting time into people and not time into project outcomes.

The result has been a healthy level of community involvement in local developments. As an activist community volunteer, Sally Lomax, explains: 'The projects—the Community Hub, the education, the BMX track, the men's shed, the tool pool—the residents have driven the changes'. And among the various community priorities, education apparently emerged early on as a key theme. As Olive Kennedy takes up the story:

> Education is important in community renewal and the people in the regional education office here have been fantastic. They have contributed a lot to the community discussions and the education and training subcommittees. We held a really well-attended public meeting at night where we looked at educational needs in the future. One of the things that came out was a concern about the high rate of absenteeism of the Wirra Wagga kids when they go to the high school at the end of year six. Often they go back to the elementary school and hang around there. They have no security at high school and they want to go back to the safety of their elementary school. Attendance is poor and we know we need better pre-school services. We hope to improve education facilities at Wirra Wagga with the amalgamation of the two existing elementary schools. Both principals have a commitment to it, but a lot of the ideas came from the community. The community needs to own [the ideas and developments] or they won't work.

The messages about the importance not only of community acceptance and participation, but also community leadership, are loud and clear. Olive summarizes:

> Most residents have a strong sense of identity with Wirra Wagga. It's their community; they have been raised there and lived there for a long, long time. What I would like to say is that the growth in confidence and self-esteem of the people during the renewal process has been amazing. . . . What's happening in Wirra Wagga is a great demonstration of the fact that if you give residents resources and allow them to develop skills they can become powerful people.

Story: Building community by engaging with education and society

As Olive Kennedy indicates, senior officials of the Regional Office of the Department of Education have been strong supporters of 'the Renewal'. Olive says that they have been 'fantastic'. They agree that the Neighborhood Renewal Program in Wirra Wagga had already become largely resident-led by the time they became involved. The regional director, Norman Jenkins, is one of the prime movers of the Wirra Wagga Community School project and his passion for the project is clearly evident during conversations with him and other members of the district education team. He states that the renewal project has been characterized by:

> Affirmative action by government to support the people. It focuses on housing and environment. And we came in and said that we should fully cooperate with the community renewal people . . . It was all resident driven—resident empowerment. We did a lot of work in trust building [but] we are a secondary agency. We felt that the whole thing was about kids and community building. We see education as being multi-contexted—and here is a micro-example in the region where we could do something. The university, police, local government were involved and people could see that, 'hang on. This is ours!' And they drove it . . . the residents identified that they wanted to change the educational environment.

One of the senior education officials, Harold Peterson, indicates the nature of the educational problems that the Wirra Wagga community faces:

> The educational subcommittee was looking at ways in which they could link people in that community back into education—lack of retention, one of the highest rates of non-continuance of students from junior high to senior high in the state, one of the lowest adult connectedness scores, a very low number of students accessing early years [education], very high absenteeism in elementary and low transference from elementary to high school. We felt that we needed a whole of community involvement and a plan.

From that point, with several senior officials directly involved, there was a series of public forums and focus group meetings at which, the officials insisted, the dialogue was about putting into practice what the residents wanted. Norman Jenkins insists that 'it's all about building a community not just a school'. He maintains that 'improving social capital and community capacity' are 'at the heart of community renewal—you build a better community if young people become empowered and if young people can see a better life in front of them'. As researchers, we have been struck by the passion and sincerity with which Norman and his colleagues speak about the urgent need for greater equity within the education system. Norman is known to speak forcefully and emotionally on this issue at briefing sessions with school principals in the region and no one doubts his sincerity when he asserts: 'This is the key factor—if young people are disenfranchised in life then their opportunities are cut off forever. You start with education.'

Direct engagement with the Wirra Wagga community certainly appears to have had an influence on Norman's thinking about local educational reform. He describes one of the community meetings, at which groups of students, parents and teachers typed suggestions for discussion into a ring of computers, as 'teary stuff! Grandparents telling us and the eight year old kids typing it in; it was heart-wrenching stuff!' He continues:

> Dads and mums had a very negative view of how the schools treated them; then we tried to turn it around: 'How do you want it to be? Turn it around'. . . . They were talking about engagement, the need for kids to feel safe came through a lot, and talk about respect—it just kept coming through. It was angry stuff . . . we workshopped all the stuff that had come up and we came up with a vision for education. Then the [Community Hub] building grew out of that. It's built on the concept of a community school. It's about re-engagement of the whole community not just the kids.

One of the main themes that emerged from public meetings and forums was that many elementary school students were reluctant to leave their elementary schools and proceed to the local campus of Provincetown High School. A number of parents, mainly mothers, refer to the Wirra Wagga High School campus as a 'scary place' for their children, in which many of them 'get lost' and 'can't cope'. Elementary school teachers talk of students who, in their first year of high school, are continually 'hanging around' their former elementary school to the point where they often get invited inside. Some of these teachers refer to the chaos, size and impersonality of high school compared with the relative order and intimacy of elementary schooling, and the lack of opportunity for the children to form relationships with the high school teachers who move from class to class. Some high school teachers speak of the 'social immaturity' of a number of the local children entering year 7 and their low levels of literacy. These teachers suggest that some of the children are simply 'not ready' for high school. The problematic transition of children from elementary to high school was impressed on the regional director by the residents. Norman recalls a critical point in the consultations:

> I was talking to the [Hillview Elementary] school president, a woman. She said her son loves it here [at the elementary school] but he doesn't want to go to [high] school next year. I said, 'What if you had something different here? If they want to go to high school, OK, but what if they have a different choice?'

The 'different choice' proposed is for students to stay on at elementary school, if they want to, for up to two additional years after completing year six. The high school has agreed to the arrangement and so the new Wirra Wagga Community School will not only include a kindergarten but will also cater for children in the first two years of high school in an elementary-like environment. Not all students will remain at the new Community School until year eight; some will proceed to high school at the conclusion of year six but might then choose to return to the elementary setting if they are not coping well in the high school environment, and some will spend time in both settings before they are ready to move fully to high school. Being able to commence their high schooling in the elementary setting, and to move between elementary and high school, is expected to make a substantial difference to the 60% of Wirra Wagga students who currently never make it to senior high school. Some of these never make it to high school at all; lots more leave during their first year at high school, and many of the rest leave during year ten. No one is sure where all these young people end up.

In fact, in our first interview with Norman Jenkins, in 2005, he referred to 'hundreds' of 'lost kids' in Provincetown, many of whom were from Wirra Wagga. He was referring to young people who had ceased attending school and whose names did not appear on the official list of any agency. They were 'lost to the system'. As we have discussed in the previous chapter, the Connexions program has been designed specifically for such young people who seek to re-engage with learning. Connexions is 'running dozens of programs out of the Wirra Wagga community—rusty panels, cooperative learning, playing monopoly, computer programming, learner driving', and, according to Paul Kilborn, the current situation is 'exciting' because running programs in the community, in places like the Wirra Wagga Community House, is for him 'the way of the future' for education. He believes the young people in the program 'have unique issues that need to be addressed in different ways and all the players know they have to turn things on their head to make this successful'. Indeed, an essential component of the Connexions approach is that the professional educators will adopt all measures to try to ensure good outcomes that meet their students' needs. As Paul's colleague, Ian Partridge, explains:

> We push the boundaries when we see the need. I've got this little boy who was just so badly beaten he would hide his face. He has a turned eye. He's going to see the [medical] specialist next Friday to fix his eye. We'll find the money somehow because it will change his life. We've got to break that cycle.

As we have seen, Ian refers to such interventions as 'engagement at the point of need,' and this example, for him, demonstrates the need for spontaneity and flexibility in the Connexions program as he follows hunches, pursues contacts through his networks and hunts down favors in the interests of the young people the Connexions team is trying to empower and to re-engage with education and with society. This approach is consistent with that of the regional director of education who also sees the renewal as being about putting people first:

> Improving social capital and community capacity building are probably at the heart of community renewal programs. You build a better community if young people become empowered and if young people can see a better life in front of them. It's not happening for these young people at present. It's also about building a better community for older people. The new Community School will be open seven days a week to the whole community and people will start to feel comfortable about education again. We have a strong view that this is a self-sustaining model because it belongs to the community. The thing about Provincetown is that there is a genuine feeling that everyone is in this together. There is a real will to do this. We have a strong relationship with the Department of Human Services, the universities and the renewal team. So the focus is on the wider good of the community—it's putting people first.

Story: Challenges for the Wirra Wagga Community School and educational professionals

In late 2006 it was announced that the principal of the larger of the two elementary schools in Wirra Wagga, Hillview Elementary, which is currently being demolished to make way for the Community Hub, had been appointed principal of the yet to be built Wirra Wagga Community School. The new school is expected to be fully operational at some point during 2008, at which time the problem of having 'lost kids' due to their uneasy transition from elementary school to high school, as discussed earlier, is expected to be largely solved through the 'different choice' proposed by Norman Jenkins. But, in addition to that, the new school will endeavor to offer education for all of the community and will include, according to the principal, Peter Cambrel, 'our own Connexions'. Peter maintains that the new school will reflect the priorities asserted by community, including the value of education for all:

> What we have now are the whiz-bang plans for a new community school based around learning communities. It's been drawn up by architects from New York and it all looks very impressive. We are working on the designs to fit the pedagogy. The new model of schooling will incorporate community-based and cooperative forms of learning. Students will be vertically grouped and there will be a big emphasis on supporting kids at various transition points in their schooling. A lot of consultation has been going on.
> *Researcher: Go backwards and talk about the reform process and the community thing.*
> First of all, it's a unique way of doing things, and it's a positive way of doing things. In communities like these they don't take kindly to big brother imposing things on them. They say: 'We're no different to others'. They are a very parochial and proud group and being a 'Wirra' is very important to them. To break out of that label, that cycle, they need some skills, and the renewal process has given them some skills. The discussions became: 'What is the main driver of change?' People identified education as being most important. When we looked at it we found we didn't have a lot of students from this area going on to higher education. I did the figures. We also had 50% or less going to pre-school. In our discussions parents told us they want better opportunities for their children. They want them to be engaged in school longer and to come out with a better knowledge of life skills—what I call the multifunctional skills. I was surprised at their response. I thought we would do more of the leading, but it's been a worthwhile experience as educators to see them take on more of the vision of what they want for their kids. They want them to have the skills to go anywhere.

The low proportion of children attending pre-school is referred to by numerous teachers at both Hillview and Rose Park schools. Prior to the school amalgamation, a teacher at Rose Park expressed the general view:

> It's a great concern that the children are not coming through kindergarten. Unfortunately, when the fees are due they just drop out. When they come to school they don't know their colors, they don't know numbers and they can't hold scissors. So we are really doing a kindergarten year in prep (the first year of elementary school). We are then so far behind that some kids never catch up.

The low level of pre-school attendance is changing due to the effort of the renewal team personnel. Harry Truebridge and Carol Georgiadis have managed to secure sponsors of kindergarten places from a number of businesses and even from the most prestigious private school in Provincetown, which, somewhat ironically, is situated just a few streets from the boundary of Wirra Wagga. Due to these 'scholarships', the pre-school attendance rate has increased from under 50% in 2005 to 90% in 2007.

Peter Cambrel confirms that, over the past ten years, only two young people from Wirra Wagga have obtained a higher education qualification. Of the families of all children who attended Hillview Elementary in 2006, only two families received income from regular employment, and 94% of the parents, a large proportion of whom are single mothers, were holders of Health Cards (the figure is 98% for all adults in Wirra Wagga). Warren Kane points out the stark reality that 'some of our young people have never seen anyone work—mum, dad, or grandma . . . A lot of children have never even thought of work'. He believes that education and the experience of seeing local parents and peers in jobs will 'enable our kids to dream'.

Marie Ovens, who is relatively new to Wirra Wagga, also wants her pupils to dream about 'alternative futures' but points out that such dreaming has to start early because of their narrow horizons:

> Our students don't have many of the experiences of everyday life that we take for granted. Lots of them have never been to the beach or seen a sheep. They find it hard to describe things. . . . We get the kids to talk about their futures and their aspirations. We have class goals and personal goals when we encourage them to think ahead about what they would like to achieve. Some talk about what they want to be when they grow up. Some want to be teachers, hairdressers, nurses and so on. Mostly they want to do something constructive.

A number of both elementary and high school teachers make reference to 'the limited experiences' of Wirra Wagga children and make attempts to broaden their horizons by including excursions and other activities in the curriculum. But teachers also speak of children's experiences of unusual kinds compared with those of middle-class kids, like having to fend for themselves, take responsibly in various ways for younger siblings, and deal with sometimes violent and chaotic domestic environments. Marie Ovens is aware of several such examples:

> They surprise you with what they don't know but sometimes they surprise you with what they do know. . . . One little kid has nine brothers and sisters to get organized before he comes to school. A little girl sets her mobile phone so she can get up because the mother is still in bed and she is so keen to come to school. These kids really want to be here and they really enjoy it. You tend to

think that these kids don't want to learn. I think I had that perception before I came here but it's definitely not the case.

Teachers at both the elementary and high schools seem to agree that many of the student problems they deal with are a result of what the principal of the Wirra Wagga campus of Provincetown High School refers to as 'a lot of out-of-school stuff coming into school'. We heard many comments about children who can unpredictably 'explode', and their sudden outbursts of anger or frustration seem to be a major behavioral management problem. An elementary teacher provides an illustrative example:

> I had an experience of this behavior on the third day I was here. I had them by myself—they sniff out someone new—when it started to hail. When we looked out the window at the huge hailstones a kid bumped into another kid and next thing they were throwing punches. Kids bring a certain amount of pent-up anger into the classroom. Mondays is usually the worst day because of family issues arising from the weekend.

As in many communities characterized by relative disadvantage, a substantial proportion of children at elementary school in Wirra Wagga are classified as being eligible for special funding because of their diagnosed 'disability and integration' needs. Teachers also refer to low levels of nutrition and personal hygiene and to issues of absenteeism, low parental skills and low parental expectations. These problems explain why retired former elementary school principal, Neil Loughran, who, as an experienced curriculum manager and student welfare counselor was employed by Peter Cambrel at Hillview Elementary prior to the amalgamation, refers to his time in Wirra Wagga as 'a baptism of fire'. Trying to turn around such problems, he maintains, is a 'slow and challenging' process. Nonetheless, he claims that some headway is being made through such measures as:

- recognizing that student safety and welfare issues have to be dealt with as a 'pre-condition for learning' and, for example, enrolling eighty students in a breakfast program as part of this emphasis
- encouraging and supporting parents to use kindergarten services and the 'scholarships' available so that children will have some grounding in learning when they enter elementary school
- implementing a 'responsibility program' that emphasizes 'getting children to understand what is appropriate social behavior'
- 'learning about consequences, verbalizing feelings and taking owner-

ship of their learning and behavior'
- developing an 'engaging and rigorous curriculum that is geared to the needs of these kids'
- making an effort to involve pupils in physical education and sports activities as a way of encouraging teamwork and improving physical fitness.

Some of the comments above seem to imply elements of deficit thinking on the part of teachers about their pupils and community, and the issues of likely professional debate and tension in the amalgamated elementary school seem to be shaping as ones related to concepts of student deficit; namely, direct instruction and student behavior management.

Story: Curriculum and control—'teachers have to earn the respect and trust of kids'

Neil Loughran is a strong believer in a 'direct instruction model of learning' for the children of Wirra Wagga, and, having been brought in by Peter Cambrel to work on the curriculum, his argument in late 2006 was that the children of Hillview Elementary School do not possess 'the knowledge and resources that middle-class kids bring to school'. Therefore, he maintains, the children need 'teacher-directed learning and individually graded programs to get up to speed'. Later on, he says, when progress has been made in the basics, more flexibility and student negotiation can be introduced into the curriculum. A number of teachers support the 'direct teaching model' advocated by Neil, particularly the highly structured literacy program, but by no means does everyone agree with it. For instance, Elizabeth Saunders, while she also generally favors a structured approach to teaching, has found the Hillview program too restrictive in her short time at the school. She says:

> I found that when I first came here it was so easy to teach. You just went bang, bang, bang, and you didn't even have to think about the lesson. It was easy, but I couldn't do it for long. I had to move away from this kind of direct instruction. . . . So my program is not so much teacher directed, although we have that in spelling and even in maths.

The problem for Elizabeth is that there is 'not enough emphasis on getting kids to think critically' when there is teacher direction, and she disagrees with the view that the need to provide grounding in literacy and numeracy justifies a structured, even rigid, program in these areas. There are other teachers, particularly at Rose Park school, who are also somewhat dismissive of 'direct instruction', which they see as characterizing a narrow approach to curriculum and pedagogy of Hillview staff. This difference in perspective was a major talking point at the combined teacher meetings in the latter part of 2006 as the schools were preparing for amalgamation. Since then, this presumed different curriculum orientation has been mentioned not only in our discussions with teachers from both schools, but also in talks with school administrative staff, parent members of both school councils, residents, and officials and volunteers at the renewal office and community house. The difference in perspective is therefore recognized right across the community as a 'major challenge' that the combined Community School will have to face up to and deal with. This level of discussion within the community about the future of elementary school curriculum and pedagogy is, in itself, indicative of increased community interest in local issues since the launch of the Neighborhood Renewal Program. There are also other examples of parent interest in their children's schooling, as Elizabeth Saunders explains:

> The culture here was that parents wouldn't take part in anything, but recently I had twenty-three out of twenty-four parents come to a parent-teacher interview. It's about how you sell it to the kids. We say to the kids, 'Show Mum and Dad what you've done'.

Parent-teacher evenings at all types of schools often suffer from poor attendance. On this occasion, the Hillview parents were invited to take part in 'three-way interviews' involving parent, teacher and student. The attendance of parents was remarkable compared with the very low attendances in the past. There was close to a hundred percent roll-up for every class. Part of the explanation for this success is thought to be the amount of interest and discussion that has been generated in the community about the imminent school amalgamation and the proposed Community Hub. Another explanation is that parents have responded in large numbers to being invited by their children to attend, and most children seem to have pressured and begged their parents to turn up. Elizabeth plans to 'strike while the iron is hot' and try to attract parents into the school again:

> I'm planning to do a maths day with parents when they can come and play games. The emphasis is on family groups so you can go and be with all of your kids. I think it's a big step to come into a school when you've not had a good experience yourself.

The parent-teacher evening provided a number of parents with an opportunity to see how much the school has changed. Two single mothers who are former pupils of Hillview Elementary and who, in 2006 were members of the School Council, say they were initially intimidated by anything to do with school but have been reassured by Peter Cambrel's warmth and charm and the general friendliness of teachers. They do not want their children to leave school early like they, themselves, did. They say they are relieved that their children's teachers are far more approachable and humane people than their own teachers were. Their memories of school are overwhelmingly of an uncomfortable place in which teachers were 'very strict and severe'. They note that there is less bullying now and much greater acceptance of difference among the pupils. A similar point is made by Natalie Jovanovich, also a local parent, who has been an integration aide (ancillary staff member who provides learning support for students with special needs) at Hillview Elementary for a number of years. She, too, is pleased that the school has a core of committed and experienced teachers who are far more supportive and understanding of the Wirra Wagga children than many teachers have been in the past.

Natalie defends the Wirra Wagga community as one that is 'proud and supportive' and in which she feels much safer than in some other parts of Provincetown. Interestingly, police data support Natalie's claim that crime rates in Wirra Wagga have dropped substantially since the commencement of the Neighborhood Renewal Program and are now relatively low. Nonetheless, Natalie says, many children carry enormous 'emotional baggage and pent-up anger' which makes them prone to 'hissy fits'. According to Natalie, it is at these times, when they are most likely to 'explode', that the children particularly need understanding rather than punitive behavioral management measures. She advocates 'sitting with a child, listening to them, encouraging them, giving them praise that they don't necessarily get from home'. She says she spends as much time addressing the 'emotional needs' of the children as their learning difficulties. This is important, she says, 'because many kids come from fractured and unstable homes [so] they need a stable and secure school environment'. On the basis of being a parent and a close observer of elementary teachers in Wirra Wagga, Natalie argues that the most important point in terms of student discipline is that 'teachers have to earn the trust and respect of kids. This won't happen by [teachers] asserting their authority. They have to model respectful behavior, work in non-confrontational ways and gain their trust'.

This fundamental pedagogical point—that teachers have to earn the trust and respect of kids—is interestingly raised here by a non-teacher. Natalie has become something of a cultural mediator and translator between pupils and the teachers, who do not, like her, reside in Wirra Wagga. It would seem apparent that in order to gain the trust and respect of their charges, the teachers must come to know them and their situations and understand their lifeworlds. This point is also implied by Norman Jenkins and Peter Cambrel, and also by the new principal of the Wirra Wagga campus of Provincetown High School, Sally Andrews, who talk about 'different kinds of teachers', 'turning education on its head', 'putting people first', 'giving kids ownership of their own learning' and 'getting away from the teacher as the focal point'. Increasingly the emphasis is shifting from school effectiveness concerns with techniques of instruction and replicating 'what works' to ethical concerns about connecting with young people and their world and 'turning things around'.

Story: Imagining alternative futures and 'avoiding the shaky knees'

At the start of the 2007 school year the two elementary schools in Wirra Wagga had amalgamated on the site of the previous Rose Park Elementary School to form the new Wirra Wagga Community School. Principal Peter Cambrel says the early days of the 'new' school have been very promising. There seems to have been general community acceptance of the merger, although a few parents did not want to be involved in the new school and moved their children to schools outside Wirra Wagga prior to the commencement of term one. The commitment of the remaining parents to the new school is indicted by the fact that almost all pupils arrived on day one in the new school uniform, the cost of which has been heavily subsidized. Staff relations are cordial and teaching teams comprising staff from both of the old schools seem to be working well so far. The foreshadowed controversy over differences in curriculum and pedagogical style between the two schools has been put on hold while the staff concentrate on implementing the amalgamation. The issue has certainly not gone away, however, as the following comment from a former Rose Park teacher demonstrates:

> We are working through the [literacy] program. But from the technical point of view I think that we still have some work to do. It's a more a literature-based approach—more prescriptive, directive. We went through the merger process [and] what we were using [at Rose Park] we don't use here anymore. What was at Hillview has just been imposed on us here.

Particularly encouraging to Peter Cambrel is the 'mingling and talking' among the two groups of parents, which seems to have promoted a great deal of dialogue about the potential benefits of the new school.

According to the Regional Director of Education, Norman Jenkins, this is the time when some 'backward stuff' is likely to happen in terms of teacher and parent morale, so the pressure is on 'to build some stability before the shaky knees happen'. A priority for Norman and his team is to support a new government literacy initiative through which two literacy specialists have been appointed to work alongside regular teachers in their classrooms. Norman expects that 'teacher capacity and teacher renewal is going to challenge some teachers; they are all on board, but some are going to [have to] rethink the way they teach and change the way they do things'. Norman emphasizes that:

> It's not just about new buildings; it's about a new process of teaching and learning. The development happens from there. Student connectedness, teacher morale; if your people culture is right, student centered, then you would hope to see some outcomes.

As well as the commencement of the amalgamated Wirra Wagga Community School, 2007 also saw the toughening of entry to the Connexions program. Peter Cambrel in late 2006 had expressed the concern that 'what teachers and principals could do is give up on a problem kid and push them out to Connexions'. He emphasizes that Connexions 'has to be structured [so] that it is targeted for the hard-core disengaged kids'. This concern about young people 'voting with their feet' and opting into Connexions rather than regular school, is being taken seriously and young people can now only transfer (or be transferred) from a school to the program after what the Regional Director calls a 'rigorous process'. Even with such restrictions, however, the Connexions program has easily made its target of 160 students and looks likely to continue to grow as more and more of the 'lost kids' find their way to it. With 160 enrolled students and still growing, Connexions can no longer be seen as a small, alternative program, and some of its staff are worried that the need to manage the large group might erode some of the program's spontaneity and individuality. Ian Partridge says, 'People say I have to write up the aims and stuff. I can't do that, it's not important'. However, Paul Kilborn, who concedes that the Connexions team is not using any particular learning model and that 'we are making it up as we go along', is becoming increasingly concerned that 'we have to demonstrate that we have a program to get them back into the mainstream'.

The Wirra Wagga campus of Provincetown High School also saw substantial changes during the 2007 school year. The new principal, Sally Andrews, supports the literacy initiative introduced by the regional director and is aware that, although a minority of her students come from the Wirra Wagga area, they make up a substantial proportion of the school's low-socioeconomic-status students. She is also aware that many of these students fail to complete year seven and that few of them make the transition to the Provincetown senior campus to undertake years eleven and twelve. Sally's career has been spent largely in schools in areas of disadvantage and she strongly expresses the view that 'we should be doing better for these kids'. She continues:

> The learning is everything for those kids. That's what it is all about. They need to have choices when they leave this school. . . . We are actually trying to run sessions where the kids talk about their learning; we have to make sure that everyone has a way of showing their parents what they are learning. I think this is a way of giving kids ownership of their own learning and it's hard for teachers to let go of this ownership. . . . In the street smarts these kids are very advanced; we don't acknowledge all the other things that these kids know.

At the Wirra Wagga campus of Provincetown High School, and at the elementary school and in the Connexions program, there seems to be an increasing interest in and commitment to the importance of building trust and establishing respectful relationships between teachers and parents and the general community as well as students. Certainly, Peter Cambrel's ideal of inclusive 'learning communities' that will operate in the Community School from 2008, will require such relationships:

> People [in the community] who have skills in the arts and computers, for example, can work with the students but there will be a staff presence. We see this as a way of engaging them. . . . Learning communities will operate and allow [a lot of] scope. Under one roof you will have three to four staff with helpers but you may also have four to five people from the community assisting as well. We'll modify the school times so these people can make use of the state of the art things that the kids have access to. When they work with the students they also learn things from the kids—and they are role models for the kids. They [pupils] are going to get more out of home grown role models than anything I can do for them. They can speak the same language with them. What we are looking at in the learning communities is getting away from the teacher as the focal point. The teacher will be the facilitator. Those people will be able to work as a team.

Throughout the community there seems to be a great deal of satisfaction with the success so far of the Neighborhood Renewal Program. There is a strong feeling in Wirra Wagga that the centrality of education reform in the process is the right way to go. There seems to be a great deal of trust towards the members of the Renewal Office and the principal of the Wirra Wagga Community School; and also towards the Regional Office of Education and the local Member of Parliament who have been very active in the process. Since the plans for the Community School have been on display and the two previous elementary schools have amalgamated, it appears that community expectations of good things to come have been raised.

Potential reform that is respectful of young lives

As we discussed in introducing this chapter, critical sociologists and policy analysts of education and community would be unlikely to have much confidence that neighborhood renewal initiatives are likely to contribute to substantial social change. And as we generally regard ourselves as critical sociologists and critical policy analysts, we must admit that we, too, were initially skeptical that the neighborhood renewal process in Wirra Wagga would be able to make a difference. We pointed out that this approach to community-building suffers from many of the same problems as earlier attempts at community development and social improvement. In particular, the approach, firstly, still seems to be caught up in deficit thinking, and, secondly, the emphasis on building social capital within communities of disadvantage does not seem to be capable of addressing the pervasive structural and class issues that make Wirra Wagga very much the kind of community that fits Sibley's (1995) description of 'geographies of exclusion'.

We remain convinced that programs like neighborhood renewal are unlikely to affect the deep, entrenched structural features of our society and economy that cause inequality and social disadvantage. But we do not accept that nothing can be done to democratically empower and, to some extent, liberate the more oppressed and marginalized in society short of bringing about profound structural change. We agree with Young (2000) that bringing about social justice requires a long and difficult journey and that we cannot wait for major social and political change to happen before commencing efforts to achieve greater democracy and social justice. As she puts it:

> The field of struggle is not level; some groups and sectors are often at a disadvantage. Fair, open and inclusive democratic processes should attend to such disadvantage. . . . [But] because disadvantaged and excluded sectors cannot wait for the process to become fair, because there are often so many contending interests and issues, oppressed

and disadvantaged groups have no alternative but to struggle for greater social justice under conditions of inequality. (Young, 2000, p. 50)

Nothing is fair or equitable about conditions in Wirra Wagga. The people who live there have been affected by social and industrial change and have been historically stigmatized as troublesome no-hopers. The schools the young people attend are likewise regarded as tough places in which to teach due to the presumed bad behavior and low motivation of students. Yet, as the above collection of stories from the field illustrates, there is evidence of a great deal of optimism and an emerging community spirit in Wirra Wagga. The achievements and outcomes in the short term have certainly been positive and encouraging, but they fall well short of the kinds of structural change that might feasibly result in genuine equity. Perhaps this is the realistic 'in between' point that we referred to earlier between the voluntarist optimism of the advocates of the theoretically thin social-capital version of community renewal and the structurally rigid skeptics who tend to dismiss policies like those of neighborhood renewal because they would seem incapable, in themselves, of bringing about change in systematic inequalities. The key point we want to make here is that aspects of the neighborhood renewal process have contributed to the emergence of a broader political process that is ongoing and, on the evidence so far, seems sustainable.

The question to be considered now is whether such developments provide genuine hope for improved livelihoods and social change in Wirra Wagga over the long term. For, again as Young (2000) points out, raising public issues through collective processes is just the beginning of the political struggle for democratic society:

> Once the issues that concern [people] are on the agenda, citizens must struggle with others over the terms in which they will engage the issues, they must struggle to get their views heard, and must struggle to persuade others (p. 50).

On the evidence presented in this chapter and the previous one, we do think there is indeed potential for extending democratic practice and political engagement in Wirra Wagga. While this community is far from having established the pre-conditions for profound structural change, a start has been made in giving voice to previously silenced citizens, given hope to community members who feel they can make a difference to the community and to their own lives and livelihoods, given respect to young people whose needs must be met by education institutions, and in extending democratic participation and engagement. Considered processes of involvement and participation are shaping the development of the 'renewal', as also is the apparent commitment to inclusion of residents in public forums, local improvement initiatives in housing, and considerations of land use and service needs. As can be seen in the stories we have presented, many residents have been telling us that they already have had input into decision-making and they believe they have made a difference. An example of an individual success story in these terms is that of Sally Lomax, who features in one of the stories in the previous chapter. Sally believes the 'renewal' has turned her life completely around. She says she was a person who so lacked motivation and hope that she often would not get out of bed for days on end. She had become 'a nothing'. After initially working as a volunteer, she now has modest paid employment in the Renewal Office and has become a committed, articulate, major player in, and source of knowledge about, the renewal and its possible direction as the following interview extract illustrates:

> Researcher: So, what has happened since we were here last?
> The community house is being restructured and they will move into the Wirra Wagga Community Hub. We're looking at the coordinator's role and breaking that up into bits rather than it all falling on one person—it's too tough. We are also looking for a youth worker, which has made us have a good look at how it works—the pay and the amount of work allocated to one person is just too much. The things that were too hard to do got left behind but they were the priority things that needed to be done. So we've looked at the Board of Management, and then the coordinator, and then we'll break it up into sections—finance, promotions, men's shed, youth center, catering. Mini coordinators will look after each area. Then we are looking to take on apprentices so that the volunteers then become paid workers. That gives people paid employment and boosts confidence to continue the work that has been taking place.

The amount of public discussion generated through residents obtaining minor house renovations has been enormous, but there has also been a substantial amount of participation in discussion about such esoteric matters as the different pedagogical practices employed at Hillview and Rose Park schools, and particularly about the option of children staying on at the new Community School for up to two years of high schooling. These discussions about current public issues feed into the forums and community committees as part of what is shaping up as participative problem-solving. There is evidence of an emerging 'inclusive deliberative democracy' (Young, 2000) that is being brought about by a wide range of people including local residents and local officials of the various agencies who are prepared to struggle to connect with each other and to do the hard work of participating and engaging with locally determined priority issues.

Although we emphasize that it is early days, we are particularly struck by the extent to which, despite the residents of Wirra Wagga obviously being less advantaged than most citizens of other areas of Provincetown, they are striving to assert their views and exert democratic influence. The obverse of this citizen struggle has been that government officials, service professionals and a number of teachers seem to have responded to, and to have encouraged, such assertion by positioning themselves as being on the side of the local people. They appear to respect community members, and they try to learn about young people and the community in order to understand the problems of cultural differences from the perspectives of the local people. They are committed to community participation and actively promote it. This is not true across the board, of course, but the fact is that many residents, who pride themselves on having 'good bullshit detectors' and an ability to 'pick a suit from a hundred paces', are convinced that, this time, the bureaucrats are genuine, that they genuinely listen, and that it is the residents who are making the decisions. The residents are rather proud that the officials have had to 'earn' their trust, and just as importantly, the officials are proud to have earned it.

Such commitment of reformist officials to the local people and their livelihoods is particularly strong in the Renewal Office, where the officials regard themselves as turning 'bureaucrat' from a dirty word to a positive word in the community. During research conversations they expressed strong commitment to reforming bureaucracies. They see themselves as activists in such reform and talk about what it might mean for democratic governance. They see themselves as policy players and it seems clear that they have encouraged, and perhaps convinced, residents such as Warren Kane and Sally Lomax to also see themselves as policy players who can make, and are making, a difference. They make it clear that they do not see themselves as simply the recipients and implementers of policy directives but as policy interpreters and reformulators who make policies meaningful and useful.

Such commitment of both residents and 'professionals' to identify with Wirra Wagga, its families, community members and young people, and to understand and respect the nature of their lives, their strengths and their problems, is not so evenly spread across school personnel, although there is evidence of similar commitment among some individual teachers and administrators. Indeed, we have never encountered such potentially radical senior education managers as Norman Jenkins, the Regional Director of Education, and a couple of his closest associates. These people are also interesting bureaucrats who are using the 'social justice' background text of Australian Labor Party education policy to create space within the neo-liberal, school-effectiveness, measurement-oriented policy template to push educators into innovative thinking even if, according to Norman, promoting greater equity means 'completely reorganizing the system we've got'. The principal of the proposed Community School, Peter Cambrel, is also encouraging staff to engage with pupils, to understand and respect them, and to work with colleagues and the community at finding better ways of engaging with and understanding the kind of educational change that will be needed not just by school students but the whole community.

This last issue touches on debates about curriculum, pedagogy and behavior management practices which are rumbling among staff of the new Community School but seem to have been deferred until the new school structure has been bedded down. We have heard sufficient serious professional consideration of these issues to anticipate that pedagogy and curriculum are going to be major topics of debate within the community of teachers, and, given the level of community discussion about the differences between the two former elementary schools, among the broader community as well. Clearly, the teachers involved in the Connexions program know where they stand on these issues and, with the encouragement of the senior education leadership, they and their colleagues are endeavoring to develop new and more engaging approaches. We saw in this chapter, and in the previous one, that these teachers support colleagues' ideas, learn together from failures, and take teaching ideas from wherever they can be found, particularly from within the community. They have an opportunity to make curriculum relevant to the young people of the community and to use local examples, local people, local organizations and local stories as curriculum resources. This might require teachers to connect with community colleagues in housing, social work, health work, and with other service professionals, volunteers and community members in exploring local issues and services in educative, inquiring and critically engaging ways. Investigations of topics such as civics, poverty, justice, environment, sustainability, health and many others could feasibly be made relevant to the lives of the young people by working across agencies with the co-participation of students and community. All of these approaches could be taken up in the Community School and in the High School as well.

It would seem that, among the participants who have been featured in the above stories of Wirra Wagga, those who have most developed a critical consciousness are perhaps the teachers in the Connexions program, Carol Georgiadis and Harry Truebridge in the Renewal Office, and Warren Kane and Sally Lomax among the residents. Norman Jenkins and Olive Kennedy might also be included in this group. Moreover, we conclude that active engagement on the side of, and with, disadvantaged communities and the residents is a now feature of the lives of these people and others, which is itself an illustration of a process of politicization within the community. Through personal, community and professional relationships, such activity can lead to deeper and wider politicization. Hence there is clearly some potential for residents, young people, teachers and service professionals to critically question what they may previously have taken for granted and to actively take a stance on issues like the purpose of schools in a democracy. The service professionals, through aligning themselves with the interests of the local community, can ultimately make themselves accountable to the community itself in a reversal of the usual authority positioning. This is what Carol and Harry advocate, and Norman and Olive also have come close to adopting such a position. Warren and Sally have got to the stage of expecting officials to accept that they are answerable to the community and that they should be guided by local concerns to act as professional activists on behalf of the community.

This political way of working is no doubt extremely difficult and requires personal courage as well as the capacity to work with delicate political relationships, ambiguous concepts and complex problems. But, as Parsons and Hailes (2004) point out, there is a fairly basic starting point for service professionals working with young people and that is to plunge in and do whatever you can. As they put it: 'we should be reminded that the critical factor is the commitment of one individual who does not give up on the young person' (p. 490). Harris and Ranson (2005) extend this point:

> [W]e propose that the stubborn relationship between social disadvantage and underachievement is more likely to be broken through localized and community-based action than through the external, dispassionate and disengaged forces of competition, control and choice. Only through systems of local governance will young people in disadvantaged communities be recognized, heard and supported. Democracy matters for the improvement of schools. But we need forms of school improvement that are localized, contextualized and above all accountable to the local needs of the community and the young people who live there.(p. 584)

The starting point for such democratic change, we suggest, may occur when schools and teachers reach out to young people and move to meet them, welcome them into schools, and validate their experiences and their lives rather than expecting them to adjust to the entrenched school and teacher paradigms (Smyth & Hattam, 2004). When this happens, teachers attempt to engage their students in relevant and interesting school experiences in which they can recognize themselves, their parents, their neighbors and their community (Angus, 2006). The process of neighborhood renewal in Wirra Wagga seems, on the evidence so far available to us, to be taking all members of the community seriously, validating their lives and their dreams, and to some extent promoting visions of more socially just alternative futures. Discourses of equity and social justice are seen to be central in this process as participants grapple with concepts of democratic possibility and the nature of democratic, equitable social institutions.

Of course, in these relatively early days it is not yet clear which players are dominating the neighborhood renewal process in Wirra Wagga, or how deep the engagement of citizens in the process actually is. Indeed, our major concerns include the reliance of the renewal on finite numbers of active volunteers, and the relative absence of men among the activists. However, we have presented sufficient stories of individual and collective agency and engagement to illustrate the fact that many community members have been actively involved, some of whom claim that their lives have changed dramatically for the better as a result. They and a number of teachers and service professionals are increasingly becoming active agents of social, educational and institutional reform. Further research will be needed to examine whether a sufficient critical mass of social and educational activists can be built such that the interests of disadvantaged people and communities can be asserted and, eventually, contribute to necessary system change.

In conclusion, we want to reiterate the point that our research in Wirra Wagga is ongoing. Important things are certainly happening in Wirra Wagga, and citizen engagement has already become an important aspect of the community and is growing. However, we emphasize again that our 'findings' in this research project are tentative. Throughout the chapters so far we have been describing and analyzing the process of community renewal and highlighting instances of progressive democratic thinking, personal and community empowerment, and democratic engagement that demonstrate the potential, which in many cases is already partially realized, for greater social and political equity in Wirra Wagga. The battle for greater social justice inevitably involves education, and the Wirra Wagga experience is indicative of the kinds of educational reforms that can make a difference. In the following two chapters we extend this discussion of the centrality of educational reform in social change by drawing upon the evidence of a large-scale research project that has been specifically concerned with making schooling more democratic in a group of schools faced with exceptionally difficult circumstances.

 FIVE

Engaging Youth and Popular Culture

Ms B is a 'cool' teacher because she has time for you and she goes out of her way to help you. 'Cool' teachers listen to you (Student).

Kids tend to engage more with popular culture. It makes it much easier to understand subcultures if you talk about the things that interest them. There aren't many texts aimed to these groups of kids (Teacher).

A teacher cannot build a community of learners unless the voices and lives of the students are an integral part of the curriculum (Peterson, 2003, p. 61).

Introduction

This chapter builds on and extends in some important new directions the idea of community-engaged learning discussed in Chapter 3. Here, we mapped some of the ways in which schools and local communities together were able to build trusting relationships and critical engagement through community-based learning. In this chapter the focus shifts to youth and popular culture which is a prominent part of young lives, and for many students, necessarily has to be included for them to invest in their learning. In particular, we want to elaborate on how it is that some teachers are able to engage students' lives and experiences in order to create a more purposeful and powerful curriculum from everyday life. Throughout our research at Bountiful Bay, which is the primary source of our storied data for this chapter, we witnessed many passionate and committed teachers, often teaching against the odds and in circumstances of diminishing resources, grappling with the complexity of young lives and changing times. Typically, we discovered teachers who were prepared to engage with students' experience, language, literature, interests, technologies, art and music. Significantly, these teachers were willing to take risks and experiment, make learning fun, respect students' knowledge and abilities, develop engaging and rigorous activities, negotiate curriculum and assessment, contextualize learning, utilize teachable moments, and build respectful relationships.

'Cool' teachers, as students described them, showed a preparedness to incorporate aspects of youth and popular culture into the curriculum (Skelton & Valentine, 1998). In pursuing 'connectionist pedagogies' (Smyth & McInerney, 2007a) relevant to the lifeworlds of students, these teachers understood that young people today are absorbed in a world of TV, popular music, movies, video games, comic books, the Internet and other aspects of popular culture or as McLaren (1995) describes it 'perpetual pedagogy' (p. 22). They appreciated how these media produce identities, create knowledge, construct meaning, and channel desire (Giroux; 2000; 2002). As Kincheloe, Slattery and Steinberg (2000) point out, the power of corporate culture 'is never greater than when it produces pleasure for children' (p. 384).

Consider for a moment the power of TV as 'the dominant mode of education in our culture' (Provenzo, 1995, p. 218). The typical child views approximately 28 hours of TV per week; when combined with other electronic media sources such as films, video games, recorded music, the total media exposure for the average child approaches nearly forty hours per week, every day of the year (p. 219). What kinds of conversations does it permit? What are the intellectual tendencies it encourages? What sort of culture does it produce? (p. 220). We have to only look at popular TV series such as the American satirical cartoons *Beavis and Butthead* or *South Park* to appreciate the impact on young male lives. In *Beavis and Butthead* two teenage boys sit all day watching TV shows and music videos which they judge as either 'cool' or 'it sucks'. For them, there is no future outside of the world of TV and the 'nihilistic masculine world-view' it promotes (Nilan, 2004, p. 313).

The point is that students today are exposed to a global info-entertainment industry that shapes identities, desires and relationships beyond the school yard. They will therefore use 'a whole different range of information cognition, thinking, and problem-solving processes beyond those required when negotiating the written text (books/literature)' (Besley, 2003, p. 173; Lankshear, & Knobel, 2003). Through these media young people find out about the world and their place in it. In other words, learning takes place across a 'multiplicity of sites', not only in schools (Giroux, 2001, p. 129; Kincheloe, 2001, p. 701). A number of teachers in this research were of the view that popular cultural artefacts and the uses young people make of them are of 'great curricular significance' (Kincheloe & Steinberg, 1998b, p. 235; Weaver, 2005).

In this chapter, we want to begin the task of mapping the pedagogy of youth and popular culture both practically and theoretically. Our purpose is to provide a lens through which to interrogate current conceptions of the curriculum with a view to reinvigorating classroom practice. Shor (1980) argues that this kind of intellectual work involves 'extraordinarily re-experiencing the ordinary' (p. 94). It means that everyday beliefs, habits, and routines become the subject matter of critical inquiry, reflection and action. In the tradition of critical engagement, teachers and students are no longer viewed as passive objects/victims but subjects/actors who are capable of changing their social realities. As Spring (1975) (cited in Shor, 1980, p. 98) writes 'To be human is to be an actor who makes choices and seeks to guide one's own destiny. To be free, to be an actor, means knowing who one is and how one has been shaped by the surrounding social world'.

In pursuing this kind of project, we have organized the chapter around a number of themes. First, we briefly allude to the changing economic, social and political forces that are impacting on young lives and the implications for pedagogy. The intent is to better understand these circumstances so that teachers might respond more appropriately to 'hybridized and globalized' youth cultures and identities in the postmodern era (Besley, 2003). We believe this will involve thinking and acting in some new ways around the question of student engagement at the beginning of the twenty-first century. Second, we will identify a repertoire of successful strategies adopted by classroom teachers committed to the pedagogy of youth and popular culture. We shall examine a number of these strategies including engaging student culture and interests; building productive relationships; pursuing rigor and integration; encouraging students as researchers; and fostering teacher collaboration, reflection and planning. Finally, we will suggest some ideas, resources and strategies that might be helpful to teachers who are interested in pursuing a socially critical approach to youth and popular culture. The aim is to extend school-based conversations with a view to enriching the pedagogy of youth and popular culture. We shall pursue a number of leads such as creating spaces for critical reflection and dialogue; stepping outside of subject disciplines; incorporating students' lives and culture into curriculum plans; and interrogating dominant constructions of youth identities.

What's happening to young lives?

We commence by acknowledging that the world of young people today is radically different from our own experience. While this observation may seem self-evident, the social institution of schooling itself has remained remarkably intact around its primary function of sifting and sorting students and maintaining social order and control. Typically, schools are organized in age-related classrooms under hierarchically organized regimes of officially sanctioned knowledge, examinations, assessment, outcomes, achievement, regulations, and accountability. Today, these things are increasingly tied to the dominant discourses of restructuring schools and teachers' work to meet the national economic and technical imperatives of a globally competitive economy (Apple, 2001; Smyth, 2001).

For now, suffice to say that within the context of the broader policy settings and dominant conversations impacting on schools and society, students themselves are experiencing a growing gap between the nature, purpose and processes of schooling and the realities of their daily lives. We believe that this disjuncture provides teachers with the spaces and resources to create some new possibilities for (re)engaging students in more critical and authentic ways connected to their lived world. As Besley (2003) observes, 'We need new ways of thinking of and working with kids, otherwise we will become irrelevant as we produce education for categories of kids that no longer exist in the postmodern world' (p. 174). Based on our conversations with teachers, there is a real desire to ensure that the curriculum be knowledge based, interdisciplinary and capable of connecting to students' lives.

Before elaborating on these pedagogies we want to paint a clearer picture of the reality of young people's lives in these changing times and how teachers might respond pedagogically. We believe it is important to get a handle on the nature of the forces impinging on the lives and identities of young people, so that teachers are better placed to help them understand and negotiate their way in an increasingly hostile and complex world. Best and Kellner (2003) get to the heart of the matter for increasing numbers of disenfranchised young people:

> For youth today, change is the name of the game and they are forced to adapt to a rapidly mutating and crisis-ridden world characterized by novel information, computer, and generic technologies; a complex and fragile global economy; and a frightening era of war and terrorism. According to dominant discourses in the media, politics, and academic research, the everyday life of growing segments of youth is increasingly unstable, violent and dangerous. . . . These alarming assaults on youth are combined with massive federal cutbacks of programs that might give youth a chance to succeed in an increasingly difficult world (p. 75).

Kincheloe (2001) argues that if teachers are going to connect to the lived world of students at the beginning of the twenty-first century, then they must understand that world (p. 62). He goes on to highlight the key characteristics of the postmodern world confronting young people today. By way of summary:

1. *The increased importance of the sign—the image—in moving everyday life and the sociopolitical sphere*: For example, 'McDonalds and Nike exert tremendous influence on moving the actions of individuals' (p. 63).
2. *An exaggeration of the power of those who hold power and its use of information to colonize human consciousness*: Consider the power of those who control telecommunications and mass media to influence 'what is heard, viewed and received by peoples around the world' (p. 65).
3. *The fragmentation of meaning and the subsequent production of social vertigo—the depoliticization of perception*: With information overload many people lose faith in their ability to make sense of anything. As a consequence, there is a retreat to the private and the removal of politics from everyday life (p. 69).
4. *The growth of cynicism in a climate of deceit*: With a loss of meaning and depoliticization, cynicism and hopelessness has reached crisis levels. 'Young people no longer look to school and work as places in which the creative spirit can be developed' (p. 73).
5. *The celebration of surface meanings; the validation of shallowness*: 'As life speeds up and intensifies products, fashions and values quickly come and go'. In this climate, meaning and commitment have been undermined. TV and mass media celebrate superficiality and shallowness at the expense of serious cultural, political and economic analysis (p. 75).
6. *The substitution of fascination for analysis; the age of spectacle*: In the post-

modern condition, 'The stimulation of the senses—entertainment-value is the core value—is the name of the game'. Corporations spend enormous amounts of money finding 'new ways to amuse the public, and to colonize human desire/libidinal energy' (p. 79).

7. *The reorganization of capital/economic power in a global context—technocapitalism supported by a neosocial Darwinism*: Technocapitalism uses consumer goods, films, TV, mass images and computerized information to shape culture and consciousness in subtle and powerful ways (p. 82). This combined with a new version of social Darwinism creates a society in which social hierarchies are viewed as natural and just (p. 84).

8. *The change of change: everything is different or at least feels that way*: Compared to the days of our parents everything is different or at least feels that way. In the postmodern condition 'everyone feels that he or she and everyone around them is going crazy' (p. 85.)

In the postmodern world described by Kincheloe, children are increasingly 'subjected to social and economic forces that exploit them through the dynamics of sexualization, commodification, and commercialization' (Giroux, 2000, p. 44). Giroux (2000) argues that as public schools are turned over to the dictates of the market, 'children find themselves increasingly isolated and removed from the discourses of community and compassion' (Giroux, 2000, p. 170). McLaren (1995) observes that 'Today's social ugliness that makes the bizarre appear normal is no longer just a surrealist fantasy' (p. 4). In a similar way, Fitzclarence and Kenway (2004) argue that 'via the globalizing processes of information exchange and rapid transit systems, violence now seems to surround us as never before' (p. 336). In this climate, 'suspicion of difference is a manifestation of an increasingly violent imagination' (p. 336).

In the context of these 'shattering shifts in economic and cultural life' (Giroux, 1994), we take Besley's (2003) point that new tools are needed to explain and understand what's happening to young lives. Drawing on Lesko's (1996) work, Besley challenges traditional taken-for-granted truths about youth and education constructed by developmental psychology: 'coming of age'; being hormonally driven; and peer orientated (p. 166). The effect of these individualized explanations has been to 'label, diagnose, categorize, calculate, normalize, judge, totals, and even pathologize young people . . .' (p. 154). The problem is that the notion of adolescence is viewed as a "natural', universal, and ahistorical stage with immutable characteristics' (p. 166). From this perspective, 'adolescents become defined as problematic, out of control and in need of constraint by adults, who assign blame to the young people themselves' (p. 166). According to Giroux (2001), youth are increasingly 'being framed as a generation of suspects' (p. 31). Like Besley (2003), we argue that this approach ignores the social processes and constructs that produce the category of adolescence and lets off the hook the 'predatory culture' (McLaren, 1995) that contributes to the problems that arise for youth and the way they are defined (p. 166). For example:

> ... having little prospect of employment stability, instead having a series of jobs that require frequent retraining; being on short-term job controls, or McJobs; having multiple part-time jobs; being unemployed at some times; working odd hours, not simply 9–5 weekdays; worries about student loans and being able to buy a house; safe sex, safe recreational drugs; saving for retirement; facing global climate change, pollution, and possible war' (Besley, 2003, pp. 173–174).

As well, it is important to comprehend how different classes of students (class, race and gender locations) experience youth and popular culture in different ways. Bourdieu's (1984) writing is especially useful in illuminating how habitus—internalized thoughts, feelings, dispositions and actions; cultural capital—knowledge, taste, ways of thinking and acting; and field—structured system of social relations—all impact on the socio-cultural practices of young people. Bourdieu's (1979) notion of cultural capital helps us to explain

> ... the unequal scholastic achievement of children originating from the different social classes by relating academic success, i.e., the specific profits which children from the different classes and class fractions can obtain in the academic market, to the distribution of cultural capital between the classes and class fractions. This starting point implies a break with the presuppositions inherent both in the commonsense view, which sees academic success or failure as an effect of natural aptitudes, and in human capital theories (p. 47).

For marginalized and alienated working class youth the experience of schooling is typically a negative one (Smyth & Hattam, 2004; Willis, 1977). It happens to be the case that the knowledge, attitudes and behaviors that characterizes the middle and upper classes—general knowledge, academic language and vocabulary, literacy, higher order numerical skills, dress, behaviors and so on—are the same as those required as one progresses through the education system. Unfortunately, the converse applies to the predispositions of students from working class backgrounds (Bourdieu & Passeron, 1981). As Connell (1993) argues, education is 'vibrantly involved in the production of social hierarchies. They select and exclude their own clients; they expand credentialed labor markets; they produce and disseminate particular kinds of knowledge to particular users' (p. 27).

In these circumstances, we should not be surprised that many young people 'no longer look to the school or to work as venues in which the creative spirit can be developed' (Kincheloe, 1995, p. 124). In Kincheloe's view, there is a crisis of motivation as evidenced by a malaise—low-quality work, absenteeism, sullen hostility, waste, alcohol and drug abuse (p. 124) and cognitive illness created by a loss of meaning and purpose in education (p. 125). According to Shor (1992), 'playing dumb' and 'getting by' are two acts of student resistance to a school culture 'that ignores their language, interest, conditions, and participation' and 'makes their subjectivity invisible' (p. 138). For these students, youth and popular culture can provide a means of challenging the formal order of schools, in which they feel devalued and disempowered (Smyth & Hattam, 2004).

In these circumstances, it makes a great deal of sense that the school curriculum should focus on investigating the everyday, informal, and popular culture that shapes student subjectivities and identities (McLaren, 1995, p. 21). McLaren puts this view well:

> What isn't being talked about in today's educational debate is the desperate need within our schools for creating a media-literate citizenry that can disrupt, contest, and transform media apparatuses so that they no longer have the power to infantilize the population and continue to create passive, fearful, paranoid, and apolitical social subjects (p. 9).

According to Giroux (1996), this kind of critically engaged pedagogy will require a different 'cartography' to help teachers address what might be called the changing conditions of youth (p. 45). In his view, it makes more sense to re-examine the role of schooling and the changing conditions of youth rather than blaming youth for the problems confronting the economy (e.g., skill shortages and lack of international competitiveness) and society in general (e.g., social malaise, sense of hopelessness, violence and insecurity). The key question becomes then, how do teachers understand, experience and respond to these sets of changing circumstances? We shall now examine some of the strategies adopted by classroom teachers involved in this research for some clues.

Connecting to students' lives and experience

In this section we want to focus on the day-to-day strategies adopted by classroom teachers to enhance student engagement through the use of youth and popular culture. Underpinning this approach is the constructivist learning theories of educational writers such as Dewey, Bruner, and Vygotsky (e.g. Dewey, 1963 [1938]). For them, knowledge is socially constructed and developed by individuals in context. Put simply, constructivist learning theories assert that learners must actively construct or generate knowledge and meaning from experience. Rather than treating students as 'depositories' or 'receptacles to be filled' with information which is often divorced from reality (Freire, 2000 [1970], p. 72), teachers and students begin to explore their own worlds, produce knowledge, generate meaning and engage in social action. Such views challenge traditional conceptions of the curriculum about what students need to know, what they might want to know, how they might learn from their own experience, and what benefits their learning might bring. In this section we want to elaborate on five strategies adopted by teachers to foster this kind of constructivist teaching and learning around youth and popular culture. These include:

- engaging students' culture and interests;
- building productive relationships;
- pursuing rigor and integration;
- encouraging students as researchers; and
- fostering teacher collaboration, reflection and planning.

Story: 'Starting from where kids are at'

Inevitably, teachers in our research commenced with the view that student culture and interests offered a valuable entrée to relevant and meaningful learning experiences for students. Lankshear and Knobel (2003) argue that it is important for teachers to know and acknowledge the kinds of things young people are 'doing and being *outside* school in order to make effective pedagogical connections to them in class' (p. 206). For instance, Ted, one of our informants, is the Manager of a Years 8–9 Arts/Humanities sub school in an outer metropolitan senior high school. He described the contradictory nature of his work. On the one hand, Ted's managerial role involved monitoring and reporting on students 'completing set tasks and satisfying the schools big focus on data and target setting'. On the other hand, he spoke about his commitment to teaching and learning as a part of the sub-school team. For him, it was all about 'starting from where the kids are at'. Ted was a keen advocate of cross curricular projects encompassing English, society and environment, art, drama and media studies. He described one project which involved students in creating a fictional rock band complete with name, CD [compact disk] titles, publicity, artwork, world tours, promotion, sound and lighting. According to Ted, this kind of engaged pedagogy allowed reluctant readers and learners to become involved as they were interested and able to connect to the magazines and literature used during the project. Ted elaborates:

> The topics I choose for English are related to music, drama and the media. The cross-curricula project we are developing this term is basically a music project. In pairs or groups of three the students are acting as publicity managers for a fictional rock band. They have to give the band a name, create identities for the members—ages, personalities, backgrounds, instruments they play—come up with a CD title and the last three singles they have written and plan a world tour for the group. S&E [Society and Environment] teachers will do some work with them on countries and places to visit as well as cultural issues; Maths will get involved through the accounting side looking at budgets etc; Science will involve some work on sound and lighting; Art—kids will design posters, logos and T-shirts: IT [information technology]—letter writing; graphic design work, e.g. CD cover and publicity labels; web page for promoting the band.
>
> When it comes to learning, start from where the kids are—what they like . . . what bands they listen to . . . what kind of music turns them on. From there they'll start talking about the style of music they want their band to do. This is an easy cross-curricula topic to do with kids because it's easy to keep them motivated. Reluctant readers will often read magazines so you have to start with what they read.

Other teachers shared similar stories about 'starting from where the students are at':

> I tap into the surf culture of the district. Boys enjoyed making an Indonesian mask. They did a cultural assignment on Indonesia in which they could write about surfing in Indonesia—had to research tourist spots and history (Teacher).
>
> Last year I had a group of troublesome year 9s. 98% of the class watched OC [Orange County] and it was impossible to stop them from talking about it on Wednesday morning. So I decided to set aside 15 minutes at the start of the lesson for discussion about the events of the previous episode. Most kids responded well but a few thought it was spoiled by having to analyze it (Teacher).

These teachers demonstrated a remarkable commitment to helping their students to read their world. Like Dewey (1944 [1916]), they shared a view that the present should generate the problems, which lead students to (re)search for meaning based on experience (p. 80). To do otherwise, Dewey argued, 'is simply to abdicate the education function' (p. 73). Furthermore, he warned that 'failure to bear in mind the difference in subject matter from the respective standpoint of teacher and student is responsible for most of the mistakes made in the use of texts and other expressions of pre-existent knowledge' (pp. 182–183). Likewise, Shor (1992) argues that to be 'democratic implies orientating subject matter to student culture—their interests, needs, speech, and perceptions—while creating a negotiable openness in class where the students' input jointly creates the learning process' (p. 16).

For example, Sonya one of the participating teachers, was able to connect to girls' passions and interests through dance performance. She was a young and enthusiastic teacher who believed that teaching and learning was about 'having fun'. She had a great passion for the performing arts, a wonderful rapport with students, an ability to tap into youth and popular culture, and a capacity to challenge students in rigorous and demanding ways. Sonya's students benefited in terms of fitness, fun, friendship, self-confidence and sense of identity. Her dance program also provided a valuable counterbalance to a masculine school culture largely centered on football. Dance offered the girls a sense of power and opportunities to express their creative talents in personally fulfilling and publicly affirming ways. Sonya tells her own story in the following narrative:

> My passion is dance. I studied dance in high school and trained as a PE [physical education] teacher. I taught dance in my very first practicum and have really enjoyed the opportunity to teach dance at this school. Dance began in a small way with 4 classes but has now grown to 8 classes with 180 students. We are hoping to introduce a year 8 class in 2006. The school's success in the Rock and Roll Eisteddfod inspired students to join the dance program. Kids had a lot of fun. We don't have any boys involved in program. A few have enrolled but haven't lasted the distance. There's still a stigma about boys and dance. We have a strong soccer and rugby culture in the school and homophobic attitudes are prevalent in the community. I like the students in our school. Their life experiences are quite amazing. They are much more streetwise and rougher around the edges than kids in other places but they give a lot of themselves in the dance program.
>
> In spite of its popular appeal, dance is still on the periphery of the mainstream curriculum. We try to get involved in the learning teams in years 8 and 9 but the cross curricula thing didn't work. Not enough time was set aside for planning and we found that some of the other teachers had rather an insular attitude towards the performing arts and other learning areas. However, we work closely with the visual arts people and support their programs where we can.

How do I engage my students? Because I'm a bit younger than the former dance teacher I think I can understand the kids a bit better. I don't talk down to them and I've got quite a bit of rapport with the girls. I use the latest music, not so much in performances but in warm-up activities. Kids love hip hop tracks so I tend to make use of that. I still make them do ballet in year 11, whether they hate it or not, but we do modern dance as well. We do lots of group work and team building. Girls feel much more comfortable performing as part of a team. They like wearing their dance tops and jackets with special logos. This style of uniform engenders a real sense of belonging and identity.

Having fun is important. The girls are with their friends and they get to dress up in costumes and do their hair and make-up. Getting up on stage and doing a performance they find is awesome. I listen to kids a lot. I like to find out what they're interested in. I'll often ask them how their soccer match went or something like that. It turns out better for me anyway because they work better for you because they think you're interested in them. You're not just one of those teachers who go, 'Oh well you're here . . . good . . . well sit down over there'. Friendship is a really important part of the dance program. There's a lot of interaction and they get a lot of confidence and self-esteem out of dance. They become more responsible and acquire a lot of team skills. They also improve their level of fitness. Because dance is an option girls are exercising choice.

I take a lot of pride in my work and I expect the girls to give me the same respect. Most hang in. Sometimes my year 11s say: 'This dance routine is too hard' but when I say: 'Okay I can give you an easier one if you like,' they invariably say: 'Oh no, we'll get it eventually.' There are some girls who would leave school without the dance program. A lot are involved in other programs but dance is what really brings them to school.

Sonya's approach to student engagement challenges the view that education is something 'done to students' (Shor, 1992, p. 20). Like Shor (1992), Sonya believed that students' culture, experience and interests should be the focus of the curriculum. According to Shor (1992), this is the only way 'to shake students out of their learned withdrawal from intellectual and civic life' (p. 20). In a similar way, the Productive Pedagogies Research project in Queensland, Australia adopted the term 'connectedness' to describe the extent to which: (i) knowledge is built on students' existing knowledge; (ii) connections are made between different bodies of knowledge (rather than compartmentalizing the curriculum); (iii) connections are made with the real world beyond the classroom; and (iv) students' knowledge and skills are developed in the context of solving real-life issues or problems (Hayes, Mills, Christie & Lingard, 2006, p. 53). Hayes, et. al. (2006) warn, however, that the study of youth and popular culture on its own is unlikely to have any long-term benefits for students unless it promotes intellectual engagement with other bodies of knowledge. We shall return to this point later in the chapter when we discuss pursuing rigor and integration and students as researchers.

Story: 'I am interested in who they are and what they do'

Teachers committed to incorporating aspects of youth and popular culture into the curriculum in these ways showed a remarkable capacity and willingness to build productive relationships with students. As noted, students talked about good teachers as being 'cool', which could be interpreted in a number of ways. For some, it was the fact that teachers don't come down on them too harshly—less authoritarian—and for others it was their ability to connect to student interests including soccer, rugby, dance or music. Many students were into surfing and hip hop music so it helped if teachers knew some of the lyrics. These teachers were not totally alien to students; they actually had something to connect to their lives. Younger teachers had a bit of an advantage because they were not that far removed from students' ages, interests and language. Students respected teachers who were willing to show support and mutual respect as one student explained 'They [teachers] give you a lot of support in all areas of your schooling. Heaps of girls would have left earlier without [teachers] taking an interest in them'. Students valued teachers who were flexible and capable of connecting to their lives.

Tom was one such teacher. He was highly regarded by his colleagues and students alike. Tom was an English teacher at a large Year 8–12 senior high school and was the youngest teacher we interviewed. We first meet Tom in a Humanities staff meeting where he made a significant contribution to a discussion about student engagement through the use of youth and popular culture. In his view, knowing about students interests was a prerequisite for curriculum development. Tom's approach was non-prescriptive which enabled him to tap into student interests in worthwhile ways. This involved revealing something of one's self in order to build productive relationships and allow students an opportunity to open up about themselves. 'Cool' teachers like Tom were able to relate to students in a personable manner without caving in to laissez faire pedagogy:

> The key thing for me is associating with the students on a personal level. I am interested in who they are and what they do. As an example, unfortunately we have a number of 'taggers' [illegal graffiti painters] in the school and if you talk about a piece to them you give them some freedom in terms of what they're

writing about in the creative writing session. One of the first things I did when I had the class was to get them to write an autobiography. This gave me an idea of who's who. Some kid's put a lot of emotion into their accounts. I also get them to read a lot in class e.g., Stephen King. They learn that a certain amount of profanity and coarse language is okay in certain circumstances. I throw in a few personal stories here and there and they see that I can be honest and open so they have a go themselves.

Emerging from this research was the significant role that the study of youth and popular culture played in creating and sustaining dialogue with students around things that mattered to them. It provided a space in the school curriculum for building relationships and forging rigorous inquiry-based learning experiences. In this task, teachers and students consistently reminded us about the relational dimension of successful teaching and learning:

It's amazing that these kids come here at all—school's a safe haven (Teacher).

It's the people who make the difference (Teacher).

It's the kids, they are great—they are honest and loyal (Teacher).

I do lots of group work and team building. Girls feel much more comfortable performing as a part of a team (Teacher).

The girls get a sense of identity through their involvement in the dance program. They like wearing their dance tops and jackets with special logos. Uniform engenders a real sense of belonging (Teacher).

I like the students. Their experiences are quite amazing. They give a lot of themselves. . . . They develop very strong bonds of friendship through school and work (Teacher).

We do a lot of work in groups. We are all equal and have to work together (Student).

Because it's a small class we get to know each other very well. We build up high levels of trust (Teacher).

Story: 'Dumbing down the curriculum does not help kids'

Teachers often spoke about the importance of creating a curriculum that was not only relevant but rigorous and integrated. For them, teaching and learning commenced with teachers' passion and commitment to a particular subject or topic and then went places. Brendan, the Manager of a highly successful Maritime Studies program at a Year 8–12 senior high school was a case in point. He originally worked as a youth education officer where he became involved in work experience programs, outdoor education and youth counseling. Brendan was a key player in the establishment of the Maritime Studies program in 1991. Brendan's background in youth counseling and experiential learning was a major asset in his work with students. Brendan spoke about his passion for maritime studies, student learning and teamwork. He was a strong advocate of rigorous community-based inquiry approaches. Brendan explains:

> Teachers' passion and having a balance of the theoretical and practical; 'hands-on' learning—kids see relationship between what they are doing in the classroom and real life e.g., maths that's relevant to yachting; and maintaining high academic standards without being text book people. Dumbing down curriculum does not help kids. We find that kids in year 10 maritime studies are taking on some complex work in physics but go back into mainstream classes where science is not very rigorous. Our kids do advanced trigonometry as part of training for boat license in year 9 and 10 but often have to put up with low-level maths in class. Kids do want to learn but the context is crucial. You also have to give them extra time if necessary and break the task down into manageable steps. Scaffolding and direct and relevant feed back is also necessary. You have to do this on an individual basis. Kids have ownership of learning.

Drawing on the Productive Pedagogies project, Brendan understood the importance of intellectual quality such as: (i) higher order thinking, (ii) deep knowledge, (iii) deep understanding, (iv) problematic knowledge, (v) substantive conversation, and meta-language (Hayes, Mills, Christie & Lingard, 2006, p. 41). In these ways he was able to use students' interests and passion to pursue a rigorous curriculum with strong cross curricular connections. This was achieved by offering programs that: (i) challenged and extended students' interests; (ii) emphasized group work rather than individualized learning; (iii) acknowledged the importance of negotiation with students; and (iv) provided opportunities for public performances of student competence.

In contrast to the current obsession with standardization, high stakes testing and back-to-basics reforms, these strategies highlight what most teachers know—that rigorous learning and improved standards will be achieved 'by enhancing—not diminishing—the authority and judgment of those who know our children best' (Meier, 2002, p. 3). Kincheloe (1993) believes that this kind of teaching and learning has a number of characteristics. It is:

- Inquiry oriented
- Socially contextualized and aware of power
- Grounded on a commitment to world making
- Dedicated to an art of improvisation
- Dedicated to the cultivation of situated participation
- Extended by a concern with critical self- and social reflection
- Shaped by a commitment to democratic self-directed education
- Steeped in sensitivity to pluralism
- Committed to action
- Concerned with the affective dimension of human beings (pp. 202–203).

It was not surprising, therefore, to hear students speak highly about teachers who were committed to these kinds of pedagogical principles and values. Students were keen to receive a rigorous and relevant education connected to their culture, interests and lives.

Story: 'They were focused and proud of their achievements'

In this section we want to elaborate on Kincheloe and Steinberg's (1998a) notion of students as researchers. For them, a good education is one that prepares students to not only 'read the world' but to change it (p. 2). This involves developing a higher level of understanding, a critical literacy that will enable them to 'learn to act in informed, socially just, and communitarian ways' (p. 3). This kind of pedagogy utilizes primary and secondary forms of research to pursue themes, questions and concerns from students' lives and experience. We agree with Greene (1999) when she says 'I would like to think of teachers moving the young into their own interpretations of their lives and their lived worlds, opening wider and wider perspectives as they do' (p. 29).

For example, Jenny was a society and environment specialist in the middle years of schooling who demonstrated a strong commitment to pursuing community-based research through integrated curricula projects, especially those which encouraged civic engagement (Noddings, 2005a). She described how her students designed a heritage trail to replace some badly faded art work along the foreshore of their local neighborhood. The project engaged students in producing pieces of creative and community-oriented public art that tapped into local culture and heritage and drew on various 'funds of knowledge' in the community (Moll, Amanti, Neff, & Gonzalez, 1992). By creating spaces for students to research significant historical themes and to organize their own displays, Jenny encouraged them to view themselves as producers of knowledge and authors of local histories. The Boardwalk Project revealed the potential of schools and students to contribute to community renewal and civic engagement around worthwhile projects. Jenny explains her work in more detail:

> Our heritage trail was supported and funded by the City Council and the local Rotary Club. Our aim was to create a series of plaques commemorating the significance of people, organizations and events in the City's history. The plaques were to be inlaid into the foreshore walk in a prominent part of the city. Artists were commissioned to work with a group of year 10 students to design and construct the murals and markers with information about pioneer families, maritime and forest industries and environmental themes. Regular society and environment curriculum was suspended for the duration of the project and a flexible timetable was introduced to facilitate sessions with the students and the artists. The artists worked with the students for at least 2–3 hours per week to provide direction and guidance.
>
> Prior to the commencement of the project students were given an overview of the City's rich history as background for their research. The class also visited the site where their work would be displayed. Students were organized in groups, with each group being responsible for researching a particular aspect of local history, such as shipping and shipwrecks, settlement and trade and the timber industry. In addition, students were given a list of prominent families and were asked to choose one that was of interest to them. The students were provided with research materials pertaining to their theme and family and used guidelines to set about researching.
>
> Research was followed up by a visit to the local museum where students could engage in displays. It is here that they gained the inspiration for their drawings from paintings, photographs models and objects that were on display. Original sketches were taken back to class where they were refined and further research was carried out. Students carried out a PowerPoint presentation displaying their designs with a summary of their meaning and significance.
>
> A presentation was made to all involved at the City Council building where students gave a short speech about their design. The students responded well to the project; they were very focused and proud of their achievements.

Jenny's story highlights the pedagogical possibilities generated by inquiry-based approaches to teaching and learning. Kincheloe (2001) elaborates on the benefits of this approach for both students and teachers:

> As they learn about issues of importance to their everyday lives, democratic social studies teachers and students connect such concerns to various knowledge bases and

develop essential intellectual skills such as reading, writing, interpreting, and communicating. In this educational context, they begin to develop awareness of themselves as social players—citizens who are shaped by social, cultural, and political forces and who have a role in molding the social sphere. They are of the social sphere; not apart from it. They produce knowledge themselves and interpret what has already been produced; they do not relegate this task to the experts (King & Darder, 1991) (p. 33).

In the tradition of Dewey, the purpose of education is not only to increase students' abilities to make meaning from their experience but to act on it and desire more learning (Shor, 1992, p. 137).

Story: 'Teachers had a license to experiment with pedagogy'

Where schools demonstrated a commitment to creating spaces for teacher collaboration, reflection and planning, innovative possibilities for student engagement were more likely. In one school we visited, a group of teachers were grappling with the question of youth and popular culture at one of their team meetings:

> When we arrived 16 teachers were seated around tables in the Humanities (Society and Environment, English, and Languages Other than English) office. The meeting was chaired by two curriculum managers. Teachers were brainstorming resources and strategies to engage kids, e.g. incorporate ideas from popular culture and TV programs like Myth Busters, Inventors, Spicks and Specks, My hero—a 'mockumentry', CNN&N, and Simpsons; make use of music; listening to students—what they are talking about? Films—a teacher explained that her students got a lot of fun and enjoyment out of the Australian comedy 'Crackerjack'; documentaries; breakfast radio programs; survey kids interests; and letters to the editor (Field observations, 26th July, 2005).

In these meetings teachers listened to and learned from each other. Some of the younger teachers in particular were able to offer newer perspectives and ideas. One teacher in the team was referred to as the 'the visual man' because he incorporated lots of animation and media-based activities into his classroom. In his words:

> Some of this is IT based but I also make use of comics. We have a very large collection of good quality comics that kids can use in class. We had a reasonably large turnover of humanities staff last year and we now have new ideas coming into the team. Lisa and I probably contribute a lot of new ideas because of our freshness (Teacher).

In general, the curriculum managers were prepared to encourage and foster innovation and risk taking. Teachers had a license to experiment with pedagogy. Both students and teachers were given freedom and choice although this tended to disappear in years 11 and 12 where the focus of teaching and learning narrowed around the Tertiary Entrance Examinations (TEE). One teacher explained to us that many students were:

> Bored with the functionalist approach in the Vocational English course. I try to give them more control over what they are doing in the classroom and work more on an individual basis with kids. I allow for free time in class as well—go outside for a walk or play some sport (Teacher).

It was clear from our conversations with teachers and students that collaboration, reflection and planning played a pivotal role in facilitating the development of productive student-learning experiences. As one student involved in a successful soccer programme explained:

> It's heaps of fun; have met good friends . . . lots of team building activities, a lot of variety, jokes, games, recognition, camps, good training and fitness programs, good coaches. With soccer you have something to look forward to every day (Student).

Whilst we witnessed many innovative and engaging practices, we do not wish to gloss over the difficulties teachers and students experience on a daily basis. Shor (1980) explains that there are significant 'interferences to critical thought' (p. 44) including traditional pedagogies which have served to 'control, instruct, monitor, reward and punish students as they acquire appropriate content' (Riveria & Poplin, 1995, p. 225). As well, student alienation and resistance; uneven levels of development; vocationalism; prior schooling; mass media; regressive ideologies e.g., racism and sexism; unattractive surroundings; language; literacy; family life; and health and nutrition can all act as obstacles in the daily lives of students (Shor, 1992, pp. 217–223). In these circumstances, there is considerable unlearning to occur before many working-class students can begin to trust an education system that has historically failed them (Connell, 1993; Teese & Polesel, 2003). Based on the evidence emerging from this study it is clear that when students' culture and interests are respected by teachers and accommodated in curriculum planning then students are more likely to engage in schooling.

Pursuing socially critical possibilities

In this section we want to suggest some ideas, resources and strategies that our research revealed about pursuing a pedagogy of youth and popular culture. To this end, the focus is on the pedagogy of possibility. What hasn't been thought about? What might be possible? What are the alternatives? What are others saying? How might we go about it? Based on the evidence presented in the previous section, the most innovative and effective strategies occurred when teachers collaborated with students, parents and the community in making professional judgments about what was in the best interests of their students. It was apparent to us and many others, that prescriptive formulas, accountability regimes and standardized solutions were unhelpful when dealing with complex matters of student engagement and learning. In this context, we want to now sketch some general principles, values and guidelines that emerge from our research related to a socially critical approach to youth and popular culture. In this task, we see this as pushing the boundaries by moving beyond current thinking and practice to explore some new possibilities for thinking and action.

Story: 'I think it's about having a team of teachers that talk to each other'

As one teacher explained to us, 'I think it's about having a team of teachers that talk to each other'. This teacher's comment highlights the importance of creating and sustaining processes for ongoing collegial conversations around questions of pedagogy. To understand the world of youth and popular culture and its pedagogical implications requires an enormous amount of teachers' time, energy and intellectual effort. As we have seen, there are no predetermined syllabuses or scripted answers for teachers working in the field of youth and popular culture. Rather, teachers require significant levels of support and resources to assist them in the task of (re)imagining and (re)inventing their own pedagogy with and for young people.

In tackling this kind of work, we believe that critically reflective practice can open up spaces for individual and/or collective teacher investigation, planning, reflection and action (Smyth, 1989; 2000; Brookfield, 1995; Bullough & Gitlin, 2001). According to Simon (1988), critically reflective practice is concerned with the moral question of 'why things are the way they are, how they got that way, and what set of conditions are supporting the processes that maintain them' (p. 2). It involves a critique of existing practices for the purpose of taking action to improve student learning for the benefit of all students, not only the privileged few. From this perspective, teachers and students become 'knowledge workers' (as opposed to technicians/civil servants) who 'research, interpret, expose embedded values and political interest, and produce their own knowledge' (Kincheloe, 2001, p. 241). According to Kemmis and McTaggart (2005) reflection becomes 'critical' when:

> We can ask whether their [teachers] understandings of their situations are less irrational (or ideologically skewed) than before, whether their action is less unproductive and unsatisfying for those involved, or whether the social relations between people in the situation are less inequitable or unjust than before. The product . . . is not just knowledge but also different histories than might have existed if participants had not intervened to transform their practices, understandings, and situations and, thus, transformed the histories that otherwise seemed likely to come into being. (p. 597)

Teachers committed to this kind of transformative intellectual work (Giroux, 1988) understand that 'education is irrevocably linked to politics and power (who gets what, when and how)' (Hartnett & Carr, 1995, p. 41) and cannot be separated from 'questions of equity, justice and even oppression' (Gitlin, 1996, p. 116). What we know, however, is that 'critical reflection is not something that can happen quickly or easily, and is not simply a process of 'implementation' after a workshop or presented as something to be 'delivered'—it has to be struggled with and worked on again, again, and again . . . !!' (Smyth, et al., 1999, p. 37). One teacher reported on some of the difficulties facing her own Learning Team:

> We got together before term 2 and we decided to use communication as our major idea because English had set its curriculum—so we tried to link into that—science and traditional societies and communication—its really, really difficult—I guess ultimately it would be lovely to say that in 2006 we will do this and this—but when you don't know what staff you are getting—and you get a transfer and the person that comes in will not fit in . . . maths is getting involved as best they can . . . maths teachers are by their nature very blinkered (Teacher).

Under these circumstances, teachers require not only the spaces for critical reflection and dialogue but a set of ideas and processes to help them think through complex issues. In our own work with teachers and schools, we have found the framework developed by Hattam, Brown and Smyth (1995) to be a useful heuristic:

- *Affiliate:* find a group of volunteers to examine rigorously some substantial educational issue.
- *Examine:* using the group find out what is going on or consult with others to find out what they think about the issue.
- *Represent:* the knowledge produced through examining the issue is represented in a form that stimulates further debate and dialogue with the wider school community.
- *Interrupt:* collectively explore alternatives, challenge myths, question practices, and locate issues in the bigger social picture.
- *Take action:* decide what can be done to incorporate the new shared understandings into practice, and then act strategically and prudently.
- *Re-examine:* within the group begin to monitor the changes and to answer the question—how will we know we have made a difference?
- *Checking out:* finally, check out with the group, how the process is going—is it beneficial for teaching and learning? How do you know? (p. 6).

In tackling this sort of critical collaborative inquiry, Wink (2005) identifies some elements that seem to work:

- Taking time.
- Tossing the texts.
- Asking, 'But why?'
- Reflecting.
- Conceptualizing and articulating our own philosophical assumptions.
- Understanding why and how beliefs change.
- Naming the power structures, critically reflecting, and acting on them.
- Relearning and unlearning.
- Acknowledging the powerful emotions of power, racism, classism, and sexism.
- Understanding and being able to articulate the new global realities.
- Challenging our long-held assumptions about teaching and learning.
- Reading hard books.
- Entering into dialogue.
- Recognizing our own power, expertise, knowledge, and role.
- Seeing with new eyes.
- Taking time and creating a safe space (p. 146).

Significantly, critical reflection of the kind advocated here, opens up the symbolic spaces where teachers can begin the task of reclaiming control over the policies and practices that are impacting on their daily lives and work (Giroux, 2004). As well, it provides an opportunity to reinsert social justice discourses back into conversations about the nature, purpose and processes of education (McInerney, 2004). Strategically, this more expansive and activist view of teacher professionalism (Whitty, 1994; Bigelow, 2006; Gale & Densmore, 2003) runs counter to the narrowly conceived efforts of government to control teachers' work through teacher-proof curricula, test driven threats and punitive forms of accountability (Nichols & Berliner, 2007).

Story: 'The curriculum is still subject/discipline orientated'

The teacher narratives alluded to in the previous section highlight the centrality of students' culture and interests in constructing a curriculum around youth and popular culture. One of the major barriers identified by teachers was the attachment to the traditional subject disciplines and its corollary timetabling. As one teacher explained it:

> We have a toxic culture because the curriculum is teacher driven as opposed to student driven. There are decisions made to appease and motivate staff rather than serve the best interest of kids. Our kids don't have a true middle school experience because the curriculum is still subject/discipline oriented. We don't have a great deal of autonomy in the teams. It's a throw back to traditional schooling methods where people feel you need to keep the lid on things. Our timetable isn't flexible enough to cater for middle schooling needs. Senior school drives timetable (Teacher).

In addressing this problem, we believe the field of cultural studies casts light on some new possibilities for engaging young people around questions of everyday life. According to Giroux (1994), cultural studies can provide teachers with an analytical lens for 'addressing the shifting attitudes, representations, and desires of this new generation of youth being produced within the current historical, economic, and cultural juncture' (p. 298). He goes on to argue that the spread of 'electronically mediated culture to all spheres of intellectual and social life has shifted the ground of scholarship away from traditional disciplines designed to preserve a 'common culture' to the more hybridized fields of comparative and world literature, media studies, ecology, society and technology and popular culture' (p. 299).

In order to help students to make sense of the world, many teachers in our research responded by crossing the boundaries of the academic disciplines (sociology, political science, economics, media studies, philosophy, history, geography, and anthropology) in pursuit of interdisciplinary approaches that critically investigate the everyday habits and routines of student's lives such as work, sport, music, school, printed text, television, cinema, art, theatre, consumer goods, advertising, and fashion (Smyth, Shacklock & Hattam, 1999) For example, one maths teacher we interviewed was able to connect to students' interest in football:

> We integrate soccer skills into the curriculum e.g., measuring the dimensions of the football fields. Most of the kids are AFL [Australian Football League] mad so when we are doing statistics we did a lot of work on player statistics. The kids loved it so much they didn't think they were doing maths. I've had to learn about footy! (Teacher).

A number of teachers commented on the benefits of negotiating the curriculum with students in these ways:

> It actually works better when the kids run it (Teacher).

> They have a purpose to what they do—they get some realism into their learning (Teacher).

> Realistically just getting them out of the classroom (Teacher).

> OBE [Outcomes Based Education] allows you to be innovative in the context of the kids and the community which you don't get in the prescriptive model which some teachers want to go back to (Teacher).

> It's really about the kids (Teacher).

With this new starting point, teachers and students begin to work collaboratively to 'gain new ways of knowing and producing knowledge that challenge the commonsense views of socio-political reality with which most individuals have grown so comfortable' (Kincheloe, 2001, p. 372). In other words, the emphasis shifts to focus on student and teacher thinking/cognition and how it serves either to inhibit or empower democratic thinking and democratic action (Kincheloe, 2005).

Story: 'As teachers we have to build up communication with kids and find out their interests'

In planning a relevant curriculum, one teacher described the need for 'creativity and flexibility and thinking outside the box'. In her view, there are many teachers 'hung up on book learning—why do we need these things—teaching things just because you had to learn them isn't a very good excuse at all'. In struggling against compartmentalization, in particular the 'blinkered nature' of maths and science subjects, this teacher found herself searching for some alternative ways of incorporating everyday life into her curriculum planning. As we mentioned earlier, another teacher was passionate about getting to know his students, 'I am interested in who they are and what they do. One of the first things I did when I had the class was to get them to write an autobiography. This gave me an idea of who's who'. The ability of teachers to investigate student culture and lives is central to the pedagogy of youth and popular culture. In addition to the many advantages of encouraging students as researchers, Kincheloe (2001) argues that there is great benefit to be gained when teachers explore the social, economic, cultural, educational, historical and political dynamics of their students and their communities. Not only does it help teachers to comprehend the forces impacting on the schools in which they work but it also helps them to understand the students they teach (p. 407). For example, Gonzalez and Moll (2002) develop the idea of 'funds of knowledge' to investigate the range of cultural and intellectual resources available to teachers and students within households in poor communities and the implications for teaching and learning.

Nespor (1998) extends this approach by enlisting students as researchers to gain new insights and perspectives. She believes that participant student inquiry can open up new questions and new understandings of students' worlds and their links to the adult world (p. 1). Nespor (1998) elaborates on how students are driven by a curiosity or desire to talk to other students about things that didn't fit into the standard narrative of school (e.g., popular music, clothes), and bigger moral questions related to tensions with adults and the difficulties of getting along in the world where power and autonomy are mediated by adults, where students are excluded from debates over the legitimacy or rightness of adult practices such as standardized testing, homework folders and so on (p. 10). By researching student culture in these ways teachers begin to see the world from multiple points.

Shor (1992) provides a list of questions to guide teachers committed to critically engaged learning through participatory research, for example:

- What do students talk about, read about, and write about? When do they read and write, for what purposes? What books do they buy or have at home?
- What do they watch on TV, read about in newspapers, and listen to on radio? Do they think the media give them an accurate picture of events? What news are they *not* getting? Can they define the politics of their newspapers? What political words are already in their vocabulary?
- What aspects of their language appear often as good choices for classroom study—repeated words, phrases, sayings, references, favorite songs, typical expressions?
- What images and texts do they have on the walls of their homes?
- How do they discuss their aspirations? What do they want from life?
- For older students—have they taken part in any political action? Do they belong to any unions or organizations? Do they vote?
- What do they say are the most important problems in society?
- What music is popular? What do they do for recreation?
- What do students hear? What clothes do they wear? What kind of housing do they live in? What kind of medical care do they get?
- For younger students—Do they show signs of neglect or child abuse? Are they read to at home? What stories do they invent or tell? What situations, themes, phrases, or characters fill up their play? What are their favorite games and toys?
- For teenage and older students, are there signs of drug and alcohol abuse? How do they get and spend money? What kinds of jobs do they hold, if any? What are their income levels? Are they sexually active? Is teenage pregnancy a problem? Do they receive effective sex education?
- If foreign born, how do they speak, write, and read English? How do they see their own ethnic identity? What do students say about other ethnic groups and races? What is the racial and ethnic makeup of their area? Do they see race relations as a problem?
- What are the typical relationships between men and women in their homes and communities? How do they see masculinity, and femininity? Do they think men and women are equal, or should be? Do women

feel free to express themselves? Do male students interrupt the women who speak in class? Are young or adult students under family pressure not to go to college? Do they experience sexual harassment in the neighborhood, school, or college?
- What about other social relationships, like those between tenants and landlords, citizens and police, workers and bosses? How do they talk about them? Which present problems?
- How do they feel about schooling? Do they think they are getting a good education? What are the local schools and colleges like? What level of education do people in their families and neighborhoods have? Are there any community-based education programs?
- What are community conditions—density, housing, religion, health care, mass transit, crime, playgrounds, sanitation, commercial and government services, race relations? (pp. 204–205).

Pursuing research as a 'jointed activity' around these kinds of questions allows teachers to see students not as 'inhabitants of foreign cultures', but as 'living in the same world, albeit differently positioned' (Nespor, 1998, p. 10). Shor (1992) argues that to study something in-depth in these ways is to research. In his view, the critical classroom functions as a research center at a number of levels:

- the teacher examines student life and language to create a curriculum situated in their themes;
- students are invited to join the teacher in studying their community and conditions, as co-researchers of their own culture; and
- once a generative, topical, or academic theme is posed as a problem for critical dialogue, students and teacher become researchers again, investigating a specific subject matter (p. 169).

As one teacher explained to us, 'as teachers we have to build up communication with kids and find out their interests. Similarly, kids also need to be able to communicate their interests with teachers' (Teacher). Underpinning this approach, is the view that subject knowledge needs to be balanced with open and democratic practices, so that while 'The teacher brings learning plans, learning methods, personal experiences and academic knowledge to class, [the teacher] negotiates the curriculum with the students and begins with their languages, themes and understandings' (Shor, 1992, p. 16). The challenge is to present knowledge in ways that 'does not silence students or sedate them' (p. 83).

Story: 'I feel a sense of pride in what I've accomplished at school'

In this study, teachers and students talked a great deal about the significance of identity and sense of belongingness. This involved friendships, relationships with teachers, trust, people taking an interest in them, and feeling valued and respected for who they are. As we pointed out, one student explained 'Heaps of girls would have left earlier without teachers taking an interest in them'. As Wexler (1992) reminds us, what matters most to young people is 'their struggle to become somebody, to establish their identity through social relations' (p. 156). For this reason, he believes that the current focus on cognitive skills, curriculum, and knowledge to the detriment of identity work has not been helpful to young people. Wexler (1992) argues that schools are one of the few public spaces left in which young people are engaged in the 'interactional work of making *meaning*' (p. 155). So while they are aware of the world of work and in varying degrees acknowledge interest and attention to the learning of school subjects, 'their central and defining activity in school is to establish at least the image of an identity . . . and this is what high school life is about' (p. 155).

In the case of a community services program for girls we observed a strong emphasis by the teachers on supporting the development of individual and group identity. Building closer relationships and gaining a better knowledge of the students' lives and circumstances was an important focus both inside and outside of the classroom. As one teacher explained 'students have their own space—a place they can call home—and time for socializing with teachers and their peers'. The students themselves acknowledged the value of their relationships with teachers and peers and appreciated the opportunities offered in the program to develop their identity during field placements. We noted the comment made by a student in Chapter 3, in the portrait, who said:

> I've worked in respite care and a hospital for disabled children. I feel a sense of pride in what I've accomplished at school. My mother is very proud of me. My parents have high expectations. They were a bit shocked about me working with disabled kids but I've learned a lot about autism, Down syndrome and other disabilities from the kids (Student).

Clearly, these kinds of experiences are central to assisting students in developing a sense of identity. Besides this important relational work going on inside schools we have argued that youth identities are increasingly being constructed, either consciously or unconsciously, by forces external to the school. With its massive apparatuses of representation and its regulation of meaning, the mass media is central to understanding how the dynamics of power, privilege, and social desire structure daily life and identity formation of young people. Therefore, it should be of great curricular interest to teachers because it opens up some new possibilities for helping young people to interrogate commonsense understandings of dominant media and consumer representations of youth, work and social life (Weiner, 2003; Smyth, Shacklock & Hattam, 1999).

Pinar (1995) makes the point that 'We are what we know.' We are, however, also what we do not know' (p. 23). In other words, young people today require the knowledge, skills and dispositions to help them interrupt dominant constructions and images of self and identity. For instance, teachers might explore how multinational corporations target niche-specific age/interest groups that are labeled in various ways e.g., pre-teens, tweenies, kidult, generation X, rappers, hip hop, homies, surfies etc., and their multiple identities, differences, desires, and buying power (Besley, 2003, p. 167). As McLaren (1997) explains, the purpose of critical pedagogy 'is to provide students with 'counter discourses' or 'resistant subject positions'—in short, with a new language of analysis—through which they can assume a critical distance from their familiar subject positions in order to engage in a cultural praxis better designed to further the project of social transformation' (p. 37).

From this perspective, according to Shor (1992), teachers can play a significant role in desocializing students 'from mass culture, from regressive values absorbed from mass media and daily life, such as racism, sexism, class prejudice, homophobia, self-reliant individualism, excessive consumerism, authority-dependence, celebrations of militarism and so on' (p. 114).

As Shor (1992) suggests, a truly democratic and empowering education is committed to helping young people understand the ways in which their self has been constructed, by whom and in whose interests. This involves questioning the dominant images and experiences of daily life and schooling that make us the people we are (p. 114). Teachers and students engaged in this kind of empowering education are interested in exploring the following kinds of questions:

- Who creates images of youth?
- What kinds of attitudes, behaviors and identities are denigrated?
- Which ones are celebrated?
- What are the effects?
- What economic, social and political conditions shape these representations?

- How have these circumstances come about?
- Who benefits?
- Who loses?
- What can be done?

Freire (2000 [1970]) argues that this kind of problem-posing education 'affirms men and women as beings in the process of *becoming*—as unfinished, uncompleted beings in and with a likewise unfinished reality' (p. 78). For him, education is an ongoing process of personal and social transformation whereby people transcend themselves, move forward and look ahead, and 'for whom immobility represents a fatal threat, for whom looking at the past must only be a means of understanding more clearly what and who they are so that they can more wisely build the future' (p. 79). In short, education is about 'making kids powerful' (Smyth & McInerney, 2007a, p. 205).

Conclusion

In this chapter we have examined the pedagogical significance of youth and popular culture as a means of engaging young people in schooling. At the outset we briefly alluded to the broader sets of economic, cultural and political forces that are currently transforming the lives of young people. As a consequence of these changing times, young people today inhabit a world characterized by novel information and computer technologies; a predatory culture based on the values of consumerism, commodification and competition; a volatile youth labor market characterized by increasing numbers of casual, part-time and low-paid jobs; an era of war, terrorism and insecurity; and a world dominated by market, corporate and media interests. Against this backdrop, we argued that it makes a great deal of sense that the school curriculum should focus on investigating the everyday, informal and popular culture that shapes students' identities and subjectivities. To this end, we examined a range of successful strategies adopted by classroom teachers who were committed to 'starting from where students are at'. These included engaging students' culture and interests; building productive relationships; pursuing rigor and integration; encouraging students as researchers; and fostering teacher collaboration, reflection and planning. We also showed how these strategies assist teachers and schools in developing a more 'socially critical' orientation towards teaching and learning about youth and popular culture. This involved creating spaces for critical reflection and dialogue, stepping outside of traditional subject boundaries, researching students' lives and culture, and interrupting dominant constructions of youth identities.

These kinds of critical pedagogies we believe can serve as a powerful antidote not only to the harm caused by imposing irrelevant and boring skill-and-drill pedagogies on students, but also the current obsession with standardization, high-stakes testing and punitive accountability regimes (Hinchey, 2004; p. 121; Meier, 2002; Lipman, 2004). Significantly, the pedagogy of youth and popular culture offers an alternative vision and practice founded on the principles and values of economic and political democracy, critical inquiry, civic engagement and 'educated hope' (Giroux, 2001, p. 125). It opens up spaces where students and teachers together can investigate questions, issues, and problems that emanate from everyday life. Like Levine (1995), we believe education should be an 'experiment in democracy' where teachers are willing and prepared 'to explore and develop student-teacher relations and curriculum content that promote high expectations, cooperation, and student initiative' (p. 53). In these ways, teachers can provide an education that is not only grounded in the lives of students but also academically rigorous, socially just, democratic, activist and capable of providing a hopeful and visionary future for all students (Bigelow, 2006, p. 7).

SIX

New Storylines That Engage Young Learners

Introduction

Throughout this book we have sought to foreground the lives, histories, experiences and aspirations of those groups marginalized and excluded from the mainstream of economic, social and civil life. Much of our focus has been on young people, especially those left behind in the education stakes as a consequence of their negative experience of schooling and the damaging impact of poverty, social dislocation and fractured relationships on their lives. Drawing on new storylines (Mishler, 2004) that engage young learners, our account has attempted to move beyond a discourse of despair to an optimistic view of the possibilities of transformative education through the intersecting notions of *critically engaged learning* and *critically engaged community capacity building*. In this task, we have pursued those places and spaces where students, teachers, community activists and researchers have been able to come together to 'make and remake their world' (Shor & Freire, 1987, pp. 98–99). By retelling some of these everyday stories, we hope that this book can make a small contribution to the ongoing struggle for social justice.

At the outset we expressed our disquiet with the pseudo 'scientific' and 'evidence-based' fetish currently driving educational policies and practice. We share Noddings' (2005b) concern that such approaches assume that knowledge and skills can be transmitted in a 'scientific' way that 'disregards the deep existential issues that motivate people to do, or not to do, the things so easily listed [for them]' (p. 47). As a counter, Noddings (2005b) advocates the need for a scheme that 'speaks to the existential heart of life—one that draws attention to our passions, attitudes, connections, concerns, and experienced responsibilities' (p. 47). In this spirit, we adopted the notion of 'portraiture' (Lawrence-Lightfoot, 2005) or 'personal narratives and life stories' (Mishler, 2004, p. 18) to help us to better understand how people 'adapt, make, and transform' culturally defined identities and the 'objective' conditions in which they find themselves (p. 18). Like Mishler (2004), we believe that this kind of 'critical analytic perspective' (p. 51) can 'serve as an opening for others to enter into dialogue' by suggesting 'new questions or methods applicable to their problems' (p. 146).

Accordingly, in the preceding chapters we have highlighted:

- The role of educators as community activists in challenging the deficit logic in relation to issues of inequality and developing more inclusive schooling arrangements for the most marginalized students;
- The capacity of schools to promote civic engagement, strengthen social networks and enhance social capital in disadvantaged communities;
- The need for education policies and practices which are respectful of the lives and circumstances of young people and which engender a sense of hope and possibility amongst students;
- The educational potential of community-based studies which draw on popular culture, new technologies and local resources to engage young people in rigorous, relevant and socially valued learning; and
- The crucial importance of critically engaged forms of learning which encourage students to challenge inequitable practices and to work for a more socially just and ecologically sustainable world.

There can be little doubt that these ideals are being undermined in neoliberal times as schools are under immense pressure to redefine themselves around utilitarian approaches to education that attach greatest weight to vocational education and to the acquisition of technical skills and competencies for the global economy (Down, 2006). According to Frymer (2005), this has reached the point in the United States where schooling is largely devoid of an educational purpose, principally because:

the now entrenched ideological linkages between school participation and competition for national superiority in a globalized economy or individual market attainment in a consumer society, have submerged the substantive ends of schooling beneath layers of instrumental rationality. (p. 12)

Instrumentalism has penetrated classrooms to the detriment of student learning. In the introduction to *Pedagogy of Freedom* (Freire, 2001), Aronowitz argues that the banking or transmission theory of knowledge is alive and well in American schools as the old notion of a liberal education has been replaced by a training model in which teachers teach to externally administered tests and students engage in meaningless rote learning:

> Where once liberal, let alone radical, educators insisted that education be at the core of an activity of self-exploration in which, through intellectual and affective encounters, the student attempts to discover her own subjectivity, now nearly all learning space is occupied by an elaborate testing apparatus that measures the student's 'progress' in ingesting externally imposed curricula and, more insidiously, provides a sorting device to reproduce the inequalities inherent in the capitalist market system. (pp. 4–5)

Railing against the pernicious influence of positivism, Kincheloe (2003, p. 5) points out that the standards movement is largely unconcerned with 'the duties of democratic citizenship, the need for social change and the issue of justice'. On this point, we agree with Giroux's (2001) argument that the moral and ethical purpose of education should be 'organized around a sense of critical public citizenship ... [and] notions of educated hope that keep alive forms of political agency capable of realizing a life outside of the dictates of the marketplace—and which are crucial to a substantive democracy' (p. 2). Instead, right wing advocates of technical standards, accountability regimes and high-stakes testing are more preoccupied with social regulation and suppression of critical reasoning rather than emancipation. They simply do not want students to question 'the facts' says Kincheloe! (2001). Although we do not wish to discount the damaging impact of this ideological movement in Australia and elsewhere today, one of the main aims of this study has been to identify the spaces for critically engaged educators to work in transformative ways with local communities to improve education for the most disadvantaged students. In what follows, we want to outline the features of critically engaged learning (many of which emerged from our ethnographic studies of Wirra Wagga and Bountiful Bay) and to engage in some reimagining of public education framed around a set of commitments to democratic practices, community capacity building and social justice.

As a way of organizing this discussion, we have endeavored to pull together—tentatively and heuristically—a schema of emergent ideas that we have represented diagrammatically in Figure 6.1:

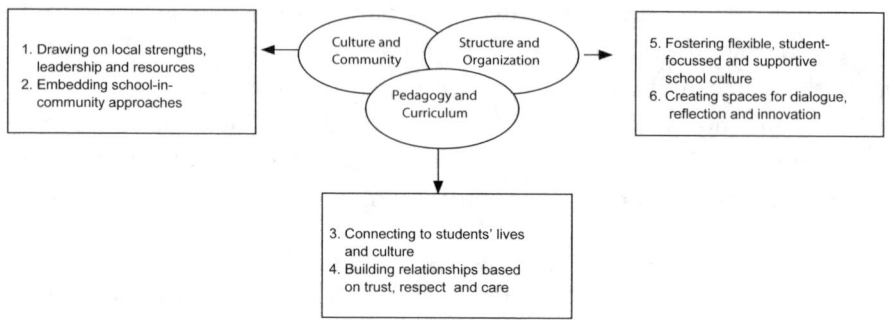

Figure 6.1: Critical engagement for school-community renewal

In Figure 6.1 we summarize three interrelated sites of thinking and action around critical engagement for school and community renewal; namely, culture and community; pedagogy and curriculum; and school structure and organization. In general terms, *culture and community* refers to those broader values, attitudes, orientations, beliefs, assumptions, behaviors and relationships that need to be created and more widely sustained to enhance critical engagement among students, teachers, community and researchers. Here we are attracted to McMurtry's (1998) notion of the 'civil commons' as a way of describing how people can act together as a community to guarantee the social conditions of 'life-capacities' for the least advantaged (p. 24). The emphasis is on how schools can create the appropriate cultural settings to work collaboratively and democratically with their communities and draw them into the educational lives of their students. By *pedagogy and curriculum* we refer to the ways in which schools are willing to connect to the lifeworlds of students and their communities. We argue that his approach opens up spaces where students and teachers can investigate together questions, issues, and problems that emanate from everyday life (Shor, 1980). By 'starting from where the students are at', teachers can provide an education that is not only grounded in the lives of students but also academically rigorous, socially worthwhile and capable of providing a hopeful future for disenfranchised and alienated students (Bigelow, 2006, p. 7). Finally, *school structure and organization* refers to the structural and organizational aspects of school life that serve to enhance relationships based on trust, respect and care rather than bureaucratic rules, regulations and control. Critically engaged schools operate in ways that de-institutionalize relationships, build a strong sense of solidarity, actively engage students' lives and voices, forge community alliances and ownership, and foster authentic teaching, learning and assessment practices in context.

In the remainder of the chapter we want to draw on the ideas in Figure 6.1 to briefly elaborate on the main elements that make up sites of school and community renewal. It should be emphasized that our intent is not to provide yet another 'to do' list for schools and teachers but rather to present a heuristic for ongoing critique, engagement and transformation.

Culture and community

'Enforced retention is no good for kids' commented a teacher in Bountiful Bay. Students from contexts that put them at an educational disadvantage require far more creative curricula and pedagogical responses than coercive policies and prescriptions embedded in the deficit discourses of conventional schooling. Sticking to the official script simply doesn't work. Many students in low socioeconomic communities experience schools as alienating institutions embodying middle class values that resonate poorly with their own backgrounds. According to Corson (1998):

> much of the cultural capital valued in school is only partly available to children who come from class, gender, or cultural backgrounds that differ from the school recognized norms (p. 11).

To put this argument another way, there is a tendency on the part of educators to ignore or devalue the assets of these communities and to impose top-down solutions to perceived problems of student engagement and school retention. Re-enchanting students with learning in these circumstances requires an orientation to education that places the individual lives, aspirations and concerns of students at the forefront of curriculum, but just as importantly, it demands a rethinking of the nature of school-community relationships. As we have described in the ethnographic studies of Wirra Wagga and Bountiful Bay, education policies that stop at the school gate are unlikely to have much impact in areas that really matter. The bigger challenge for schools is to work *with*, rather than *against*, local communities to:

- Develop curriculum that is more responsive to students' lives and cultures, as well as being accessible to adult members of the community;
- Build social networks that open up educational and vocational pathways for young people;
- Revitalize democracy at the grassroots level through participatory forms of decision making in local community organizations; and
- Develop integrated programs (health, welfare, adult education) that contribute to long-term community capacity building.

The task of re-engaging excluded youth involves a restoration of the social, political and economic order such that school and community renewal go hand-in-hand. Drawing on the experiences of Wirra Wagga and Bountiful Bay, two of the key elements of this broader democratic project as indicated in Figure 6.1, include:

1. *Drawing on local strengths, leadership and resources*
   Community renewal, as exemplified in Wirra Wagga emphasizes the capacity of communities (with external support) to improve the quality of life for citizens by drawing on local strengths, leadership and resources. The idea of capacity building, as opposed to community development challenges the paternalism embedded in many public policies and programs where outside experts rather than residents steer changes supposedly in the interests of the less privileged. Appropriating Singh (2003), community renewal incorporates the following principles and concepts:

- *Place based*—flexibility, local knowledge and 'local solutions' to 'local problems'.
- *Asset based*—all communities have a reserve of skills, talents, gifts, and resources, but they also have constraints that limit what is possible in capacity building.
- *Engaged citizenship*—building local skills and knowledge to increase community participation.
- *Local ownership*—an emphasis on local democracy, local ownership, organic leadership and grassroots initiatives.
- *Collective action*—residents identify their long-term hopes and goals for the neighborhood and develop solutions toward a shared vision or common good.
- *Relationship building*—networks enhance social capital, promote dia-

logue and civic engagement and help to develop a sense of agency.
- *Comprehensive and integrated approach*—the neighborhood is viewed in a holistic manner. Services and initiatives are created and administered in recognition of other programs in the neighborhood and where possible coordination or collaboration occurs.

Critically engaged learning of the kind we are describing here is embedded in the social, political and cultural lives of students and their communities. It expresses itself in a concern for the social life of young people, their households and neighborhoods and acknowledges 'the important role of indigenous, traditional and culturally based knowledge in schools [as] a valuable educational resource for the learner' (Dei, 1993, p. 253). For learning to have real meaning and purpose it needs to be grounded in the communal life and concerns of students (Vibert and Shields, 2003, p. 234) and the bigger issues confronting society. A critical pedagogy of engagement positions the school as a community asset that can work collaboratively with local residents to build a better community.

2. *Embedding school-in-community approaches*
    Schooling takes place in a social and community context but all too often the officially sanctioned curriculum takes little heed of the culture, family background and local influences on children's lives. School structures, programs and norms are typically imposed on students with little or no consultation with the communities they are intended to serve. The education of young people is everybody's business and cannot be achieved without the cooperation and active involvement of parents, teachers, students and community groups. Community-engaged schools exhibit some of the following features:

- *Learning extends beyond the walls of the classroom*—social networks assist students to find ways to learn in and about the community in which they live. The school is seen as a community resource and major contributor to community capacity building.
- *Communities take ownership and responsibility*—school 'belongs to' rather than 'relates to' the community (Smith et. al, 1998). There is a strong culture of inclusion and participatory decision making. Parents and community are actively cultivated into the school as a 'rich resource' rather than seen as being a deficit. Community talents and strengths are identified and fostered (Kretzmann & McKnight, 1993).

- *Accommodating the social conditions of life of students and their families*—schools are embedded in the social, political and ethical lives of students and their families. Community-engaged schools demonstrate a preparedness to hang in with students who face complex and challenging lives. The focus is on developing an 'ethic of care'—'care for self, care for intimate others, care for associates and distant others' (Noddings, 2005b, p. 47).
- *Reconstituting individual and community identities*—schools play a key role in (re)constituting individual and cultural identities by stepping outside of the language of pathologizing practices. When teachers, community activists and parents assert their individual and collective agency, communities are able to 'push back' against alienating, demeaning and disempowering policies and practices.

A critically engaged approach to school and community capacity building is committed to the principles and values of dialogue, public participation, communal engagement and democracy. The evidence arising out of this research indicates that when schools and communities are reconnected in these ways there is a greater likelihood that the aspirational goals of disadvantaged communities might be realized.

Pedagogy and curriculum

Ted, one of the participants in this study, summed it up pretty well when he said it was all about 'starting from where the kids are at'. Whilst this might seem self evident to teachers committed to progressive educational practices, advocates of neo-liberal and neo-conservative reforms have unashamedly attempted to reshape education around increasingly narrow instrumentalist approaches to teaching and learning through greater emphasis on vocationalism, national curricula, testing, appraisal, auditing, back-to-basic reforms, behavior management, and so on. Based on the stories of teachers, students, parents and community activists involved in this research it is apparent that these sorts of muscular policies and practices are not only ineffectual but also damaging to students, families and communities put at disadvantage. What we have witnessed in both Wirra Wagga and Bountiful Bay is evidence of an alternative approach to education grounded in the daily lives and struggles of students, teachers and community activists. This provides us with a renewed sense of hope and optimism about how things might change for the better 'by enhancing—not diminishing—the authority and judgment of those who know our kids best' (Meier, 2002, p. 3). By way of summary, this kind of engaged learning has two main features, as indicated in Figure 6.1:

3. *Connecting to students' lives and culture*
   Connecting to students' lives and culture is based on the assumption that knowledge is socially constructed and developed by individuals in context. Rather than treating students as 'depositories' to be filled with information often divorced from reality, teachers and students begin to explore their own worlds, produce knowledge, generate meaning and engage in social action (Freire, 2000 [1970]). In the tradition of John Dewey, teachers share a view that the present should generate the problems, which lead to students and teachers collaboratively investigating experience. As Singh (2007) explains, significant progress is likely to occur when teachers connect school knowledge to the learner's background, passions, culture, language, needs and interests. Beginning with the familiar, teachers are able to broaden students' horizons and move to more powerful representations of knowledge. There are a number of aspects to this kind of engaged learning:

- *Giving students a say in what they learn and how*—schools are organized in ways that take seriously what students have to say and how they want to learn. By actively listening to students the focus shifts from 'doing for (or to)' to 'working with' students on issues of common interest (Smith et. al, 1998). The idea of the 'school as an experiment in democracy' opens up new possibilities for 'student-teacher relations and curriculum content that promote high expectations, cooperation, and student initiative' (Levine, 1995, p. 53).
- *Incorporating youth and popular culture into the curriculum*—teachers recognize the curricular significance of cultural artifacts emanating from everyday life. 'Cool' (Skelton & Valentine, 1998) teachers appreciate the importance of youth and popular culture—TV, music, movies, video games, the Internet, fashion and art—in shaping students subjectivities and identities. These teachers comprehend the need to create a 'media-literate citizenry that can disrupt, contest, and transform media apparatuses' (McLaren, 1995, p. 9).
- *Making the curriculum challenging, rigorous and fun*—teachers appreciate that the curriculum should not only be relevant and socially worthwhile but challenging, rigorous and fun. Standards are high and the

pedagogical structure is explicit. Students are 'treated as responsible, capable human beings who should expect to do a lot and do it well' (Shor, 1992, p. 21).

- *Learning is collaborative, hands-on and inquiry based*—teachers and students together (co)research themes, questions and issues from students' lives and experiences (Kincheloe & Steinberg, 1998c). Drawing on local 'funds of knowledge' (Moll, et. al., 1992) students undertake community-based learning informed by the actual and immediate events in their lives. Teachers are prepared to engage students in real-world experiences, step outside the traditional subject disciplines, investigate 'multiple perspectives' (Sleeter, 2005) and celebrate learning through the use of public performance.
- *Encouraging students to think about big questions*—teachers are willing to engage students in thinking about the big questions and ideas confronting society at the beginning of the 21st century (Hutchinson, 1996). Controversial issues related to politics, justice and the environment are not avoided but addressed as a part of the curriculum.

Putting students' lives and culture at the center of the curriculum makes a great deal of sense in these uncertain and exploitative times. If we are going to help students to make sense of their world critically then we must necessarily tangle with the everyday, informal and popular culture that so powerfully shapes their subjectivities and identities. In doing so, education reclaims its emancipatory intent by interrogating commonsense understandings of dominant media and consumer representations of young people, work and social life. Failure to engage with the present, says Dewey (1944 [1916]), 'is simply to abdicate the education function' (p. 73).

4. *Building relationships based on trust, respect and care*
Throughout this study we were reminded about the relationally intensive nature of schools, and how schools that are successfully engaging young lives are particularly adept at building relationships founded on trust, respect and care (Smyth, 2007; Smyth & Fasoli, 2007). We argue, however, that the issue is not simply one of care, respect, regard for others and interpersonal relationships, although these are obviously extremely important—rather, it is a case of how students are enabled too relate to one another, to their teachers, school leaders and members of the community. Equally important, but often not thought about in the same way, is how young people are inducted into the process of

relating to bigger and more important social ideas, issues and questions—how they analyze them, how they interrogate information, how they make knowledge transfer, and how they develop ethical positions regarding socially important questions that require them to prudently and courageously take a position. In short, we believe that both aspects—the interpersonal as well as ideational relationships—both play a crucial part in engaging students in school, firing their imaginations, and sustaining the will to want to continue formal learning.

In moving towards these aspirations we can identify a number of conditions that are conducive to creating and supporting relational schools of this kind:

- *The de-institutionalization of relationships* (Osterman, 2000)—which is to say, removing the distant and impersonal way schools insulate themselves from the way they relate to students and community through rules, policies and bureaucratic procedures.
- *Emphasizing the creation of capabilities*—which as Sen (1992; 1999; 2002) argues, is about assisting people to: (i) identify the kind of lives they want to lead; (ii) providing them with the skills and knowledge to do that; and (iii) helping them understand and confront how their political, social and economic conditions will allow or impede them.
- *Building relational trust* (Bryk & Schneider, 2002)—in the form of social exchanges that bring with them 'respect', 'personal regard for others', 'competence', and 'integrity', and the set of mutually interrelated dependencies that come with these and that constitute a valuable organizational and institutional resource.
- *Divesting ownership of decision making over learning* to learners who have a meaningful stake in what and how they learn, and how that learning is assessed and reported upon.
- *Humanizing relationships* (Noguera, 1995; Bartolome, 1994)—so that fear, threats and retribution are removed as the basis for learning, and as a consequence a climate is created in which it is safe to take risks.
- *Eliminating the stress that comes with inequality* by deconstructing hierarchy (Spring, 2007, p. 50) and banishing harmful competition—so that energy, emotion and learning time are not dissipated in dealing with the extraneous and unhealthy effects of competition; and
- *Having an improvisational view of teaching* (Smyth, 2005)—that goes beyond the arbitrary imposition of standards, and that instead licenses and legitimates courageous, exploratory and experimental approaches.

Put most directly, from the point of view of students, there can be 'no learning without relations' (Bingham & Sidorkin, 2004). The evidence in both Wirra Wagga and Bountiful Bay is compelling. When teachers place the interests of students first by providing them with relevant and meaningful learning experiences, then schools become far more hospitable and engaging places.

Structure and organization

To create truly democratic schools, we must start by ensuring that all students are treated fairly. In other words, schools must operate in ways that protect the 'personal right and dignity' of all students as well as the 'common good' (Beane, 2005, p. 9). According to Bernstein (1996), this involves the institutionalization of three interrelated rights in schools: (i) the right to individual enhancement so that students experience new possibilities beyond individual and cultural stereotypes and identities; (ii) the right to be included as well as the right to be separate and autonomous; and (iii) the right to participate not only in shaping the discourses but also the practices and outcomes of schooling (pp. xx–xxi). Locating matters of school structure and organization in the context of these broader democratic ideals and aspirations enables us to move beyond the limited story of regulatory, top-down, and managerial discourses to a more 'purposeful and intentional' approach geared to critically engaged learning. At heart, this means restoring 'schools as democratic public spheres' (Giroux 1997, p. 218) where the ideals of 'social cohesion, empathy, caring, respect, reciprocity, and trust' (Beckmann & Cooper, 2004, p. 11) become the cornerstones of school structure and organization. Towards this end, we want to return to Figure 6.1 and to briefly discuss the two key features that comprise a more democratic approach to school structure and organization.

5. *Fostering a flexible, student-focused and supportive school culture*
   When the starting point for conversations is around students' interests, culture, experience and needs rather than the interests of management, bureaucrats, politicians or business, we believe an educative and socially just orientation to schools is more likely. As one teacher put it, 'It's really about the kids'. There are a number of structural and organizational arrangements that are conducive to this kind of relational work:

- *Fostering relationships and dialogue is more important than regulation by policy*—schools take students seriously and acknowledge their voices in decision making. Students themselves feel like they are listened to, respected and treated as young adults. Adult relationships are modeled for students in the context of their learning, and parents are actively welcomed and cultivated into the culture of the school and have a major say in deciding curriculum priorities.
- *Developing flexible approaches to teaching and learning*—in the form of flexible timetabling, activities, pathways, choices and assessment. There is greater emphasis on personalized learning centered on student interests and passions as well as real-world learning experiences.
- *Forging a whole of community approach to supporting students*—by taking a holistic approach to education with an emphasis on inter-agency connections and sharing of knowledge across the community. The focus is on student welfare and support with a strong ethic of care. Prominent attention is given to safety, care and community (Smith et al., 1998).
- *Establishing an ethical commitment to justice and a 'fair go'*—so that students and their needs are at the center of all decision making.
- *Creating a sense of student ownership, identity and belonging*—by getting to know students, which is typically achieved by having smaller classes and in which teachers get to know their students' lives. From the point of view of students, it means having teachers who are passionate, committed and enthusiastic.
- *Having a pleasant built environment*—in which students, their families and community can take pride. When students are provided with equitable resources in respect of school buildings, facilities and maintenance there is likely to be a stronger sense of ownership, self-worth and achievement in comparison to their wealthier counterparts.

These orientations together provide a framework for rethinking the structure and organization of traditional high schools. The emphasis in on how administrative arrangements can serve the interests of students by building a school culture founded on relational trust, collaboration and learning rather than regulation, control, direction and policing.

6. *Creating spaces for dialogue, reflection and innovation*
   Many of the stories portrayed in this book highlight the powerful effects of school-community dialogue, collaboration, reflection and plan-

ning. Where schools are willing to create spaces for teacher dialogue and reflection then innovative possibilities for student engagement are more evident. This is not to say, however, that the problems of student engagement are simply a matter of getting individual teachers to be more innovative, although this helps. Our argument is that these matters are far more complex and cannot be divorced from the deeply entrenched structural inequalities of the economy and society. As Teese (2006) points out, the work of disadvantaged schools (and teachers) cannot be viewed in isolation from the whole school system. In other words, disadvantaged schools contribute 'to the success of the rest of the system, partly by what they do for the most demanding pupils and partly by what they surrender in the form of teacher resources, pupil mix and operating conditions' (p. 4). In reality, disadvantaged schools are 'condemned to innovate' because 'it is in these schools that nothing can be taken for granted regarding a child's readiness for school, his or her language skills, attitude to work in a classroom, respect for others, and comprehension of what is meant by the notion of the 'craft' of being a pupil' (p. 8). So what is going on in these schools? We might say:

- *Supporting innovation and risk taking*—in circumstances where traditional approaches to schooling do not work. School leaders encourage innovation and risk taking in order to find productive ways of engaging students. Students and teachers are given the freedom and choice to experiment with hands-on community-orientated learning programs around students' interests.
- *Organizing small learning teams*—to facilitate dialogue and reflection around things that work! There is a greater sense of distributed leadership and ownership of student learning based on curriculum expertise and knowledge. Those closest to students are encouraged to take responsibility for students' learning and welfare.
- *Reinventing policy locally*—to ensure that the interests and needs of teachers and students are protected from the worst excesses of centrally mandated policies and practices. There is a clear sense that political and bureaucratic interferences and prescriptions are not helpful and simply result in more accountability and work without the resources to do the job.
- *Talking up the vision*—of the school and community by creating a spirit of ownership, pride and collegiality in achievements, no matter how

small. Success is encouraged and publicly acknowledged. Students themselves appreciate teachers who choose to stay in the school, trust them and commit to the future.
- *Searching out opportunities and connections*—to enhance students learning in the community. Teachers go out of their way to find resources, support, and learning opportunities to address the interests and needs of their students. This often involves additional fund raising, extra curricular activities, excursions, project learning, and parental contact.

While dialogue, reflection and innovation are to be encouraged as a necessary first step, we argue that these conversations must also be 'critical' and connected to the broader vision of producing democratic relationships in schools and between schools and their communities. In Chapter 1, we explained that this critical democratic engagement involves 'a preparedness to recognize existing inequalities, to challenge authoritative discourses, to confront injustices, and to not accept the status quo'. Our central argument is that in 'communities blighted by exclusion' both *critically engaged learning* and *critically engaged community capacity building* have to occur in unison.

What next?

Re-enchanting students with learning in the ways we have described is a necessary step towards critically engaged forms of learning and community capacity building. However, we suggest that a good deal of what passes for 'progressive schooling' corresponds to an interpretive/student-centered view of learning that accords primacy to notions of individual choice, autonomy and student-initiated curriculum (Vibert & Shields, 2003). What is largely missing from this discourse is a critical perspective that encourages teachers and students to question the established order and work for the common good rather than self-interest. Viewed through a critical/transformative lens:

> The purpose of education is not so much preparatory . . . but to take up, examine and work on the world as it presents itself to students (and teachers) here and now. A critical lens commits educators to take seriously a number of concerns: the democratic purposes of schooling; the inevitability of the political dimensions of education and teaching; the importance of dealing explicitly with issues of race, class, gender, and all embodiments of social difference as a concern for social justice . . . From a critical perspective, engagement in learning and school life is a form of engagement with the world at large (Vibert & Shields, 2003, p. 228)

It is a measure of how far conservative interests have penetrated schools that many so-called 'controversial topics' such as the Iraq war, terrorism, violence, consumerism, work, poverty, biotechnology and so on are out-of-bounds for student investigation, a phenomenon which Flinders (2005) refers to as a 'null curriculum'—that which schools do not teach. It may well be that some schools view a study of these topics as a distraction from their academic mission in an era of standards and high-stakes testing, or perhaps the influence of the New Right is so pervasive that these topics are untouchable if not 'unteachable'. However, given the precarious condition of our planet, the increasing likelihood of global conflict and the threats to democracy we see an urgent need for these topics to become part of the official curriculum. Contemporary moves towards uniform curriculum, standardized testing and national benchmarks are more likely to inhibit debate and stifle creativity when it comes to resolving these complex and pressing issues. Furthermore, we contend that these top-down instrumentalist policies serve to deny the histories, cultures, voices, interests, dreams, and aspirations of those students, families and communities excluded from the mainstream of economic, social and civic life. If we are intent on building a more democratic society then we need to take seriously Giroux's (2005) advice that 'a critical pedagogy of democracy does not begin with test scores but with questions' (p. 67).

If we could sum up in a few words what we have been trying to convey in this book it would be the idea of making young people 'powerful people' (Smyth & Fasoli, 2007, p. 281). Critically engaged learning and community capacity building as we have described it, aims to achieve this, not in the oppressive sense of students being able to exercise control or domination over others, but rather in a positive way that increases their agency, autonomy and a capacity for critical reflection and social action. This is likely to occur when students are accorded a high level of respect and trust, have an active voice in what happens in schools, and exercise a high level of ownership of learning. Creating the conditions for such learning is vitally important for young people living in communities that have been excluded from the mainstream of economic and civil life. These 'forgotten people', as one of our informants described them, have been rendered voiceless through the ways the pathologizing discourses and paternalistic practices of neo-liberal policies have done their work on these communities. Because young people's identities and aspirations are so intimately connected to the neighborhoods in which they live, the task of making them powerful is inseparable from the broader challenge of making communities powerful. Given the entrenched and structured inequalities pervading disadvantaged communities, this is something, which cannot be achieved without the political will and enormous financial commitment on the part of governments. Ultimately communities become empowered through social, cultural and economic opportunities and services that are readily available to other members of society. Notwithstanding the difficulties, the optimistic stories of individual and collective agency and engagement from Wirra Wagga and Bountiful Bay point to the possibilities of school and community renewal improving the educational opportunities and life chances for young people in difficult circumstances.

Appendix A

Summary of Interviews: Bountiful Bay Education District High Schools

	Casuarina Heights	Banksia Hill	Marine Park	Enterprise	Totals
Principal	1	1	1	1	4
Deputy Principal	1	1	1	3	6
Assistant Principal			1		1
Manager / Head of Department	1	6	7	2	16
Teacher	6	5	2	9	22
Psychologist	1				1
Parent		2	2		4
Student	6	7	2		15
Industry Manager			1		1
Totals	16	22	17	15	70

Interviews varying in length from 30 to 90 minutes were conducted at the school sites and amounted to approximately 50 hours overall.

The research involved approximately 12 hours of participant observation of classroom teaching, staff / faculty / leadership team meetings, school assemblies, parent information evening, and structured workplace learning.

Appendix B

Summary of Interviews: Wirra Wagga Schools and Community (February 2006–March 2007)

School principal / head of school	7
Teacher	15
Ancillary staff	4
Parents / School Council reps.	8
Students	15
Education Administrator	5
Project Manager	1
Wirra Wagga resident	6
Former resident	1
Wirra Wagga Renew team member	4
University Research Coordinator	2
Member of Parliament	1
Total	**69**

Interviews 45–60 minutes in length were conducted at participants' work sites and amounted to 60 hours overall. The sites included two elementary schools, one middle school, Community House, neighborhood renewal center, District

Education Office, parliamentary office and University School of Education.

The research involved approximately 10 hours participant observation of classroom teaching, staff meetings and community education programs as well as guided tours of education facilities and neighborhood renewal projects.

References

Alvesson, M., & Deetz, S. (2000). *Doing Critical Management Research*. London: Sage Publications.
Amin, A. (2002). Ethnicity and the multicultural city: living with diversity. *Environment and Planning, 34*(6), 959–980.
Angus, L. (1993). The sociology of school effectiveness. *British Journal of Sociology of Education, 14*(3), 333–345.
———. (2006). Educational leadership and the imperative of including student voices, student interests and students' lives in the mainstream. *International Journal of Leadership in Education, 9*(4), 369–379.
Anyon, J. (2005a). *Radical Possibilities: Public Policy, Urban Education and a New Social Movement*. New York: Routledge.
———. (2005b). What 'counts' as educational policy? Notes towards a new paradigm. *Harvard Educational Review, 75*(1), 65–88.
Apple, M. (2001). *Educating the 'Right' Way: Markets, Standards, God and Inequality*. New York & London: Routledge/Falmer.
Atkinson, E. (2000). In defence of ideas, or why 'what works' is not enough. *British Journal of Sociology of Education, 21*(3), 317–330.
Attwood, G., Croll, P., & Hamilton, J. (2003). Re-engaging with education. *Research Papers in Education, 18*(1), 1–21.

Ayers, W. (2004). *Teaching the Personal and the Political: Essays on Hope and Justice*. New York: Teachers College Press.

Ball, S., Maguire, M., & Macrae, S. (2000). *Choice, Pathways and Transitions Post-16: New Youth, New Economies in the Global City*. London & New York: Routledge/Falmer.

Bartolome, L. (1994). Beyond the methods fetish: toward a humanizing pedagogy. *Harvard Educational Review, 64*(2), 173–194.

Bastian, A., Fruchter, N., Gittell, M., Greer, C., & Haskins, K. (1985). Choosing equality: the case for democratic schooling. *Social Policy, 15*(3), 34–51.

Beane, J. (1990). *A Middle School Curriculum: From Rhetoric to Reality*. Columbus OH: National Middle School Association.

———. (2005). *A Reason to Teach: Creating Classrooms of Dignity and Hope*. Portsmouth, NH: Heinemann.

Beckmann, A., & Cooper, C. (2004). 'Globalisation', the new manageralism of education: rethinking the purpose of education in Britain. *Journal of Critical Education Policy Studies, 2*(2), 1–14.

Berliner, D. (2006). Our impoverished view of educational research. *Teachers College Record, 108*(6), 949–995.

Bernstein, B. (1961). Social structure, language, and learning. *Educational Research, 3*, 163–176.

———. (1996). *Pedagogy Symbolic Control and Identity: Theory, Research, Critique*. Bristol, PA: Taylor & Francis.

———. (2004). Social class and pedagogic practice. In S. Ball (Ed.), *The RoutledgeFalmer Reader in Sociology of Education* (pp. 196–217). London & New York: Routledge Falmer.

Besley, A. (2003). Hybridized and globalized: youth cultures in the postmodern era. *Review of Education, Pedagogy and Cultural Studies, 25*, 153–177.

Bessant, J. (2002). Risk and nostalgia: the problem of education and youth unemployment in Australia—a case study. *Journal of Education and Work, 15*(1), 31–51.

Best, S., & Kellner, O. (2003). Contemporary youth and the postmodern adventure. *Review of Education, Pedagogy and Cultural Studies, 25*, 75–93.

Bigelow, B. (2006). Getting to the heart of quality teaching. *Rethinking Schools, 20*(2), 6–8.

Bingham, C., & Sidorkin, A. (2004). The pedagogy of relation: an introduction. In C. Bingham & A. Sidorkin (Eds.), *No Education Without Relation* (pp. 1–4). New York: Peter Lang Publishing.

Bohn, A. (2006). A framework for understanding Ruby Payne. *Rethinking Schools, 21*(2).

Bomer, R., Dworin, I., May, L., & Semingson, P. (2008). Miseducating teachers about the poor: a critical analysis of Ruby Payne's claims about poverty. *Teachers College Record, 110*(11).

Boomer, G. (Ed.). (1982). *Negotiating the Curriculum: A Teacher-Student Partnership*. Sydney: Ashton Scholastic.

Bourdieu, P. (1979). Cultural reproduction and social reproduction. In J. Karabel & A. Halsey (Eds.), *Power and Ideology in Education* (pp. 487–511). New York: Oxford University Press.

———. (1984). *Distinction: A Social Critique of the Judgement of Taste*. Cambridge, MA: Harvard University Press.

Bourdieu, P., & Passeron, J. (1981). *Reproduction in Education, Society and Culture* (2nd ed.). London: Sage Publications.

Brookfield, S. (1987). *Developing Critical Thinkers: Challenging Adults to Explore Alternative Ways of Thinking and Acting*. Milton Keynes, England: Open University Press.

Brookfield, S. (1995). *Becoming a Critically Reflective Teacher*. San Francisco: Jossey-Bass.

Brown, R. (1990). Social science and the poetics of public truth. *Sociological Forum*, 5(1), 57–74.

Bryk, A., & Schneider, B. (2002). *Trust in Schools: A Core Resource for Improvement*. New York: Russell Sage Foundation.

Bullough, R., & Gitlin, A. (2001). *Becoming a Student of Teaching: Linking Knowledge Production and Practice*. New York: RoutledgeFalmer.

Carr, W. (2003). Educational research and its histories. In P. Sikes, J. Nixon & W. Carr (Eds.), *The Moral Foundations of Educational Research: Knowledge, Inquiry and Values* (pp. 6–17). Maidenhead, England: Open University Press/McGraw Hill Educational.

Carter, P. (1996). *The Lie of the Land*. London: Faber and Faber.

———. (2007). *'Care at a distance': affiliations to country in a global context*. Introductory lecture to the 'Landscapes and Learning Symposium', Monash University, Gippsland, 14 August.

Cass, B. (2007, August). *Social inclusion; a broader perspective*. Paper presented at the the Benevolent Society workshop on 'Growing our Caring and Inclusive Community'.

Chaskin, R. (2001). Building community capacity: a definitional framework and case studies froma comprehensive community initiative. *Urban Affairs Review*, 36(3), 291–323.

Chavez, R., & O'Donnell, J. (Eds.). (1998). *Speaking the Unpleasant: the Politics of (non) Engagement in the Multicultural Education Terrain*. Albany: State University of New York Press.

Comer, J., & et al. (Eds.). (1996). *Rallying the Whole Village*. New York: Teachers College Press.

Commission on Poverty Participation and Power. (2000). *Listen Hear: The Right to be Heard*. Bristol: Policy Press.

Connell, R. (1993). *Schools and Social Justice*. Toronto: Our Schools/Our Selves Education Foundation.

Corson, D. (1998). *Changing Education for Diversity*. Buckingham: Open University Press.

Counts, G. (1932 [republished 1978]). *Dare the Schools Build a New Social Order?* Carbondale, Ill: Southern Illinois University Press.

Cox, E. (1995). *A Truly Civil Society*. Sydney: Australian Broadcasting Corporation.

Cummins, J. (2002). Empowering minority students: a framework for intervention. *Harvard Educational Review*, 71(4), 649–675.

Dei, G. (2003). Schooling and the dilemma of youth disengagement. *McGill Journal of Education*, 38(2), 241–256.

del Tufo, S., & Gaster, L. (2002). *Evaluation of the Commission on Poverty, Participation and Power*. York, England: The Joseph Rowntree Foundation.

Dewey, J. (1944 [1916]). *Democracy and Education*. New York: Free Press.

———. (1959). School and society. In M. Dworkin (Ed.), *Dewey on Education* (pp. 33–90). New York: Teachers College Press.

———. (1963 [1938]). *Experience in Education*. New York: Collier.

Di Bartolo, L. (2005). Educational polarisation in Brisbane: Rawls's least advantaged and the myth of choice. *Australian Educational Researcher*, 32(3), 63–82.

Down, B. (2006). A critical pedagogy of vocational education and training in schools and communities struggling with the shifts in the global economy. *Learning Communities: International Journal of Learning in Social Contexts*, 3, 94–120.

Edwards, R. (2006). A sticky business? Exploring the 'and' in teaching and learning. *Discourse:*

Studies in the Cultural Politics of Education, 27(1), 121–134.

Evans, S., & Boyte, H. (1986). *Free Spaces: The Sources of Democratic Change in America*. Chicago & London: University of Chicago Press.

Fear, F., Rosaen, C., Bawden, R., & Foster-Fishman, D. (2006). *Coming to Critical Engagement: an Autoethnographic Exploration*. Lanham, MD: University Press of America.

Featherstone, J. (1989). To make the wounded whole. *Harvard Educational Review, 59*(3), 367–378.

Ferrari, J. (2007, 12 December). Top charity shifts focus to educaton. *The Australian*, p. 7.

Field, J., & Olafson, L. (1998). Caught in the machine: resistance, positioning, and pedagogy. *Research in the Middle Level Education Quarterly, 22*(Fall), 39–55.

Fielding, M. (2006). Leadership, radical student engagement and the necessity of person-centred education. *International Journal of Leadership in Education, 9*(4), 299–314.

Fitzclarence, L., & Kenway, J. (2004). Gunshots that were heard around the world: towards anti-violence pedagogies in schools. In J. Allen (Ed.), *Sociology of Education: Possibilities and Practices* (pp. 322–342). Southbank, Victoria: Social Science Press.

Flinders, D. (2005). Adolescents talk about the Iraq war. *Phi Delta Kappan, 87*(4), 320–323.

Foley, D. (1997). Deficit thinking models based on culture: the anthropological protest. In R. Valencia (Ed.), *The Evolution of Deficit Thinking: Educational Thought and Practice* (pp. 113–131). London & Washington: Falmer Press.

Foucault, M. (1980). *Power/Knowledge: Selected Interviews and Other Writings 1972–1977*. New York: Pantheon.

Fraser, D., & Petch, J. (2007). *School Improvement: A Theory of Action*. Melbourne: Office of School Education, Department of Education, Victoria.

Freire, P. (2000 [1970]). *Pedagogy of the Oppressed*. New York: Continuum.

———. (1994). *Pedagogy of Hope: Reliving Pedagogy of the Oppressed*. New York: Continuum.

———. (2001). *Pedagogy of Freedom: Ethics, Democracy, and Civic Courage*. Lanham, MD: Rowman & Littlefield.

——— (2004). *Pedagogy of Indignation*. Boulder, CO: Paradigm Press.

Fruchter, N. (2007). *Urban Schools, Public Will: Making Education Work for All Our Children*. New York: Teachers College Press.

Frymer, B. (2005). Freire, alienation, and contemporary youth: toward a pedagogy of everyday life. *InterActions: UCLA Journal of Education and Information Studies, 1*(2), 1–16.

Gale, T., & Densmore, K. (2003). *Engaging Teachers: Towards a Radical Democratic Agenda for Schooling*. Maidenhead, UK: Open University Press.

Giroux, H. (1988). *Teachers as Intellectuals: Toward a Critical Pedagogy of Learning*. Granby, MA: Bergin & Garvey.

———. (1994). Doing cultural studies: youth and the challenge of pedagogy. *Harvard Educational Review, 64*(3), 278–308.

———. (1996). Is there a place for cultural studies in colleges of education? In H. Giroux, C. Lankshear, P. McLaren & M. Peters (Eds.), *Counternarratives: Cultural Studies and Critical Pedagogies in Postmodern Spaces* (pp. 41–58). New York: Routledge.

———. (1997). *Pedagogy and the Politics of Hope: Theory, Culture and Schooling*. Boulder, CO: Westview Press.

———. (2000). *Stealing Innocence: Youth, Corporate Power and the Politics of Culture*. New York:

St Martin's Press.

———. (2001). *Public Spaces, Private Lives: Beyond the Culture of Cynicism*. Lanham, MD: Rowman & Littlefield.

———. (2001). Introduction: Critical education or training. Beyond the commodification of higher education. In H. Giroux & K. Myrsiades (Eds.), *Beyond the Corporate University: Culture and Pedagogy in the New Millennium* (pp. 1–12). Lanham, MD: Rowman & Littlefield.

———. (2002). *Breaking into the Movies: Film and the Culture of Politics*. Oxford: Blackwell.

———. (2004). *The Terror of Neoliberalism: Authoritarianism and the Eclipse of Democracy*. Boulder, CO: Paradigm Press.

———. (2005). *Border Crossings: Cultural Workers and the Politics of Education*. New York & London: Routledge.

Gitlin, A. (1996). Teacher education: what is good teaching, and how do we teach people to be good teachers? In J. Kincheloe & S. Steinberg (Eds.), *Thirteen Questions: Reframing Education's Conversation* (pp. 110–119). New York: Peter Lang Publishing.

Gonzales, N., & Moll, L. (2002). Cruzando el Puente: building bridges to funds of knowledge. *Educational Policy, 16*(4), 623–641.

Goodman, J. (1992). *Elementary Schooling for Critical Democracy*. Albany: State University of New York Press.

Goodman, J., & Kuzmic, J. (1997). Bringing a progressive pedagogy to conventional schools: theoretical and practical implications from Harmony. *Theory into Practice, 36*(2), 79–86.

Gorski, P. (2005). Savage unrealities: uncovering classism in Ruby Payne's framework. Unpublished MS, Graduate School of Education, Hamline University, St. Paul, MN.

———. (2006). The classist underpinnings of Ruby Payne's framework. *Teachers College Record, 9 February* (12322).

Gotham, K. (2003). Toward an understanding of the spatiality of urban poverty: the urban poor as spatial actors. *International Journal of Urban and Regional Research, 27*(3), 723–737.

Greene, M. (1999). *Releasing the Imagination: Essays on Education, the Arts, and Social Change*. San Francisco: Jossey-Bass.

Greig, A., Lewins, F., & White, K. (2003). *Inequality in Australia*. Port Melbourne, Vic: Cambridge University Press.

Gruenewald, D. (2003). Foundations of place: a multidisciplinary framework for place-conscious education. *American Educational Research Journal, 40*(3), 619–654.

Gulson, K. (2005). Renovating educational identities: policy, space and urban renewal. *Journal of Education Policy, 20*(2), 141–158.

———. (2007a). 'Neoliberal spatial technologies': on the practices of educational policy change. *Critical Studies in Education, 48*(2), 179–195.

———. (2007b in press). Temporary fixations: education policy and the politics of place. *Journal of Education Policy*.

Gulson, K., & Symes, C. (Eds.). (2007). *Spatial Theories of Education: Policy and Geography Matters*. New York: Routledge.

Gulson, K., Symes, C., & Sumsion, J. (2007). Knowing one's place: space, theory, education. *Critical Studies in Education, 48*(1), 97–110.

Haberman, M. (1991). The pedagogy of poverty versus good teaching. *Phi Delta Kappan, 73*(4),

290–294.

Harris, A., & Ranson, S. (2005). The contradictions of education policy: disadvantage and achievement. *British Educational Research Journal, 31*(5), 571–587.

Hartnett, A., & Carr, W. (1995). Education, teacher development and the struggle for democracy. In J. Smyth (Ed.), *Critical Discourses on Teacher Development* (pp. 39–53). London: Cassell.

Hattam, R., Brown, K., & Smyth, J. (1995). *Sustaining a Culture of Debate About Teaching and Learning.* Adelaide: Flinders Institute for the Study of Teaching.

Hayes, D., Lingard, B., & Mills, M. (2000). Productive pedagogies. *Education Links, 60,* 10–13.

Hayes, D., Mills, M., Christie, P., & Lingard, B. (2006). *Teachers and Schooling Making a Difference: Productive Pedagogies, Assessment and Performance.* Sydney: Allen & Unwin.

Hinchey, P. (2004). *Becoming a Critical Educator: Defining a Classroom Identity, Designing a Critical Pedagogy.* New York: Peter Lang Publishing.

Hirsch, D. (2006). *Where Poverty Intersects with Social Exclusion: Evidence and Features of Solutions.* York, England: Joseph Rowntree Foundation.

Hursh, D. (2005). Neo-liberalism, markets and accountability: transforming education and undermining democracy in the United States and England. *Policy Futures in Education, 3*(1), 3–15.

Hutchinson, F. (1996). *Educating Beyond Violent Futures.* London & New York: Routledge.

Joseph Rowntree Foundation. (2007). *Experiences of Poverty and Educational Disadvantage.* York, England: Joseph Rowntree Foundation.

Kelly, P. (1999). Wild and time zones: regulating the transitions of youth at risk. *Journal of Youth Studies, 2*(2), 193–211.

———. (2007). Governing individualized risk biographies: new class intellectuals and the problem of youth at risk. *British Journal of Sociology of Education, 28*(1), 39–53.

Kemmis, S., & McTaggart, R. (2005). Participatory action research; communicative action and the public sphere. In N. Denzin & Y. Lincoln (Eds.), *Sage Handbook of Qualitative Research 3rd Edition* (pp. 559–603). Thousand Oaks, CA: Sage Publications.

Kincheloe, J. (1993). *Toward a Critical Politics of Teacher Thinking: Mapping the Postmodern.* Westport, CT: Bergin & Garvey.

———. (1995). *Toil and Trouble: Good Work, Smart Workers, and the Integration of Academic and Vocational Education.* New York: Peter Lang Publishing.

———. (2001). *Getting Beyond the Facts: Teaching Social Studies/Social Sciences in the Twenty-first Century* (2nd ed.). New York: Peter Lang Publishing.

———. (2003). *Teachers as Researchers: Qualitative Inquiry as a Path to Empowerment.* London: RoutledgeFalmer.

———. (2005). *Critical Constructivism.* New York: Peter Lang Publishing.

Kincheloe, J., Slattery, P., & Steinberg, S. (2000). *Contextualizing Teaching.* New York: Longman.

Kincheloe, J., & Steinberg, S. (1998b). Making meaning and analyzing experience—student researchers as transformative agents. In J. Kincheloe & S. Steinberg (Eds.), *Students as Researchers: Creating Classrooms That Matter* (pp. 228–244). London: Falmer Press.

———. (1998a). Students as researchers: critical visions, emancipatory insights. In J. Kincheloe & S. Steinberg (Eds.), *Students as Researchers: Creating Classrooms That Matter* (pp. 2–19).

London: Falmer Press.

———. (Eds.). (1998c). *Students as Researchers: Creating Classrooms That Matter*. London: Falmer Press.

Kostogriz, A. (2006). Putting 'space' on the agenda of sociocultural research in education *Mind, Culture and Activity, 13*(3), 174–188.

Kostogriz, A., & Peeler, E. (2007). Professional identity and pedagogical space: negotiating difference in teacher workplaces. *Teaching Education, 18*(2), 107–122.

Kozol, J. (1992). *Savage Inequalities: Children in America's Schools*. New York: Harper Perennial.

———. (2005). Confections of apartheid: a stick and carrot pedagogy for the children of our inner-city poor. *Phi Delta Kappan, 87*(4), 364–375.

Kretzmann, J., & McKnight, J. (1993). *Building Communities from the Inside Out: A Path Toward Finding and Mobilizing a Community's Assets*. Evanston IL: Institute for Policy Research, Northwestern University.

Lankshear, C., & Knobel, M. (2003). *New Literacies: Changing Knowledge and Classroom Learning*. Buckingham, England: Open University Press.

Lather, P. (1998). Critical pedagogies and its complicities: a praxis of stuck places. *Educational Theory, 48*(4), 487–497.

Lawrence-Lightfoot, S. (1983). *The Good High School*. New York: Basic Books.

———. (2000). *Respect: An Exploration*. Cambridge, MA: Perseus Books.

———. (2005). Reflections on portraiture: a dialogue between art and science. *Qualitative Inquiry, 11*(1), 3–15.

Lawrence-Lightfoot, S., & Davis, J. (1997). *The Art and Science of Portraiture*. San Francisco: Jossey-Bass.

Lesko, N. (1996). Denaturalizing adolescence: the politics of contemporary representations. *Youth and Society, 28*(2), 139–161.

Levine, D. (1995). Building a new vision of curriculum reform. In D. Levine, R. Lowe, B. Peterson & R. Tenorio (Eds.), *Re-thinking Schools: An Agenda for Change* (pp. 52–60). New York: The New Press.

Levinson, B., Foley, D., & Holland, D. (Eds.). (1996). *The Cultural Production of the Educated Person: Critical Ethnographies of Schooling and Local Practice*. Albany: State University of New York Press.

Lewis, O. (1961). *The Children of Sanchez*. New York: Random House.

Lilley, D. (2005). Evaluating the 'comunity renewal' response to social exclusion on public housing estates. *Australian Planner, 42*(2), 59–65.

Lipman, P. (2004). *High Stakes Education: Inequality, Globalization, and Urban School Reform*. New York: Routledge.

Lipsky, M. (1980). *Street-level Bureaucracy: Dilemmas of the Individual in Public Service*. New York: Russell Sage Foundation.

Lister, R. (2004). *Poverty*. Cambridge, MA: Polity Press.

Marcus, G. (1998). *Ethnography Through Thick and Thin*. Princeton, NJ: Princeton University Press.

Martin, J. (1992). Critical Thinking for a Humane World. In S. Norris (Ed.), *The Generalizability of Critical Thinking: Multiple Perspectives on an Educational Ideal* (pp. 163–180). New York: Teachers College Press.

Massey, D. (1984). *Spatial Divisions of Labour*. London: Macmillan.

———. (2005). *For Space*. London: Sage.

McClenaghan, P. (2000). Social capital: exploring the theoretical foundations of community development. *British Educational Research Journal, 26*(5), 568–583.

McFadden, M., & Munns, G. (2000). *Chance, illusion and engagement*. Paper presented at the annual meeting of the Australian Association for Research in Education, Sydney.

McInerney, P. (2004). *Making Hope Practical: School Reform for Social Justice*. Flaxton, Qld: Post Pressed.

McKnight, J., & Kretzmann, J. (1996 Revised). *Mapping Community Capacity*. Evanston, IL: Institute for Policy Research, Northwestern University.

McLaren, P. (1995). *Critical Pedagogy and Predatory Culture: Oppositional Politics in a Postmodern Era*. New York: Routledge.

——— (1997). *Revolutionary Multiculturalism: Pedagogies of Dissent for the New Millennium*. Boulder: CO: Westview Press.

McMahon, B., & Portelli, J. (2004). Engagement for what? Beyond popular discourses of student engagement. *Leadership and Policy in Schools, 3*(1), 59–76.

McMurtry, J. (1998). *Unequal Freedoms: the Global Market as an Ethical System*. Toronto: Garamond Press.

McPeck, J. (1981). *Critical Thinking and Education*. New York: St. Martin's Press.

Mediratta, K., Fruchter, N., et al. (2001). *Mapping the Field or Organizing for School Improvement: A Report on Education Organizing*. New York: Institute for Education and Social Policy, New York University.

Mediratta, K., Fruchter, N., & Lewis, A. (2002). *Organizing for School Reform: How Communities Are Finding Their Voices and Reclaiming Their Public Schools. A Report*. New York: New York University, Institute for Education and Social Policy.

Meier, D. (2002). *In Schools We Trust: Creating Communities of Learning in an Era of Testing and Standardization*. Boston: Beacon Press.

Melaville, A., Berg, A., & Blank, M. (2006). *Community-Based Learning: Engaging Students for Success and Citizenship*. Washington, DC: Coalition for Community Schools.

Millar, P., & Kilpatrick, S. (2005). How community development programmes can foster re-engagement with learning in disadvantaged communities: leadership as process. *Studies in the Education of Adults, 37*(1).

Mills, C., & Gale, T. (2001). *The 'ideal': what does this mean for schools and their communities*. Paper presented at the annual meeting of the Australian Association for Research in Education conference, Fremantle.

———. (2004). Parent participation in disadvantaged schools: moving beyond attributions of blame. *Australian Journal of Education, 48*(3), 268–281.

Mishler, E. (2004). *Storylines: Craftartists' Narratives of Identity*. Cambridge, MA: Harvard University Press.

Moll, L., Amanti, C., Neff, D., & Gonzalez, N. (1992). Funds of knowledge for teaching: using a qualitative approach to connect homes and classrooms. *Theory into Practice, 31*(2), 132–141.

Nespor, J. (1998). The meanings of research: kids as subjects and kids as inquirers. *Qualitative Inquiry, 4*(3), 1–13.

Ng, J., & Rury, J. (2006). Poverty and education: a critical analysis of the Ruby Payne phenomenon, *Teachers College Record* (Vol. July 18, 12596).

Nichols, S., & Berliner, D. (2007). *Collateral Damage: How High Stakes-Testing Corrupts America's Schools*. Cambridge, MA: Harvard University Press.

Nilan, P. (2004). 'Reality TV?' School students and popular culture. In J. Allen (Ed.), *Sociology of Education: Possibilities and Practices* (pp. 306–321). Southbank, Victoria: Social Science Press.

Nixon, J., Allan, J., & Mannion, G. (2001). Educational renewal as democratic practice: 'new' community schooling in Scotland. *International Journal of Inclusive Education*, 5(4), 329–352.

Noddings, N. (2005a). Place-based education to preserve the earth and its people. In N. Noddings (Ed.), *Educating Citizens for Global Awareness* (pp. 57–68). New York: Teachers College Press.

———. (2005b). *The Challenge to Care in Schools: An Alternative Approach to Education*. New York: Teachers College Press.

Noguera, P. (1995). Preventing and producing violence: a critical analysis of responses to school violence. *Harvard Educational Review*, 65(2), 189–213.

Orner, M. (1996). Teaching for the moment: intervention projects as situated pedagogy. *Theory into Practice*, 35(2), 72–78.

Osei-Kofi, N. (2005). Pathologizing the poor: a framework for understanding Ruby Payne's work. *Equity and Excellence*, 38(4), 367–375.

Osterman, K. (2000). Students' need for belonging in the school community. *Review of Educational Research*, 70(3), 323–367.

Parsons, C., & Hailes, J. (2004). Voluntary organizations and the contribution to social justice in schools: learning from a case study. *Journal of Education Policy*, 19(4), 473–495.

Payne, R. (1998 [2005]). *Framework for Understanding Poverty*. Highlands, TX: Aha Process Inc.

Payne, R. (2002). *Hidden Rules of Class and Work*. Highlands, TX: Aha Process Inc.

Payne, R., DeVol, P., & Smith, T. (2006). *Bridges Out of Poverty: Strategies for Professionals and Communities*. Highlands, TX: Aha Process Inc.

Peck, J., & Tickell, A. (1994). Searching for a new institutional fix: the after-fordist crisis and global-local disorder. In A. Amin (Ed.), *Post-Fordism: A Reader* (pp. 280–315). Cambridge, MA: Blackwell.

Peterson, B. (2003). One teacher's journey. In L. Christensen & S. Karp (Eds.), *Rethinking School Reform: Views from the Classroom* (pp. 60–75). Milwaukee, WI: Rethinking Schools.

Pinar, W. (1995). The curriculum: what are the basics and are we teaching them? In J. Kincheloe & S. Steinberg (Eds.), *Thirteen Questions: Reframing Education's Conversations* (pp. 23–30). New York: Peter Lang Publishing.

Polletta, F. (1999). 'Free spaces' in collective action. *Theory and Society*, 28(1), 1–38.

Portelli, J., & McMahon, B. (2004). Why critical democratic engagement? *Journal of Maltese Education Research*, 2(2), 39–45.

Portelli, J., & Vibert, A. (2002). A curriculum of life. *Education Canada*, 42(2), 36–39.

Provenzo, E. (1995). Media and schools: what is the effect of media on the educational experience of children? In J. Kincheloe & S. Steinberg (Eds.), *Thirteen Questions: Reframing Education's Conversations* (pp. 217–226). New York: Peter Lang Publishing.

Putnam, R. (2000). *Bowling Alone: The Collapse and Revival of American Community*. New York:

Simon & Schuster.

Quinn, J. (2005). Belonging in a learning community: the re-imagined university and imagined social capital. *Studies in the Education of Adults, 37*(1).

Riveria, J., & Poplin, M. (1995). Multicultural, critical, feminine, and constructive pedagogies seen through the eyes of youth: a call for the revisioning of these and beyond: toward a pedagogy for the next century. In C. Sleeter & P. McLaren (Eds.), *Multicultural Education: Critical Pedagogy and the Politics of Difference* (pp. 221–244). Albany: State University of New York Press.

Sammons, P., Hillman, J., & Mortimore, P. (1995). *Key Characteristics of Effective Schools: A Review of School Effectiveness Research*. London: Education Resources Information Centre.

Samoff, J. (Ed.). (2003). *Institutionalizing International Influence*. Lanham, MD: Rowman and Littlefield.

Sen, A. (1992). *Inequality Re-examined*. Cambridge, MA: Harvard University Press.

———. (1999). *Development as Freedom*. Oxford: Oxford University Press.

———. (2002). *Rationality and Freedom*. Cambridge, MA: Harvard University Press.

Shirley, D. (1997). *Community Organizing for Urban School Reform*. Austin: University of Texas Press.

———. (2002). *Valley Interfaith and School Reform*. Austin: University of Texas Press.

———. (2007). Book review of Anyon 'Radiical Possibilities: Public Policy, Urban Education, and a New Social Movement'. *Urban Education, 42*(5), 502–507.

Shor, I. (1980). *Critical Teaching and Everyday Life*. Chicago: University of Chicago Press.

———. (1992). *Empowering Education: Critical Teaching for Social Change*. Chicago: University of Chicago Press.

———. (1993). Education is politics: Paulo Freire's critical pedagogy. In P. McLaren & P. Leonard (Eds.), *Paulo Freire: A Critical Encounter* (pp. 25–34). London: Routledge.

Shor, I., & Freire, P. (1987). *Pedagogy for Liberation: Dialogues on Transforming Education*. Westport, CT: Bergin and Garvey.

Sibley, D. (1995). *Geographies of Exclusion: Society and Difference in the West*. London & New York: Routledge.

Simon, R. (1988). For a pedagogy of possibility. *Critical Pedagogy Networker, 1*(1), 1–4.

Simon, R., Dippo, D., & Schenke, A. (1991). *Learning Work: A Critical Pedagogy of Work Education*. New York: Bergin & Garvey.

Singh, P. (2007). *Bounded and fluid contexts and identities—implications for pedagogies of lifelong learning*. Paper presented at the the 4th International Centre for Research in Lifelong Learning conference, Sterling, Scotland.

Singh, S. (2003). *Neighbourhood strengthening through community*. Retrieved 24 December, 2007, http://www.comm-org.wisc.edu

Skelton, T., & Valentine, G. (Eds.). (1998). *Cool Places: Geographies of Youth Cultures*. London & New York: Routledge.

Sleeter, C. (2005). *Un-standardized Curriculum: Multicultural Teaching in the Standards-based Classroom*. New York: Teaches College Press.

Smith, C., & Turley, A. (2007, 29 October). Our forgotten poor. *The Age*, p. 13.

Smith, G. (1996). Ties, nets and an elastic bund: community in the postmodern city. *Community Development Journal, 31*(3), 250–259.

———. (2002). Place-based education: learning to be where we are. *Phi Delta Kappan, 83*(8), 584–595.

Smith, W., & et al. (1998). *Student Engagement in Learning and School Life: National Project Report*. Montreal: Office of Research on Educational Policy, McGill University.

Smyth, J. (1989). A critical pedagogy of classroom practice. *Journal of Curriculum Studies, 21*(6), 483–502.

———. (2000). Reclaiming social capital through critical teaching. *Elementary School Journal, 100*(5), 491–511.

———. (2001). *Critical Politics of Teachers' Work: An Australian Perspective*. New York: Peter Lang Publishing.

———. (2005). Policy research and 'damaged teachers': toward an epistemologically respectful paradigm. In F. Bodone (Ed.), *What Difference Does Research Make and for Whom?* (pp. 141–159). New York: Peter Lang Publishing.

———. (2006). Schools and communities put at a disadvantage: relational power, resistance, boundary work and capacity building in educational identity formation. *Learning Communities: International Journal of Learning in Social Contexts, 3*, 7–39.

———. (2007). Teacher development against the policy reform grain: an argument for recapturing relationships in teaching and learning. *Teacher Development: An International Journal of Teachers' Professional Development, 11*(2), 221–236.

Smyth, J., & Fasoli, L. (2007). Climbing over the rocks in the road to student engagement and learning in a challenging high school in Australia. *Educational Research, 49*(3), 273–295.

Smyth, J., Hattam, R., Cannon, J., Edwards, J., Wilson, N., & Wurst, S. (2000). *Listen to Me, I'm Leaving: Early School Leaving in South Australian Secondary Schools*. Adelaide: Flinders Institute for the Study of Teaching; Department of Employment, Education and Training; and Senior Secondary Assessment Board of South Australia.

———. (2004). *'Dropping Out', Drifting Off, Being Excluded: Becoming Somebody Without School*. New York: Peter Lang Publishing.

Smyth, J., & McInerney, P. (2007a). *Teachers in the Middle: Reclaiming the Wasteland of the Adolescent Years of Schooling*. New York: Peter Lang Publishing.

———. (2007b). 'Living on the edge': a case of school reform working for disadvantaged adolescents. *Teachers College Record, 109*(5), 1123–1170.

Smyth, J., McInerney, P., Hattam, R., & Lawson, M. (1999). *Critical Reflection on Teaching and Learning*. Adelaide: Flinders Institute for the Study of Teaching.

Smyth, J., Shacklock, G., & Hattam, R. (1999). Doing critical cultural studies: an antidote to being done to. *Discourse: Studies in the Cultural Politics of Education, 20*(1), 73–89.

Soja, E. (2000). *Postmetropolis: Critical Studies of Cities and Regions*. Cambridge, MA: Blackwell.

Solomon, Y., & Rogers, C. (2001). Motivational patterns in disaffected school students: insights from pupil referral unit clients. *British Educational Research Journal, 27*(3), 331–345.

Spring, J. (1975). *A Primer of Libertarian Education*. New York: Free Life.

———. (2007). *A New Paradigm for Global School Systems*. Mahwah, NJ: Lawrence Erlbaum & Associates.

te Riele, K. (2006). Youth 'at risk': further marginalizing the marginalized? *Journal of Education Policy, 21*(2), 129–145.

Teese, R. (2004). *Class war and the war on class: the two faces of neo-conservative research in the*

Australian media. Paper presented at the Radford Lecture, Australian Association for Research in Education.

———. (2006). Condemned to innovate. *Griffith Review, 11*, 1–13.

Teese, R., & Polesel, J. (2003). *Undemocratic Schooling: Equity and Quality in Mass Secondary Education in Australia*. Melbourne: Melbourne University Press.

Thrupp, M. (1999). *Schools Making a Difference: Let's Be Realistic*. Buckingham, England: Open University Press.

———. (2001). Sociological and political concerns about school effectiveness research: time for a new research agenda. *School Effectiveness and School Improvement, 12*(1), 7–40.

Tierney, W. (1993). *Building Communities of Difference: Higher Education in the Twenty-First Century*. South Hadley, MA: Bergin and Garvey.

Tilley, C. (1994). *A Phenomenology of Landscape: Places, Paths and Monuments*. Oxford, UK: Berg.

Troman, G., Jeffrey, B., & Raggl, A. (2007). Creativity and performativity policies in primary school cultures. *Journal of Education Policy, 22*(5), 549–572.

Troman, G., & Woods, P. (2001). *Primary Teachers' Stress*. London & New York: Routledge/Falmer.

Vadeboncoeur, J., Hirst, E., & Kostogriz, A. (2006). Spatializing sociocultural research: a reading of mediation and meaning as third space. *Mind, Culture and Activity, 13*(3), 191–204.

Valencia, R. (Ed.). (1997). *The Evolution of Deficit Thinking. Educational Thought and Practice*. London: Falmer Press.

Vibert, A., & Shields, C. (2003). Approaches to student engagement; does ideology matter? *McGill Journal of Education, 38*(2), 221–240.

Vinson, T. (2007). *Dropping Off the Edge: The Distribution of Disadvantage in Australia*. Richmond, Vic: Jesuit Social Services & Catholic Social Services Australia.

Warren, M. (2005). Communities and schools: a new view of urban school reform. *Harvard Educational Review, 75*(2), 133–173.

Warren, M., Thompson, J., & Saegert, S. (2001). The role of social capital in combating poverty. In S. Saegert, J. Thompson & M. Warren (Eds.), *Social Capital and Poor Communities* (pp. 1–28). New York: Russell Sage Foundation.

Weaver, J. (2005). *Popular Culture*. New York: Peter Lang Publishing.

Webb, R., & Vulliamy, G. (2006). *Coming Full Circle: The Impact of New Labour's Education Policies on Primary 'School Teachers' Work*. London: Association of Teachers and Lecturers.

Weiner, E. (2003). Beyond 'doing' cultural studies: towards a cultural studies of critical pedagogy. *Review of Education, Pedagogy and Cultural Studies*(25), 1.

Wexler, P. (1992). *Becoming Somebody: Toward a Social Psychology of School*. London: Falmer Press.

Whitty, G. (1994). *Deprofessionalising Teaching? Recent Developments in Teacher Education in England*. Occasional Paper No. 22, The Australian College of Education. Deakin: The Australian College of Education. .

Willis, P. (1977). *Learning to Labor: How Working Class Kids Get Working Class Jobs*. Westmead, England: Gower.

Wink, J. (2005). *Critical Pedagogy: Notes from the Real World*. New York: Pearson.

Wishart, D., Taylor, A., & Shultz, L. (2006). The construction and production of youth 'at risk'. *Journal of Education Policy, 21*(3), 291–304.

Wood, G. (1992). *Schools That Work: America's Most Innovative Public Education Programs*. New York: Dutton.
Yankelovich, D. (1991). *Coming to Public Judgement: Making Democracy Work in a Complex Society*. New York: Syracuse University Press.
Young, I. (2000). *Inclusion and Democracy*. Oxford: Oxford University Press.
Zou, Y., & Trueba, H. (Eds.). (2001). *Ethnography and Schools: Qualitative Approaches to the Study of Education*. Lanham, MD: Rownam & Littlefield.

Author Index

A

Allan, J., 59
Alvesson, M., 17, 18,
Amanti, C., 21, 67, 73, 132, 158
Amin, A., 3,
Angus, L., x, 85, 86, 115
Anyon, J., 26, 31, 58
Apple, M., 120,
Atkinson, E., 87, 88,
Attwood, G., 46,
Ayers, W., 60, 68,

B

Ball, S., 46,
Bartolome, L., 159

Bastian, A., 77,
Bawden, R., 5, 7
Beane, J., 72, 160,
Beckmann, A., 160
Berg, A., 71,
Berliner, D., 57, 139
Bernstein, B., 64, 65, 87, 160,
Besley, A., 119, 120, 122, 123, 145
Bessant, J., 89
Best, S., 120
Bigelow, B., 139, 147, 152
Bingham, C., 160
Blank, M., 71
Bohn, A., 32
Bomer, R., 32
Boomer, G., 71,
Bourdieu, P., 87, 123
Boyte, H., 24, 31
Brookfield, S., 17, 136

Brown, K., 137
Brown, R., 24
Bryk, A., 60, 159
Bullough, R., 136

C

Cannon, J., ix, 47
Carr, W., 88, 137
Carter, P., 2, 8
Cass, B., 37
Chaskin, R., 67
Chavez, R., 27
Christie, P., 128, 131
Comer, J., 30
Commission on Poverty Participation and Power., 39
Connell, R., 87, 123, 135
Cooper, C., 160
Corson, D., 153
Counts, G., 22
Cox, E., 77
Croll, P., 46
Cummins, J., 85

D

Davis, J., 8
Deetz, S., 17, 18,
Dei, G., 155,
del Tufo, S., 39
Densmore, K., 139
DeVol, P., 32
Dewey, J., 66, 67, 78, 87, 125, 126, 127, 134, 157, 158
Di Bartolo, L., 57
Dippo, D., 75
Down, B., x, 150
Dworin, I., 32

E

Edwards, J., ix, 47
Edwards, R., 88
Evans, S., 24, 31

F

Fasoli, L., 47, 158, 164
Fear, F., 5, 7,
Featherstone, J., 9
Ferrari, J., 20
Field, J., 59, 60
Fielding, M., 59
Fitzclarence, L., 122
Flinders, D., 164
Foley, D., 32,33
Foster-Fishman, D., 5, 7
Foucault, M., 82
Fraser, D., 86, 87, 88
Freire, P., 70, 72, 76, 125, 146, 149, 151, 157
Fruchter, N., 23, 26, 77
Frymer, B., 150

G

Gale, T., 54, 73, 139,
Gaster, L., 39
Giroux, H., 118, 119, 122, 123, 124, 137, 139, 147, 151, 160, 164
Gitlin, A., 136, 137,
Gittell, M., 77
Gonzalez, N., 21, 67, 68, 73, 132, 141, 158
Goodman, J., 60, 70, 75
Gorski, P., 32,
Gotham, K., 25,
Greene, M., 132
Greer, C., 77
Greig, A., 58

Gruenewald, D., 72, 76
Gulson, K., 1, 2, 3,

H

Haberman, M., 59,
Hailes, J., 114
Hamilton, J., 46,
Harris, A., 114
Hartnett, A., 137
Haskins, K., 77
Hattam, R., ix, 8, 47, 115, 123, 124, 137, 140, 145,
Hayes, D., 67, 128, 131
Hillman, J., 86,
Hinchey, P., 86, 147,
Hirsch, D., 52,
Hirst, E., 25
Holland, D., 33
Hursh, D., 85
Hutchinson, F., 158

J

Jeffrey, B., 28
Joseph Rowntree Foundation., 30, 31,

K

Kellner, O., 120
Kelly, P., 89
Kemmis, S., 137
Kenway, J., 122
Kilpatrick, S., 83
Kincheloe, J., 118, 119, 121, 122, 124, 131, 132, 133, 137, 140, 141, 151, 158,
Knobel, M., 119, 125
Kostogriz, A., 25, 26, 27

Kozol, J., 3, 58
Kretzmann, J., 31, 41, 42, 67, 155
Kuzmic, J., 60, 70

L

Lankshear, C., 119, 125
Lather, P., 41
Lawrence-Lightfoot, S., 8, 9, 150
Lawson, M., 139
Lesko, N., 122
Levine, D., 147, 157
Levinson, B., 33,
Lewins, F., 58,
Lewis, A., 26
Lewis, O., 32
Lilley, D., 83, 84,
Lingard, B., 67, 128, 131
Lipman, P., 147
Lipsky, M., 42
Lister, R., 37

M

Macrae, S., 46,
Maguire, M., 46,
Mannion, G., 59
Marcus, G., 18
Martin, J., 45
Massey, D., 3, 25
May, L., 32
McClenaghan, P., 83
McFadden, M., 64, 65
McInerney, P., ix, x, 8, 34, 47, 59, 75, 118, 139, 146
McKnight, J., 31, 41, 42, 67, 155
McLaren, P., 118, 122, 123, 124, 145, 157
McMahon, B., 4, 45
McMurtry, J., 152
McPeck, J., 45

McTaggart, R., 137
Mediratta, K., 26
Meier, D., 59, 131, 147, 157
Melaville, A., 71
Millar, P., 83
Mills, C., 54, 73
Mills, M., 67, 128, 131
Mishler, E., 149, 150
Moll, L., 21, 67, 68, 73, 132, 141, 158
Mortimore, P., 86
Munns, G., 64, 65

N

Neff, D., 21, 67, 73, 132, 158
Nespor, J., 141, 143
Ng, J., 32
Nichols, S., 139
Nilan, P., 118
Nixon, J., 59
Noddings, N., 132, 150
Noguera, P., 159

O

O'Donnell, J. 27
Olafson, L., 59, 60
Orner, M., 74
Osei-Kofi, N., 32, 40, 84
Osterman, K., 159

P

Parsons, C., 114
Passeron, J., 123
Payne, R., 32
Peck, J., 23, 26
Peeler, E., 27
Petch, J., 86, 87, 88
Peterson, B., 117

Pinar, W., 145
Polesel, J., 86, 87, 135
Polletta, F., 24, 25
Poplin, M., 135
Portelli, J., 4, 45, 46
Provenzo, E., 118
Putnam, R., 82, 83

Q

Quinn, J., 83

R

Raggl, A., 28
Ranson, S., 114
Riveria, J., 135
Rogers, C., 46
Rosaen, C., 5, 7
Rury, J., 32

S

Saegert, S., 52
Sammons, P., 86
Samoff, J., 33
Schenke, A., 75
Schneider, B., 60, 159
Semingson, P., 32
Sen, A., 159
Shacklock, G., 140, 145
Shields, C., 155, 163
Shirley, D., 26, 35
Shor, I., 60, 72, 76, 119, 124, 127, 128, 134, 135, 142, 143, 145, 149, 152, 158
Shultz, L., 89
Sibley, D., 16, 109
Sidorkin, A., 160
Simon, R., 75 136
Singh, P., 65, 157

Singh, S. 154
Skelton, T., 118, 157
Slattery, P., 118
Sleeter, C., 158
Smith, C., 3
Smith, G., 72, 73, 84
Smith, T., 32
Smith, W., 155, 157, 161
Smyth, J., ix, x, 8, 34, 47, 57, 59, 115, 118, 120, 123, 124, 136, 137, 140, 145, 146, 158, 159, 164,
Soja, E., 25
Solomon, Y., 46
Spring, J., 119, 159
Steinberg, S., 118, 119, 132, 158
Sumsion, J., 1, 2, 3
Symes, C., 1, 2, 3

T

te Riele, K., 89, 90
Taylor, A., 89
Teese, R., 86, 87, 135, 162
Thompson, J., 52
Thrupp, M., 85, 86
Tickell, A., 23, 26
Tierney, W., 54
Tilley, C., 1, 2
Troman, G., 28, 29
Trueba, H., 33
Turley, A., 3

V

Vadeboncoeur, J., 25
Valencia, R., 31
Valentine, G., 118, 157
Vibert, A., 46, 155, 163
Vinson, T., 55
Vulliamy, G., 29

W

Warren, M., 52, 57, 58, 76, 78
Weaver, J., 119
Webb, R., 29
Weiner, E., 145
Wexler, P., 144
White, K., 58
Whitty, G., 139
Willis, P., 87, 123
Wilson, N., ix, 47
Wink, J., 138
Wishart, D., 89
Wood, G., 68, 78
Woods, P., 29
Wurst, S., ix, 47

Y

Yankelovich, D., 5, 7
Young, I., 109, 110, 111

Z

Zou, Y., 33

Subject Index

A

Aboriginal elders, 68
Aboriginal Liaison Officer, 14, 69
Aboriginal students, 13, 14
Aboriginality, 54
absenteeism, 95, 96
accepted ways of thinking and acting, 24
accommodation, 4
accountability, 22, 82, 85, 86, 139, 147, 151, 162,
accountable to the community, 114
action plan, 11, 36
action, 119, 132
active agents, 27, 71
active choices, 46
active citizen, 5
active contributors to civic life, 66
active voice, 164
actively listening, 30, 157
activism, 20, 115
activist view of teacher professionalism, 139
affirmative action by government, 96
age of spectacle, 121
agency, 32, 52, 62
aggravation and distraction, 47
alienated students, 152
alienated working class youth, 123
alternative visions, 25
ambiguous and complex problems, 114
ameliorating the symptoms, 20
Anglo-Celtic ancestry, 10
aspirations towards education and work, 51
assertive group identity, 24
assets of low socioeconomic communities, 67, 154
assets, 32
at risk, 6, 13, 18, 67, 89

attendance, 95
Australia, 9
Australian Labor Party, 113
Australian Research Council, ix
authentic teaching, learning and assessment, 153
authenticity, 9
authoritarian and patronizing approaches, 61
authoritative discourses, 5
authorizing locally produced knowledge, 73
autobiography, 141

B

backgrounds of disadvantage, 22
back-to-basic reforms, 131, 156
banking knowledge, 151
behavior management, 56, 59, 103, 105, 156
being appropriately skeptical, 17
being treated like children, 58
belongingness, 77
benevolent and patronizing intention, 89
best practice, 86
big thinkers in education, 87
bigger moral questions, 141
blaming the victim, 4
blind adherence to rules and regulations, 48
Boardwalk Project, 133
boundaries as sites of learning, 26
boundary crossing, 9
breakfast program, 14
building community trust, 82
building community, 96
building on what students bring to school, 68
building relationships, 125, 130, 146
bull shit detectors, 44, 112
bullying, 46, 105
bureaucratic insurgent, 44
bureaucratic redtape, 50
bureaucratization and standardization, 68

C

capabilities-oriented institution, 28
capacity building, x, 12, 39, 76, 154, 164
capacity of people in poverty, 39
capacity of people to rejuvenate communities, 38
capacity to listen, 11
cardholders, 44
care at a distance, 2
care, 46, 153, 157, 160
careful empirical work, 17
celebration of surface meanings, 121
Central Park East High School, 78
challenging assumptions, 17
challenging inequitable practices, 150
challenging the existing social order, 17, 31
circumstantial activism, 18
citizen engagement, 115
citizen struggle, 112
citizens, 42
civic education, 55, 71
civic engagement, 54, 77, 79, 132, 133, 147, 150
civic pride, 36
civic responsibility, 71, 74, 75
civics, 113
civil commons, 152
class prejudice, 145
class, 54, 55, 57 85, 87, 163
clients, 42
Coastal Studies Program, 14
co-curriculum programs, 55
coercive policies, 153
collaboration, 161
collaborative learning, 5
collaborative, reflection and planning, 125
collaboratively investigating experience, 157
collecting data, 16
collective action, 154
collective agency and engagement, 164
collegial conversations around pedagogy, 136
collegiality, 162

commodification, 146
common culture, 139
common good, 160, 163
common sense, 81
communal views, 5
communitarian, 132
communities blighted by exclusion, 163
communities of difference, 54
communities put at a disadvantage, 2, 156
communities that are 'done to', 55
community acceptance, 95
community activism, 7, 20, 26, 27, 53, 249, 156
community alliances, 153
community and school renewal, 35
community as a resource for learning, 30, 54, 66, 71
community assets, 11
community building, 57, 77, 79, 84, 109
community capacity building, 4, 11, 57, 76, 83, 96, 151, 154, 155
community connectedness, 71
community consultation, 94
community development, 82, 99, 109
community empowerment, 93, 115
community engaged learning, 117
community engaged schools, 155, 156
community engagement, 12, 54, 67, 68
community house, 10, 12, 38, 44, 92, 111
community hub, 91, 95, 97, 99
community identity formation, 38, 43, 44
community involvement, 95
community knowledge, 12
community leadership, 95
community meetings, 97
community minded advocates, 23
community organizing, 24, 26
community ownership, 34, 39
community partnership, 92
community pride, 35
community projects, 11
community renewal, 11, 19, 23, 25, 27, 35, 36, 38, 43, 51, 53, 84, 91, 96, 115, 133, 154

community resources, 56
community school, 78
community service, 12, 77, 79
community strengths, 21, 37
community studies, 55, 63, 64
community voice, 23
community, 21, 27, 28, 81
community-based learning, 14, 16, 54, 70, 73, 76, 117, 132, 150, 158
compartmentalization, 128, 141
compensatory education, 59
competition, 146, 159
competitive assessment, 65
complexity, 18, 32
compliant, 4
computer club, 40
computing skills, 40
confidence and self-esteem, 48
confronting wider causes, 18
connectedness to community, 5, 71
connectedness, 67, 128
connecting personal achievement to public purpose, 71
connecting to students' lives, 19, 79, 120, 124, 152, 157
connectionist pedagogy, 60, 70, 74, 118
Connexions, 47, 48, 49, 50, 51, 52, 90, 98, 99, 100, 107, 108, 113, 114
conservative interests, 4, 164
constructing spaces, 6
constructivist learning, 125
consumerism, 146, 164
contesting inequalities, 26
contexts of disadvantage, 6
contextual histories, 7
control, 28, 29
'cool' teachers, 118, 129, 157
cooperation, perseverance and persistence, 49
co-operative relationships, 31
co-ownership, 6
co-researchers, 143
counter discourses, 145
counter hegemonic ideas, 24
counter narratives, 10, 21, 34, 38, 53

counter perspectives, 81, 82
countervailing policy tendency, 28
courage, 22, 114
courageous, exploratory and experimental approaches, 159
Courtyard Project, 61, 62
creating capabilities, 159
creating data, 16
creative learning, 28
creative spirit, 124
creativity of the worker, 28
creativity, 29
crime rates, 105
critical, 17
critical and authentic, 120
critical classroom, 143
critical collaborative inquiry, 138
critical democratic engagement, 46, 163
critical democratic engagement, 6, 7, 45
critical democratic practice, 5
critical engagement for school and community renewal, 152
critical engagement, 5, 30, 60, 117, 113, 119, 152, 156
critical ethnography, 18
critical inquiry, 119, 147
critical literacy, 132
critical pedagogy, 72, 76, 124, 145, 147, 155, 164
critical perspective, 150, 163
critical policy analysts, 109
critical public citizenship, 151
critical reflection, 120, 137, 139, 146, 164,
critical research, 17
critical scholars, 84
critical social science, 17
critical sociologists, 57, 109
critical spaces, 27, 28
critical spectators, 45
critical theorists, 17
critical thinking, 103
critical tradition, 16
critical transformative, 163
critical understanding, 72
critically educative process, 45
critically engaged citizens, 54
critically engaged community capacity building, 4, 149, 163, 164
critically engaged learning, 4, 19, 23, 62, 64, 70, 74, 78, 142, 149, 150, 151, 155, 160, 163
critically engaged schools, 153
critically minded educators, 23
critically reflective practice, 132, 136
cross curricular, 15, 125, 126, 131
cultural and intellectual resources, 141
cultural anthropology, 32
cultural awareness, 69
cultural capital, 123
cultural exchange programs, 13
cultural praxis, 145
culture and community, 152
culture of poverty, 32, 33, 35, 40
current orthodoxy, 82
curriculum and control, 103
curriculum for life, 46
curriculum in the community, 74
curriculum leadership, 15
curriculum relevance, 66
curriculum, pedagogy and behavior management, 113

D

dance performance, 127
de facto policy makers, 42
debilitating cycle of educational disadvantage, 24
declining enrolments, 15
deconstructing hierarchy, 159
deep existential issues, 150
defamilarization, 18
deficiency oriented social service model, 67
deficit discourse, 10, 153
deficit logic, 21, 81, 84, 150
deficit prism, 65
deficit thinking, 89, 103, 109
deficit views, 5, 18, 56, 66, 67

deficit, 6, 30, 31, 89, 155
de-institutionalized relationships, 31, 33, 34, 38, 47, 52, 62, 153, 159
deliberative democracy, 111
democracy matters, 114
democratic citizenship, 151
democratic engagement, 23, 115
democratic governance, 112
democratic practice, 110
democratic reform, 91
democratic relationship, 163
democratic schools, 160
democratic space, 20
democratic thinking and action, 140
democratically empower, 109
demolition, 11
demonize, stigmatize and pathologize, 57
demonizing discourses, 10
Department of Housing, 40
dependence, 26
depersonalization, 33
depoliticization, 121
devaluing identity, 85
diagnosed learning difficulties, 11
dialogic decision making, 60
dialogic space, 21
dialogue with students, 72
dialogue, reflection and innovation, 163
didactic teaching, 65
different cartography, 124
dignity, 32, 35
dilemmas, contradictions and paradoxes, 42
direct instruction, 103, 104
direction, hope, possibility and purpose, 34
disability, 11, 54, 55
disadvantage, ix, 11, 27, 30, 46, 65
disadvantaged schools, 18, 162
disadvantaged young people, 4
disaffected students, 66
discipline policies, 47
discomfort, 27
disconnect from young people's lives, 59
discourse and pedagogic practices, 64
discourse of creativity, 28
discourse of despair, 149
discourses of community and compassion, 122
discourses of equity, 115
disengaged students, 77
disparities in income distribution, 57
disrupting social reality, 17, 157
distributed leadership, 6, 162
distribution of disadvantage, 55
diversity, 32
dominant discourses, 120, 121
dominant ideology, 21
dominant policy response, 55
domination, 25, 26
'down on its luck', 43
drawing on local strengths, 154
dropping off the edge, 55
drug dealing, 38
dumbing down the curriculum, 130
dysfunctional families, 10

E

early school leavers, 42, 89
early years education, 96
educated hope, 147, 151
educational disadvantage, 3, 13, 18, 20, 26, 30, 31, 54, 55, 56, 58, 64, 153
educational engagement, 34, 39,
educational inequality, 82
educational organizing for school reform, 23
educational policy contradictions, 28
educational policy, 7
educational reform, 21, 81, 87
educational rigor, 22
educationally marginalized, 18, 29
effective schools, 85, 86
elaborated code, 64
electronically mediated culture, 139
eligible for special funding, 102
emancipation, 46, 151
emotional needs of children, 105
empower residents, 83
empowering education, 145

enforced retention, 153
engage in social action, 125
engage students in real-world experiences, 158
engage with the lifeworlds of students, 70
engaged citizenship, 154
engaged learning, 4, 157
engaged pedagogy, 66, 126
engagement at the point of need, 99
engagement with difference, 67
engagement, 97
engaging and rigorous curriculum, 103
engaging policy, 7
enriched view of schooling, 5
enterprise education, 78
enterprising activities, 15, 16
entrenched racism, 75
entrenched structures, 77
environment, 113
environmental education, 71
equality of educational opportunity, 30
equitable society, 57
equity, justice and democracy, 88
ethic of care, 59, 156, 161
ethical positions, 158
ethnic groups, 15
ethnicity, 54
ethnographic studies, 151, 153
ethos of volunteering, 11
everyday curriculum, 19
everyday lives, 17, 140
evidence-based, 9, 85, 86, 88, 150
excluded and marginalized, 27
excluded communities, 7, 20, 21, 55
excluded from policy discourse, 57
exclusion and marginalization, 2, 27, 37
exclusionary structures, 56
exercising choice to leave school, 46
exiled from school, 42
exotic species, 37
expand horizons, 79
expanding opportunities, 52
experiential learning, 47, 131
experiment in democracy, 147
expert judgments, 7
exploding structural arrangements, 24
extraordinarily re-experiencing the ordinary, 17, 119

F

fake ownership, 36
family background, 54
family trauma, 54
fault lines of opportunity and risk, 9
feeling valued and respected, 144
ferals, 91
flawed logic, 85
flexible approaches, 161
flexible timetable, 66, 133
fluid approaches, 25
foregrounding lives of young people, 60
forgotten people, 93, 164
forgotten poor, 3
forms of representation, 24
forums and community committee, 111
Foucault, 59
fractured lives of students, 56
free space, 24, 25, 31
free-floating oppositional consciousness, 24
Freire, 70
friendships, 144
fun, 135
functionalist approach, 135
funds of knowledge, 20, 21, 33, 69, 73, 77, 132, 141

G

gated school, 2
gender, 163
generate meaning, 125
generation of suspects, 123
generative themes, 71
genre stretching, 24
genre thickening, 24
geographies of exclusion, 16, 109

getting by, 124
giving ownership over learning, 106
giving students a say, 157
giving voice, 9
global capitalism, 55
global info-entertainment, 118
globalization, 10, 57
globalizing processes, 122
globally competitive economy, 120
government (public) schools, 9
government assistance, 11
government intervention, 92
government knows best policies, 55
government speak, 36
great place to live, 12
grounded in communal life, 155
group work, 130, 131
growing educational divide, 57

H

habitual ways, 28
habitus, 123
'hand up not a handout', 37, 83
hands-on approach, 62, 63
hands-on community-oriented learning, 162
hanging in, 15
harassment, 46
health cards, 101
healthy skepticism, 9
heritage and cultural studies, 71
heritage trail, 132, 133
hermetically sealed, 54
hidden curriculum, 64
hierarchical structure of high schools, 58
high concentration of socially disadvantaged students, 87
high drop-out rates, 58
high expectations, 86
high levels of uncertainty and unpredictability, 42
high school, 97, 98
high stakes testing, 131, 147, 151, 164

history and pride in community, 35
history of outside agencies, 44
holistic, community-based approach, 69
home backgrounds, 29
home grown role models, 108
homework center, 15
homophobia, 127, 145
horticultural program, 73
Housing Commission, 91
humanizing relationships, 159
hybridized and globalized identities, 119

I

ideational relationships, 158
identity and sense of belongingness, 144
identity formation of young women, 51
identity work, 144
identity, 144
ignorance and prejudice, 10
ill health, 54
imaging the whole, 18
imagining alternatives, 31
improvisation, 132, 159
inclusion and participatory decision making, 155
inclusive democratic processes, 109
incorporating students' lives, 120
Indigenous Australians, 10, 68
individual and collective agency, 115
individual and cultural stereotypes, 160
individual and group identity, 144
individual learning plans, 15, 49
individual pathology, 89
indoctrination, 4
industrial model, 48
inequalities, 5, 27, 37, 57, 109
inhibiting debate and stifling creativity, 164
injustices, 5
innovation, 28
inquiry oriented, 132
inspection, 28
institution of schooling, 46

institutional barriers to learning, 54, 61
institutional boundary between family and school, 59
institutional character and culture, 8
institutional fix, 24
institutional norms, 47
institutional practices, 89
institutional relationships, 33, 37, 40, 42
institutionalization, 33, 49, 77
institutionalized distance, 77
instrumental theory of action, 87
instrumentalism, 151
integrated approach, 12, 155
integrated curriculum, 15
intellectual and civic life, 128
inter-agency connections, 161
interconnectedness, 79
interdisciplinary approaches, 140
interferences to critical thought, 135
intergenerational unemployment, 55
internal resources of community, 42
internal strengths, 33
international economic competitiveness, 28, 124
interrogate commonsense understanding, 145
interrogating dominant constructions, 120, 145, 159
interrupting asymmetry, 17
invest in their learning, 118
investigatory probes, 18
investment from governments, 12
Iraq war, 164
irrelevance of curriculum, 46
islands of democracy, 75
'it's really about the kids', 160

J

Jesuit Social Services, 55
joined-up government, 83, 92
just social order, 17
justice and a 'fair go', 161

justice, 113

K

'knowing when your job is done', 45
knowledge industries, 28
knowledge transfer, 159
knowledge workers, 137

L

lack of connectedness to school, 58
language code, 64
leadership, 42, 43, 46, 86
league tables, 28
learn in and about the community, 155
learning communities, 108
learning contracts, 47
learning outside formal structures of schooling, 47
learning portfolios, 47
learning teams, 127, 162
learning through public performance, 157
legitimacy, 9
liberal, progressive, student-oriented, 5
license to experiment, 135
'lie of the land', 8
life-capacities for least advantaged, 152
lifeworlds of students, 118, 156
limited experiences, 101
listening stance, 43
literacy and numeracy, 47
lived experience, 6, 27, 121
lives and identities of young people, 120
lives histories, experiences and aspirations, 4
local accommodation, 3
local as a point of entry, 72
local civic contribution, 42
local community as a source of knowledge, 70
local educational reform, 97

local funds of knowledge, 2, 68
local histories and community contexts, 68
local leadership, 79, 83,
local literacies, 55
local ownership, 68, 154
local service agencies, 83
local voices, 2, 21
located in students' daily worlds, 46
lock down mode, 22
Lone Tree project, 78
long standing community institutions, 25
long term sustainability, 11
loss of meaning and purpose, 124
loss of power and agency, 38
lost kids, 107
lost to the system, 98
low levels of education, 55
low levels of home ownership, 55
low proportion of children in pre-school, 100
low self-esteem, 14
low socioeconomic status, 86. 108

M

makers and interpreters of history, 70
making meaning, 144
making schools accountable, 57
making young people powerful, 146, 164
management and leadership, 82
managerialism, 22
mandated solutions, 57
mapping and analyzing the community, 31, 67
mapping complex spaces, 18
mapping the pedagogy of youth, 119
marginalization, 7
marginalized and excluded communities, 21
marginalized youth, 90
maritime industries, 14
Maritime Studies Program, 131
market attainment, 151
masculine school culture, 127

master client relationship, 45
McJobs, 123
media based activities, 134
media literate citizenry, 124
medical metaphor, 33
men's shed, 10, 95
merit pay, 28
metal detectors, 22
metaphor, 25, 27, 32
middle class institution of schooling, 57
middle class, 30, 46, 59, 64, 67, 84, 85, 102, 103, 123, 153
middle school, 14, 139
middle years of schooling, ix, 15, 56, 59, 132
militarism, 145
minimal parental education, 54
minimizing risk, 89
misleading simplicity, 24
monitoring learning progress, 47
multi agency approaches, 29
multiple communities, 46
multiple constituencies, 7
multiple forms of disadvantage, 29, 30
multiple identities, 25
multiplicity of sites, 119
multi-sited ethnography, 18, 19
myths, 10

N

narrative portraits, 9
narratives, 8, 150
narrow instrumentalist approaches, 156
national benchmarks, 85, 164
national superiority in a globalized economy, 151
national testing, 28, 67
native's point of view, 17
natural order, 87
navigating a pathway, 16
needs of individual students, 15
needs oriented approach, 79
needs survey, 67

200 ❖ Critically Engaged Learning

negative labeling, 91
negotiated curriculum, 71
negotiated learning, 47, 48, 58, 131
neighborhood identity, 10
neighborhood meetings, 11
Neighborhood Renewal Project, 10
neighborhood renewal, 10, 11, 21, 82, 83, 84, 90, 92, 104, 108, 115
neoliberal policies, 10, 55, 82, 83, 93, 150, 156, 164
neutral discourses, 81
new institutional fix, 23, 26
New Right, 164
new social order, 22
newcomers accepted, 10
null curriculum, 164

O

object of pity, 37
official curriculum, 164
official script, 153
one-size-fits-all approach, 29
ongoing assessment, 71
opportunities and connections, 163
opportunity structure, 31
oppositional behavior, 59, 60
ordinary citizens, 24
othering discourse, 37, 55
Outcomes Based Education, 140
over romanticize, 35
ownership of learning, 29
ownership, 7, 28, 29, 30, 43, 62, 93, 108, 153, 155, 159, 161, 164

P

paradigms, 24
parental background, 29
parental choice, 57
parent-teacher interview, 104, 105

participant observation, 19
participative problem solving, 111
participatory decision making, 79
partnership with government, 83
passive assistance, 20
passive spectator, 5
past ineffectual efforts, 44
pastoral care, 15
paternalistic practices, 85, 154, 164
pathological view of disadvantage, 21, 34
pathologizing disadvantage, 34, 53
pathologizing discourses, 156, 164
pathologizing the poor, 84
pathway planning, 49
patronizing, 32
Payne, 33, 35, 40
pedagogical, 7, 64, 74, 75, 133, 136, 152
pedagogy of poverty, 59
pedagogy of youth and popular culture, 119, 136, 141, 147
peer groups, 54
performance and development culture, 85
performance gaps, 86
performance management, 28
performance targets, 85
performativity, 28, 29
performing arts, 127
permeable boundaries, 45
person centered approach to schooling, 59
personal and social transformation, 146
personalized learning around student interests, 161
personalized learning contracts, 47
personalized timetables, 49
pervasive mythologies, 31
'pick a suit', 112
place and space, 1, 2, 3, 16, 20, 25, 27
place-based learning, 21, 54, 72, 154
place-making, 2
playing dumb, 124
pleasant built environment, 161
pluralism, 132
policy discourse, 81
policy interpreters, 112
policy orthodoxy, 82

policy players, 112
political engagement, 110
political, global and social forces, 7
politicization within the community, 114
politics without guarantees, 3
poor attendance, 58
poor health, 55
popular culture, 16, 72, 129, 157
portraiture, 8, 9, 150
positivism, 151
poverty, 3, 10, 12, 12, 25, 30, 31, 32, 34, 37, 39, 42, 52, 54, 55, 56, 57, 75, 84, 85, 93, 113, 164
power of paradox, 9
power, 1, 6, 16, 41, 44, 45, 59, 84, 88, 121, 132, 141, 145
powerful people, 95
predatory culture, 123, 146
pre-schooling, 11, 101
previously silenced citizens, 110
privatization, 93
privileging education policy, 88
problem posing education, 146
problem solving by outside experts, 67
problematic transition, 97
producers of knowledge, 133
Productive Pedagogies Research project, 128, 131
productive pedagogies, 67
productive relationships with students, 129, 135
professional activists, 114
professional judgment, 79, 136
Program for Students with Disabilities, 86
programmatic formulae, 42
progressive democratic thinking, 115
prominent themes, 20
pseudonyms, 19
pseudo-scientific, 86, 150
public goods, 77
public housing, 10, 82
public judgment, 7
public meetings, 97
public policy, 79
Puente project, 68

punctuality, 48
puncturing simplistic stereotypes, 34, 43
purposeful and powerful curriculum, 118
purposeful engagement, 65
push back against disempowering policies and practices, 156
putting people first, 99, 106

Q

Queensland School Longitudinal Study, 67
questioning dominant practices, 17

R

racial background, 57, 163
racism, 145
raising school leaving age, 56
rallying whole village, 30
real world learning, 161
rebuilding and repairing computers, 40
reciprocity, 84, 160
reconnecting young people to schooling, 11, 12
reconstituting identities, 42, 156
reduced access to communication technologies, 55
re-engage with learning, 47, 49, 50, 153, 163
re-engaging students, 3, 4, 21, 42, 120
re-engaging whole community, 97
reflection, 87, 88, 199
reforming bureaucracies, 112
regressive ideologies, 135
re-imagining and reinventing pedagogy, 136
re-imagining relationships, 26
re-inventing policy locally, 162
relational corrosion, 33
relational nature of schools, 62, 157
relational power, 52
relational practices, 7, 88
relational schools, 159

relational trust, 60, 159, 161
relational work, 144, 160
relationship building, 39, 154
relationship to teachers, 62
relationships, 2, 5, 15, 22, 24, 25, 27, 31, 45, 46, 53, 97, 114, 119, 144, 152, 153, 157, 161
relevance, 15, 28, 29, 49
relevant curriculum, 53, 141
religion, 54
reluctant readers, 126
Renewal Office, 114
Renewal Team, 94
renovation of communities, 3, 39
repair and restoration, 4
repertoire of teachers' thinking, 88
research imaginary, 18
researching student culture, 141
resident stories, 53
resilient and caring community, 10
resistance, 59, 145
resourceful nature of community, 31
respect for background differences, 30
respect, 19, 22, 32, 35, 37, 38, 46, 48, 55, 59, 60, 66, 70, 90, 103, 105, 106, 153, 157, 160, 164
respectful of young lives, 20, 21
respectful relationships, 108
respectful structures, 48, 60
responsive to students' lives, 154
restoration of social, political and economic order, 154
restricted public transport, 55
restricted, 65
revitalization of communities, 3, 76
revitalizing grassroots democracy, 154
revitalizing inner-city neighborhoods, 57
rich resource, 155
rigor, 15, 157
rigorous and integrated, 130
rigorous and relevant education, 130, 132
rigorous community-based inquiry, 131
rigorous, relevant and socially valued learning, 150
risk taking, 159, 162

role of the outsider, 44
rote learning, 151
rust belt, 20

S

school and classroom cultures, 19
school and community boundaries, 21
school and community capacity building, 55, 156
school and community portraits, 9
school as a community asset, 54, 155
school as a resource for community building, 76
school as an experiment in democracy, 157
school based conversations, 119
school business partnerships, 54, 68
school council, 105
school effectiveness, 21, 54, 79, 82, 85, 86, 87, 90, 106, 113
school reform for disadvantaged young people, 23, 25
school retention, 9, 12, 13, 15, 54, 56, 57, 73, 96, 153
school structure, 152
school uniforms, 47
school-community dialogue, 19
school-community engagement, 53
school-community relations, 56, 79, 153
school-in-community, 155
schooling as alienating and irrelevant, 70
schools as 'toxic' places, 90
schools as alienating institutions, 153
schools as controlling and coercive places, 30
schools as democratic public spheres, 160
schools as prisons, 48
scripted teaching, 136
second chance, 49
security guards, 22
self and identity, 145
self-analysis, 9
self-determination, 6
self-scrutiny, 9

self-worth, 161
semiotic denseness, 24
semi-structured interviews, 19
sense of belonging, 16
sense of community, 15
sense of pride, 37
sense of wholism, 18
service learning, 55, 71, 77, 78
sexism, 145
sexualization, commodification and commercialization, 122
shame of the nation, 3
single mothers, 101
sites of pedagogic acquisition, 21, 65
situated participation, 132
situated pedagogy, 74
skill-and-drill pedagogies, 147
skills and wisdom of community organizations, 67
skills audit of local area, 92
skills within community, 83
soccer, 135
social action, 76, 164
social and cultural fabric, 54
social and economic advantages, 88
social and industrial change, 110
social and political equity, 115
social and political forces, 4
social capital, 29, 76, 77, 82, 83, 84, 90, 96, 99, 109, 110, 150
social change, 110
social cohesion, 82, 160
social control, 89
social Darwinism, 122
social disadvantage, 114
social entrepreneurship, 83
social exclusion, 7, 10, 16, 24, 54, 55
social geography, 16
social hierarchies, 122, 123
social immaturity, 97
social improvement, 109
social inclusion, 21, 52, 81
social injustice, 27
social institution of schooling, 4, 120
social justice, 7, 89, 90, 109, 113, 115, 139, 149, 151, 163
social positioning, 17
social power, 28
social relations, 144
social sphere, 134
social ties, 83
social transformation, 88, 145
socially critical, 20, 23, 24, 27, 31, 53, 76, 119, 136, 146,
socially just, 75, 132
societal power structure, 85
socio-cultural practices of young people, 123
socio-economic disadvantage, 7
sociological machinery of school, 58, 59, 64
socio-political reality, 140
socio-spatial relations, 16, 25
solidarity, 28, 153
sorting, 58
space-as-container ontology, 25
spaces for collaboration, reflection and planning, 134
spaces for critically engaged educators, 151
spaces for dialogue, 35, 62, 161
spatial aspects, 37
spatial boundaries, 25
spatial contexts, 84
spatial history, 2
spatial turn, 25
speaking the unpleasant, 27
spectator citizenry, 45
standardization, 131, 147
standardized solutions, 136
standardized testing, 72, 141, 164
standards, 29, 72, 85, 151
standards-based curricula, 67
starting from where students are at, 126, 146, 152, 156
stereotypical portrayals, 34, 39, 40, 55
stigma and stereotyping, 21, 36, 39, 43, 55, 94, 110
stigmatize and demonize, 37, 48, 84
storylines, 149
streaming, 58
street smart, 108
street-level bureaucrats, 42

street-level problems, 26
strengths and capacities in communities, 21, 32, 68
structural adjustments to economy, 12
structural and class issues, 109
structural change, 46, 91, 110
structural features, 84, 90, 109
structural inequalities, 75, 90, 162
structure of the high school, 60
structured inequalities, 164
structured literacy program, 103
struggle to 'become somebody', 144
student achievement, 85
student alienation and resistance, 135
student care and safety, 29
student connectedness, 107
student engagement, 4, 9, 12, 13, 15, 54, 56, 73, 75, 119, 124, 128, 136, 153
student identity, 64
student meaning, making 134
student negotiation, 103
student ownership, 74, 161
student resistance, 124
student safety and welfare issues, 102
student subjectivities and identities, 124, 157
student voice, 5, 30, 58, 161
student-focused and supportive school, 160
student-led approach to learning, 59
students as depositories, 157, 125
students as researchers, 141, 146
students at risk, 81
students with special needs, 105
students, 16
students' culture and interests are respected, 135
students' existing knowledge, 128
students' lives and experience, 132
students' personal problems, 89
study of locally produced texts and artifacts, 70
studying community and conditions, 143
sub-schools, 14, 15
substance abuse, 38, 47
substitution of fascination for analysis, 121
sustainability, 113

systematic inequalities, 84, 110
system-driven accountability, 16

T

taking responsibility, 34
'taking you as you are', 48
talk-fests, 43
target setting, 28
teacher capacity and renewal, 107
teacher collaboration, 146
teacher directed learning, 103
teacher narratives, 139
teacher proof curricula, 139
teacher stress, 56
teachers' tacit knowledge, 88
teachers' work, 75
teaching as technical work, 71
team building activities, 135
team meetings, 134
technical and expert values, 5
Technical and Further Education (TAFE), 14
technical intervention strategies, 89
technical skills and competencies, 150
technicians/civil servants, 137
technologies of exclusion, 58
telecommunications and mass media, 121
temporary constellations of trajectories, 3
temporary fixations, 3
terrorism, 164
Tertiary Entrance Examinations (TEE), 135
The Smith Family, 20
theoretically thin, 45, 86, 110
theory kicks in, 18
thickening concept of engagement, 45
three-way interviews, 104
tightly coded descriptions, 24
timetable, 47, 139
token participation, 36
top-down policies, 153, 164
top-down, and managerial discourses, 160
toxic culture, 22, 139

traditional pedagogies, 135
traditional subject disciplines, 139, 157
transformative and democratic, 45, 76, 149
transformative intellectual, 137
transforming lives of young people, 146
transience, 54
transition points in schooling, 11
tree planting project, 77
trickle-down effects, 3
true partnership, 45
trust, 16, 22, 44, 46, 52, 83, 84, 95, 96, 103, 105, 106, 108, 112, 117, 153, 157, 160, 163, 164

U

uncertain and exploitative times, 157
underachievement, 85, 114
understandable suspicions, 44
understanding of the significant community issues, 66
understanding students' lives, 30, 106
undeserved put downs, 37
unexamined shibboleths, 21
uni-dimensional, 40
uniform learning outcomes, 72
urban school reform, 26, 57, 76
utilitarian concerns, 88
utilize and value community assets, 53

V

valued learning pathway, 48
vernacular theories of knowledge, 77
VET [Vocational Education and Training], 14
victim-blaming, 27, 32
vision, 43, 162
vocational education, 15, 135, 150
vocational orientation, 64
voiceless, 164
voices and stories of informants, 18, 21, 28

voluntarist discourse of renewal, 84
voluntarist optimism, 110
voluntary work, 64
volunteer burnout, 36
voting with their feet, 017

W

wastage of working class potential, 64
welfare dependency, 10, 12, 13, 55, 82, 83
welfare-to-work policies, 55
'what works', 88
who benefits and who loses, 28
whole of community approach, 83, 94, 161
wider perceptions of the community, 38
wired for failure, 48
wonderland, 84
work against the grain, 28
work placement programs, 15, 75, 79
work-based studies, 71
workforce participation, 12
working across boundaries, 18
working class students, 135
working class, 65
world making, 132

Y

young educational destinies, 21
young people's identities, 54, 107
youth and popular culture, 7, 20, 22, 117, 118, 120, 123, 124, 125, 128, 129, 130, 134, 146, 157
youth identities, 120
youth unemployment, 12

Adolescent Cultures, School & Society

Joseph L. DeVitis & Linda Irwin-DeVitis
GENERAL EDITORS

As schools struggle to redefine and restructure themselves, they need to be cognizant of the new realities of adolescents. Thus, this series of monographs and textbooks is committed to depicting the variety of adolescent cultures that exist in today's post-industrial societies. It is intended to be a primarily qualitative research, practice, and policy series devoted to contextual interpretation and analysis that encompasses a broad range of interdisciplinary critique. In addition, this series will seek to provide a pragmatic, pro-active response to the current backlash of conservatism that continues to dominate political discourse, practice, and policy. This series seeks to address issues of curriculum theory and practice; multicultural education; aggression and violence; the media and arts; school dropouts; homeless and runaway youth; alienated youth; at-risk adolescent populations; family structures and parental involvement; and race, ethnicity, class, and gender studies.

Send proposals and manuscripts to the general editors at:
>Joseph L. DeVitis & Linda Irwin-DeVitis
>The John H. Lounsbury School of Education
>Georgia College & State University
>Campus Box 70
>Milledgeville, GA 31061-0490

To order other books in this series, please contact our Customer Service Department at:
>(800) 770-LANG (within the U.S.)
>(212) 647-7706 (outside the U.S.)
>(212) 647-7707 FAX

or browse online by series at:
>WWW.PETERLANG.COM